"A Winner by Any Standard provides any young person with a unique yearlong opportunity for personal growth."

—**Alice Mitchell**, founder and director of the nationally recognized *UpBeat* peer-leadership program

"By encouraging the next generation to be more open-minded, proactive and introspective, the author makes it possible for them to attain true success in life."

—**William Silva, Ph.D**, parent, recipient of the Milken National Educator Award

"This is the kind of information many adults wish they'd heard growing up. It provides an advantage."

—**Michael J. Balinskas**, parent of former students, Vice-President of Business Development and Acquisitions for Xcelecom

"Mr. G is a role model who young people relate and respond to."

—**Lisa Zaccagnino**, former student, interning for *The Today Show*

"A Winner by Any Standard promotes the personal habits needed for any individual to live effectively...habits that require work and persistence, and are therefore not widely practiced in society."

—**Carl Ajello III**, parent, lifelong friend, Attorney

"This book hits on what young people of today live, and speaks to their intrinsic desire to grow, evolve and contribute."

—**Zachary Leghorn**, former student, National Merit Scholar

"A Winner by Any Standard will help counteract the culture that young people of today are forced to grow up in."

—**Rebecca Charamut-Cass**, parent of former student, A Decade of Volunteer Leadership

"Mr.G challenges each of us to challenge ourselves."

—**Kelly J. Foy**, former student, cancer survivor, U.S. Student Ambassador

"This book does it all: promotes sound character and citizenship, develops social and emotional aptitude, and provides the next generation with an all-important sense of direction and purpose."

—**Keith Roeder, Psy.D**, parent, Clinical Psychologist

"This book serves as a road map for charting and navigating one's own extraordinary life journey."

—**Carol Virostek, Ph.D**, parent, former Connecticut State Teacher of the Year

A Winner by Any Standard

A Personal Growth Journey for Every American Teen

Rob Garofalo, Jr.

Teen Winners Publishing
BERLIN, CONNECTICUT

First printing 2004

ISBN 0-9740356-4-5
LCCN 2003104207

This book is dedicated to every one of
my past and present students.
May it provide you with
guidance, hope, and inspiration
as you journey through life.

Table of Contents

Acknowledgments

Many thanks to all who contributed to the creating and launching of this book. To the talented Leslie Virostek, who transformed a 400-page rough draft into a clean, organized manuscript; the team of Sue Collier and Kate Deubert, for performing such a thorough copyediting job; Cathy Bowman, for her creative design sense and overall expertise; the inspirational Marilyn Ross, who took a personal interest in even the smallest project details; Deb Ellis and Lurina Thieman, for the unending levels of patience and professionalism they demonstrated.

And lastly, thank you to my wife, Kris, for her steadfast support throughout this seven-year process—and, most fittingly, for her daily example of living as "a winner by any standard."

THE DEFINITION

"A WINNER BY ANY STANDARD" IS ANY YOUNG PERSON WHO IS INTENT ON GROWING AND EVOLVING INTO A TRUE INDIVIDUAL.

THEREFORE, HE HAS GOALS AND DREAMS, AND DOESN'T BACK DOWN FROM A CHALLENGE.

SHE ALSO MAINTAINS PERSPECTIVE ON WHAT'S TRULY IMPORTANT IN LIFE—THINGS LIKE STANDING FOR SOMETHING, ENJOYING EACH DAY, BUILDING MEANINGFUL RELATIONSHIPS, AND STRIVING TO MAKE AN INDIVIDUAL DIFFERENCE IN THE WORLD.

THE WORLD NEEDS MORE OF THEM.

Dreams can often become challenging, but challenges are what we live for.

—Travis White

Above all, challenge yourself. You may well surprise yourself at what strengths you have, what you can accomplish.

—Cecile M. Springer

Introduction

Have you noticed the adult tendency to hand down advice as one-line declarations? *Believe in yourself; enjoy the process; stay away from drugs; be more positive*—and on and on. You've probably heard them all. But if these messages are so important, why are they presented to young people in such an inadequate, lifeless way?

Hello, my name is Rob Garofalo, but you can think of me as Mr. G, just as my students in class do. I became a teacher some 12 years ago with the intent of preparing the next generation to not only learn effectively, but also to live effectively. So whenever I present advice, I make sure to first add lots of life and substance to it. My personal observations, reflections, anecdotes, and favorite inspirational quotes all help to explain ideals to young people in a way that's both meaningful and relevant to their lives. Then, rather than expect the advice to be blindly accepted by all, I leave it up to each individual to decide whether or not it's something of value—something worthy of being incorporated into his or her own life. (As you'd predict, this approach has proven far more effective than the parroting of one-liners.)

My students also respond positively to me because they sense how much I care—about them as individuals and about making the world a better place through them. It helps, too, that I have tremendous respect for all who are growing up in these complex times. (I'm sure there's a teacher in your own life who can be described in such ways.)

This, my first book, is a compilation of the same attempts I've made in class, the same words of wisdom I've been sharing with students over the years.

I encourage you to approach these 52 messages with an open-minded respect, for each one can help you to develop inner power, the very power that leads to feeling confident about yourself and your place in the world.

You may start feeling you know yourself better than ever before, or seeing with greater clarity what is truly important in life. Perhaps you'll figure out what it is you want to stand for, the type of person you want to become. Who knows, with this newfound sense of self in place, you may even come to realize that you possess the power to accomplish anything you put your mind to. You do possess the power to shape yourself and, in the process, shape the world—don't let anyone tell you differently.

If you do find any of my book's weekly messages to be of personal value, you will need to extend your efforts beyond merely reading about them. To apply an ideal to real life and actually make it a part of who you are is quite the challenge, one that requires both thought and action. That is why I have included a helpful Life App (short for Life Application) section at the end of each chapter. The question is, *Are you up to the challenge?* My hope, and belief, is you are—52 times over.

As you make your own decision each week, keep in mind that for any of us to unlock our full potential as human beings; to create truly rich, fulfilling lives; and to become winners by any standard, we must consistently challenge ourselves to learn and grow. Truth be told, this is not an easy way to travel through life—the path is laden with hard work, obstacles, and failure—but those who do choose the less traveled path anyhow discover the rewards of doing so to be both numerous and everlasting. If you are interested in gaining the inspiration, as well as the insight, required to chart and navigate just such an extraordinary life journey, then this book is for you. Enjoy it.

I can't tell you how hopeful I am that these positive changes take place in your life. Partly because in a world teeming with negative, unfulfilled people, I consider it a personal mission to make effective living more the rule than the exception. And partly because lots of folks feel your generation in general isn't capable of doing what it takes to succeed at life. They don't believe you can even maintain your focus long enough to learn—unless, of course, there is nonstop action, jokes, or gratuitous violence involved.

I know from my own experiences, however, that when the material being presented is meaningful and relevant to your lives, and the person delivering it truly cares, your generation is as willing and capable of learning as any. And it just so happens this book *was* written from the heart and consists of nothing but what *you* live: school, sports, music, personal image, emotions, television, friends, heroes, dreams, etc.

Finally, although *A Winner by Any Standard* is set up to have you concentrate on tackling one challenge per week, feel free to use it as a guidebook or manual. For example, on those days you're feeling down and out, take a look at Searching for the Bright Side and Living with a Grateful Heart. When somebody is giving you a hard time and getting on your nerves, refer to Thickening Your Skin. Or when you find yourself eagerly anticipating—or dreading—the future, read Following Your Dreams and Taking Risks. You get the idea. And keep in mind that, while I've written these advisements for every young person of your generation and beyond, I want you to read each one as if it were just the two of us having a heart-to-heart.

Remember then, my student, you help to shape yourself as well as the entire world, each and every time you accept a challenge. So turn the page and *challenge yourself to reflect…to take action…to grow…and to become a winner by any standard.* You can do this.

WEEK 1

Never Giving Up

We can do anything we want to do if we stick to it long enough.

—Helen Keller

Many of life's failures are people who did not realize how close they were to success when they gave up.

—Thomas Edison

If at first you don't succeed, keep on sucking till you do succeed.

—Curly Howard

Travel back in years to the time you first learned how to ride a bike. Even if you can't recall the exact details of the experience, it's safe to say that despite the frustration—and any physical pain caused by a cut-up knee or two—it never even occurred to you to give up.

This means, my student, when you were—what?—five years old, you knew that to succeed at learning to ride a bike you had to pick yourself up each time you fell. Well, guess what? What you knew when you were five years old is still true. Learning anything new involves a struggle, but that certainly doesn't mean you should give up when the going gets rough. Your present challenge is to bring this wisdom to the forefront of your mind and to begin applying it to all areas of life.

Where better to get started than in school, a place in which new skills and concepts are regularly introduced? In my own classes, my students and I matter-of-factly refer to the initial stages of the learning process as "the struggle phase." As in: "Mr. G, I'm still in the struggle phase on this algebra concept. Can you explain problem number three again?"

Mind you, I'm not claiming this fresh perspective eliminates all feelings of frustration and inadequacy. But what I am saying is when young people like yourself are made aware of the process, they are infinitely more likely to give strong effort, remain determined, and come to trust in themselves. Consequently, when learning something new they are far less likely to feel stupid and give up.

Personally, I can't help wishing someone had let me in on this rather basic lesson of life. Perhaps my parents and teachers assumed young people should be able to figure it out on their own—who knows? The fact is I didn't and it showed.

I was the kid who rarely stuck with anything challenging. And because I'd let the daunting feelings of futility and inadequacy get the best of me, I evolved into your typical quitter. Quitting, as you know, is easy—and tempting; you just do it and presto, no more frustration, no more feelings of inadequacy, and no more embarrassment. (Come to think of it, no more boo-boos on your knees either.) The funny thing is I didn't realize how much it had cost me until I got older and saw all that others were capable of and had accomplished.

For example, when I hear friends of mine playing a musical instrument with skill and passion, I can't help regretting my hasty choice to give up on sax lessons. Or when I see the progress my brother has made with his golf game, I find myself wishing I too had worked through my initial flaws and continued to practice over the years. (Well, at least I came to recognize the error of my ways late as opposed to never.)

Now that you are clear about it being completely normal to struggle when trying something new—and about how painful it can be to look back and wonder what might have been—you hold a distinct advantage over the many who think like I did. This does not, however, guarantee you will always meet with personal success and avoid the temptation to quit. Indeed, there will be exasperating times when your hard work and persistence don't seem to be paying off. But before you give in to the disappointment, I want you to remember another of life's most fundamental truths: *Each individual possesses different strengths and weaknesses.*

If you find you are putting in all the necessary effort to improve, but still making far less progress than others, you have simply happened upon a personal weakness. (You can actually use it as a cue to be even more diligent—and patient—with your efforts.) Conversely, when you're breezing through the struggle phase with relative ease and quickness, you can add yet another personal strength to your already impressive list.

Make no mistake, this basic point about each of us possessing different strengths and weaknesses—like the learning-to-ride point—is a frequently overlooked one. Young people especially, tend to beat themselves up when they try something new and discover they're not very good at it. You'd think with all the strength-weakness evidence in life, they would know better than to react this way.

In school, do you not know students who struggle mightily in art class but excel in phys ed or music? Do you not know individuals who are genius-like in algebra and other math subjects but couldn't write creatively if their lives depended on it? Wouldn't you even agree a professional basketball player who tried his hand at another sport, say, soccer or baseball, would almost surely stink up the field—or to be more diplomatic—fail to perform at an equally elite level? Clearly, we *all* have different strengths and weaknesses.

With this point now established, I want you to also recognize just because you happen to be weak in certain areas does not mean you always will be. No, it is entirely possible that with a mix of determination and grit, what was once a weakness can eventually be transformed into yet another personal strength. If you were to ask any person who now performs at an advanced level—professional athletes and musicians included—about their early experiences, the vast majority would back up my claim.

Michael Jordan, for one, was cut from his high school JV basketball team. (I know it's difficult to fathom, but it's true.) If not for his ability to turn frustration into inspiration, and a personal resolve to spend countless hours improving upon his weaknesses, he would have never become the international icon he now is. Can you imagine that? Never hearing of the man who provided an insane amount of thrills and inspiration to millions and millions of people? Well, if he had given up on developing his weaknesses, that's precisely what the reality of the situation would be.

A friend of mine from junior high also provided—albeit unwittingly—a prime example of grit and stick-to-itiveness. Despite the fact he loved to play baseball, Derek was the kind of hitter opposing teams welcomed to the plate. (He was considered that much of a sure out.) No amount of encouragement from teammates or instruction from coaches seemed to change the fact he rarely made contact with a pitch.

One day, Derek revealed to me that each and every time he warmed up in the on-deck circle, self-doubt would begin to creep into his mind. By the time he made his way into the batter's box, he would be thinking only of how many pitches it would take to seal his fate. Clearly, any shred of confidence he once had was gone and it was widely believed to be only a matter of time before he would give up.

In retrospect, it's a wonder Derek hadn't thrown in the towel earlier. Although he had always been a good glove man, his hitting weaknesses had persisted since our Little League days. And we all know just how easy and tempting it is to quit.

But to Derek's credit he refused to take the easy way out. He recognized that his struggle phase was lasting far longer than most people's and then used it as a cue to step up his efforts. That summer, rather than being at the batting cages on a once-in-a-while basis, we were there daily. We also videotaped each other's swings for the first time ever, studied the mechanics of countless major-leaguers, and began to research—at his dad's urging—the importance of a positive attitude. (Success, after all, is determined as much by attitude as it is by ability.)

In time, Derek began to walk into the batter's box with new and improved technique as well as new and improved thoughts. And while his "I'm going to rip the cover off the ball" mind-set didn't work every time, he did improve markedly.

By high school, he had turned himself into an all-around solid hitter. Mind you, he didn't turn out to be the MJ of the baseball world or anything, but he did eventually become a three-year starter on his college team—a remarkable accomplishment considering his earlier performance. But even more significantly, Derek, having never given up while transforming a nagging weakness into a personal strength, was the best *he* could possibly be.

For additional examples of people who absolutely refused to quit as they battled through personal weaknesses, hardships, and initial failures, look no further than our own country's history. The lives of Helen Keller, Martin Luther King, Jr., Walt Disney, and Abraham Lincoln—among others—not only define, but breathe eternal life into the ideals of determination, fortitude, and never giving up. The final results of their noble struggles did nothing less than change our world for the better—the ultimate in human accomplishment.

Each of these individuals, including my old friend from junior high, had a hand in teaching me this, the inspirational alternative to giving up: *Each time life knocks you down, learn something and get back up even hungrier than before. Success, after all, has no other choice but to give in to rare displays of resolve and grit.*

Remember then, my student, when trying something new—whether it be in school or in the arena of life, at the age of 5 or 15—it's supposed to be a struggle...*so challenge yourself to never give up*. You can do this.

LIFE APP

THINK BACK TO SOMETHING YOU ONCE REALLY WANTED TO DO BUT GAVE UP ON, SAYING "I QUIT" AT THE FIRST SIGN OF FRUSTRATION. WITH THIS *STRUGGLE PHASE* INSIGHT NOW IN THE FOREFRONT OF YOUR MIND, YOU ARE EQUIPPED TO GIVE WHATEVER IT WAS ANOTHER SHOT.

THIS TIME AROUND, THOUGH, SCRATCH AND CLAW YOUR WAY THROUGH THE AWKWARDNESS. BE PATIENT AND BELIEVE IN YOURSELF, FOR YOUR LONG LIST OF PERSONAL STRENGTHS ATTESTS TO THE FACT YOU'VE WORKED YOUR WAY THROUGH BEFORE. AND EVEN IF THINGS DON'T END UP WORKING OUT THE WAY YOU'D HOPED, AT LEAST THIS TIME AROUND YOU'LL BE ABLE TO MOVE ON—AND SOMEDAY LOOK BACK—WITH ZERO REGRETS.

WEEK 2

Making Your Own Choices

Think for yourself. Whatever is happening at the moment, try to think for yourself.
—Jean Rabat

Your life is the sum result of all the choices you make, both consciously and unconsciously. If you can control the process of choosing, you can take control of all aspects of your life. You can find the freedom that comes from being in charge of yourself.
— Robert F. Bennett

It is always your next move.
— Napoleon Hill

As obvious as it may sound, many people don't realize that our choices are what shape our lives.

At present, the choices with the greatest potential impact on your future would include how hard you're working in school, the types of outside interests you're developing, how you're treating others, and who you're hanging out with. Now reflect for a moment, my student. When it comes to these areas of life, are you the one at the controls, the one calling all the shots? Or are you surrendering your most powerful right—the right to make your own choices?

One of the big reasons I ask is that adolescents have more to overcome with regard to thinking for themselves than members of any other age group. In fact, many adults tend to forget just how influential and unrelenting a group of friends can be.

To illustrate just how formidable a foe peer pressure can be, look no further than the ever-increasing number of your peers using alcohol, cigarettes, and illegal drugs. These trends are especially relevant, not to mention destructive, because nothing compromises the ability to think for oneself more than drugs. If you don't believe it, ask any smoker.

Nicotine simply doesn't allow most people in its grips to escape—no matter how sincere or determined the choice to quit happens to be.

As for alcohol, check out any newspaper on any given day. It doesn't matter where you live, you will find an example of how drinking contributed to a fight, an arrest, or a death. And as you might expect, our prison population consists largely of individuals who made choices while under the influence. Tragically, a significant number wouldn't have made the same ill-fated decisions if they hadn't handed over their control to a drug. Nevertheless, the bad choices were made and they are now left to pay the price, for a long time to come.

Another collection of people who allow their power of choice to be undermined are those who drive while under the influence. For as long as alcohol and vehicles have coexisted, some have brazenly chosen to combine the two. On more occasions than any of us would want to believe, drunk drivers subsequently wake up in hospital beds to a law officer standing over them. Then, upon being informed they're under arrest for causing an accident that took the lives of innocent people, they respond incredulously: "What? There must be some mistake. I would remember something like that; this can't be real!" How pathetic. They can't even recall the incident, let alone their own choice to drive drunk.

The sad fact of the matter is no drinker thinks he or she is going to be the one who ends up causing a crash. The alcohol simply provides a false sense of invincibility, thus impairing an individual's ability to choose. I mean, think about it. Would anyone actually decide to get behind the wheel if they believed they were about to become just another statistic, the next headline in a tragic newspaper story? Of course not. So the half-blind choice to drive under the influence is made. And whether the decision is remembered or not isn't relevant; they instantly become responsible for any horrible event that results.

Hearing about such realities, my student, should prompt you to think long and hard before ever giving up control of your choice-making powers...to anyone or any thing. And remember, while negative peer pressure may be a formidable foe, it *can* be defeated. All it takes—in a head-to-head encounter, if you will—is a little insight on your part.

First, you enter into play your unique awareness of how choices shape lives. This serves to get you out of the blocks and off to a running start. When you then take into account that those who let others choose for them are essentially surrendering their most powerful right, you gain even more of an inside track. Lastly, and just in time for the crucial stretch run, you consider that when you decide to go along with the group—whether it be for the sake of fun or camaraderie—you the individual are left to suffer the consequences alone.

Make no mistake, when you do manage to think for yourself in the face of peer pressure, these are the very moments in which you develop and grow as a person. Oh yes, as much as anything else, it helps to define you as the strong, confident individual you are becoming—someone who has enough intelligence and guts to listen to his own heart, to trust her own instincts, even when it means others will be upset. Moreover, you will be left feeling more self-reliant and "in charge" than ever before. Consequently, the tough choices awaiting all young people won't seem so tough to you.

Remember then, my student, we are each responsible for—and destined to—live the life that our own choices shape...*so challenge yourself to make your own choices.* You can do this.

LIFE APP

THIS WEEK WILL UNDOUBTEDLY PRESENT AN OPPORTUNITY TO APPLY WHAT WE'VE DISCUSSED. MAKE THE COMMITMENT TO YOURSELF TO NEVER AGAIN HAND OVER YOUR CONTROLS. REMEMBER, YOU CALL ALL THE SHOTS.

IMAGINE, FOR EXAMPLE, A GROUP OF FRIENDS ASKING IF THEY CAN COPY YOUR HOMEWORK. WHAT ARE YOU GOING TO DO WHEN YOU KNOW YOUR CHOICE COULD LAND YOU IN SERIOUS TROUBLE? WELL, YOU CAN SHRUG AND SIMPLY STATE YOUR OWN LINE OF CHOICE, E.G., "SORRY, I ALWAYS MAKE MY OWN DECISIONS AND I DON'T WANT TO DO THIS" OR "HEY, IT'S MY LIFE AND I'M THE ONLY ONE AT THE CONTROLS."

JUST REALIZE THAT OTHERS WHO MAY BE ACCUSTOMED TO YOUR GOING ALONG WITH THEM, OR BELIEVE THEY KNOW WHAT'S BEST FOR YOU, WILL REACT IN DIFFERENT WAYS. TAKE COMFORT IN THE KNOWLEDGE THAT ANYONE WHO ENDS A FRIENDSHIP SIMPLY BECAUSE YOU REFUSE TO GO ALONG WAS NOT A TRUE FRIEND TO BEGIN WITH—AND CERTAINLY NOT WORTHY OF YOUR LOYALTY. WHILE, ON THE OTHER HAND, IF SOME IN THE GROUP RESPECT YOUR CHOICE AND ADMIRE YOUR STRENGTH, YOUR CONNECTION TO THEM WILL ONLY GROW STRONGER.

NOW GO SHAPE YOUR LIFE.

WEEK 3

Living with a Grateful Heart

All happy people are grateful. Ungrateful people cannot be happy...
—Dennis Pager

For today and its blessings, I owe the world an attitude of gratitude.
—Clarence E. Hodges

Gratitude unlocks the fullness of life. It turns what we have into enough, and more...
—Melody Beattie

To speak gratitude is courteous and pleasant, to enact gratitude is generous and noble, but to live gratitude is to touch heaven.
—Johannes A Gaertner

If you or someone close to you has been through a life-threatening situation (like a serious illness or accident), you know firsthand just how clear and focused your perspective becomes.

All of a sudden, thoughts of what's truly important and meaningful take control of your mind. Your heart begins to swell with gratitude for all that's good and right in life. Every waking day becomes more of a gift. Each present moment becomes more precious. Even the smallest details of day-to-day life—routine things you often took for granted (e.g., eating a meal with your family or receiving a phone call from a friend)—begin to take on special significance.

But come on, should it really take a near tragedy to wake us up and focus the lenses through which we see things? Of course not, my student. Each of us needs to choose to live more gratefully now.

Now, I'm not claiming that living with a grateful heart is as easy to do as it sounds. On the contrary, I believe it to be quite the challenge. After all, it seems natural, does it not, for each of us to become accustomed to having around all the good things we have in our lives—family members, friends, our possessions, a roof overhead, food on the table, our health, etc. We can easily wind up in an unappreciative comfort zone if we fail to keep tabs on our habits of thought.

Perhaps the ease with which we come to take things for granted helps to explain the mixed-up way in which many perceive day-to-day life. Have you noticed, for example, that no matter how many good things happen in a day—and much of what we experience in a typical day *is* positive, or at least acceptable—people still focus their energies on the one or two negative events that take place? It's safe to assume that even if you've managed to ace a test, enjoy the respect and friendship of others, and win a game—all in a single 24-hour period—you'll still be left thinking and talking mostly about what went wrong, e.g., the incorrect answer you gave, the dirty look one person shot you, or the infield pop-up you hit. Hard to figure, eh?

At one point, my wife and I had developed this habit of zeroing in on negatives. Each night over dinner, we'd end up discussing all that had gone wrong that day: the traffic we hit, the crowd at the grocery store, the student who acted out, the rude note from a parent, the unexpected bill, and on and on. With all the practice, we were getting pretty good at harping on negatives.

It wasn't until after I wrote this particular advisement that we finally began to wake up and refocus our lenses. For the first time we realized we were actually choosing unhappiness, and what's more, that we had no excuse whatsoever for acting ungratefully—not when we were reaping so many personal blessings in a world where millions are suffering from disease, poverty, starvation, and war.

Now, with new habits of thought in place, our nightly conversations have come to reflect far more grateful living. In fact, not a meal goes by without our first offering thanks and then recounting any positives from the day, e.g., a student's accomplishment, the respect of a parent, the friendliness of a neighbor, and on and on. Like anyone else, we still need to get negative things off our chest now and again, but overall, what we choose to think about and discuss is far more balanced. And let me tell you, this simple shift in focus has infused our hearts with higher levels of both happiness and hopefulness.

Isn't it time for you too to establish and enjoy the attitude of gratitude, to finally refocus your own lenses by putting forth a conscious and consistent mental effort? You can get started today with the simple yet empowering practice of listing all that is good and right in your life.

Just remember to include the more "fundamental" gifts, like having a family, a home, food on the table, a loving pet, clothes on your back, good friends, good health, etc. And then there are the more "individual" gifts to add, like your level of intellect, athleticism, perspective on life, dreams, faith, artistic talents, and other personal strengths.

Once your thinking emphasis begins to shift to a more positive direction, you can begin to apply the attitude of gratitude to your daily experiences. (Be sure to list these day-to-day things as well.) For example, instead of focusing on how tired you are when you wake up in the morning, give thanks for the warm bed and the roof over your head—not to mention the fact you're alive and healthy. Rather than gripe about the weekend chores awaiting you, concentrate on the free time you'll enjoy upon completing them. Instead of perseverating over the awful day you had, be grateful for the chance you have to start fresh tomorrow. Or when you're down about a trip coming to an end, shift your thoughts over to how fortunate you are to travel, and to the new memories you'll possess for a lifetime.

In time, you'll find your lenses focusing in on even the smallest details of day-to-day living. You may even start noticing, appreciating, and giving thanks for such things as the smell of your mom's perfume, a favorite song playing on the radio, the glow of a friend's smile, being able to buy new clothes, the calm and quiet of your backyard at night, the sensation of biting into a piece of fruit, or the sound of rain falling outside your bedroom window.

As you come to see, think, and live more gratefully, you can rest assured that you'll not only be surprised by just how much there is to appreciate, but also by how much you end up benefiting. Indeed, there are major upsides to living with a grateful heart:

- Simply put, you become a happier person.
- You stand out in the crowd as that rare someone who sees the big picture and lives each day to the fullest.
- You empower others in your life to become happier, more satisfied, more optimistic people.
- Every day becomes more of the true gift it's meant to be.
- Every life experience—new or routine—becomes more enjoyable and memorable.

- You take more pleasure and inspiration from even the smallest details of life.
- You discover that the habit of focusing in on what's good and right can empower you to overcome even life's biggest challenges.
- You're guaranteed to succeed at finding positives in people and situations—just as those who look for negatives are guaranteed to succeed.
- The quality of your relationships vastly improves. (After all, people know when they're being—or not being—taken for granted and respond accordingly.)
- Inevitable problems and hassles don't seem insurmountable anymore; you handle the stress involved with more perspective and dignity.
- When you prove yourself capable of living gratefully, you open the floodgates for even more good to rush into your life. (Conversely, those who do not appreciate all they are blessed with aren't likely to receive more. And even if they were to, their habits of thought would leave them feeling empty, and again, yearning for more.)
- You personally benefit and grow from searching out the good in others. For example, when you focus on the redeeming qualities of your teachers, you yourself become a more receptive and higher-achieving student. When you focus on the redeeming qualities of your parents, your home becomes a more positive, peaceful place. And when you focus on the redeeming qualities of your friends, you become more loyal and fun to be around.
- Finally, you come to the profound realization that you already have everything you really need to be happy; that you are a wealthy person in the truest sense.

Remember then, my student, the habit of focusing your lenses on what's good and right about life is *the* essential component to becoming a happy, hopeful, truly rich individual…*so challenge yourself to live with a grateful heart*. You can do this.

LIFE APP

IN ADDITION TO LISTING WHAT YOU ARE GRATEFUL FOR EACH DAY, WHY NOT BECOME THE RARE TYPE OF INDIVIDUAL WHO LEADS BY EXAMPLE AND BRINGS TO LIFE FOR OTHERS THE CONCEPT OF GRATEFUL LIVING?

FOR INSTANCE, WHEN TALKING TO THOSE CLOSE TO YOU ABOUT THEIR DAY, YOU CAN MAKE A POINT OF ASKING WHAT WENT *RIGHT* FOR THEM—ANY NICE PEOPLE, GOOD FORTUNE, OR POSITIVE INSPIRATION TO SPEAK OF? DON'T TAKE NO FOR AN ANSWER.

WHEN THESE SAME PEOPLE INSIST ON COMPLAINING, REMIND THEM THAT BECAUSE NO LIFE SITUATION OR PERSON IS PERFECT, THE SEARCH FOR NEGATIVES WILL ALWAYS END IN SUCCESS.

BE MORE GENEROUS WITH THE DOLING OUT OF HANDSHAKES, HUGS, SMILES, AND COMPLIMENTS.

WHEN SOMEONE ELSE—INCLUDING YOUR MOM OR DAD—DOES SOMETHING FOR YOU, LOOK THEM IN THE EYE AND SAY, "THANK YOU, I REALLY APPRECIATE WHAT YOU DID."

OFFER TO SAY GRACE BEFORE MEALS, POINT OUT POSITIVE ALTERNATIVES WHEN PLANS UNEXPECTEDLY FALL THROUGH, VOLUNTEER TO RECAP THE MEMORIES OF A FAMILY TRIP, ETC.

MAKE NO MISTAKE ABOUT IT, BY APPROACHING LIFE FROM THIS PERSPECTIVE, YOU CREATE A WIN-WIN-WIN SITUATION. FIRST, BY PROMPTING OTHER PEOPLE TO LEAD MORE GRATEFUL LIVES, YOU'RE GIVING THEM THE GREATEST GIFT ANYONE CAN GIVE. SECOND, YOU'RE CERTAINLY HELPING TO MAKE YOUR SMALL CORNER OF THE WORLD A BETTER PLACE TO BE. AND LAST, BUT NOT LEAST, YOU ARE BECOMING MORE IN TOUCH WITH ALL THAT'S GOOD AND POSITIVE ABOUT PEOPLE AND LIFE!

WEEK 4

Looking Inward

The ability to accept responsibility is the measure of the man.

—Roy L. Hunt

The vast possibilities of our great future will become realities only if we make ourselves responsible for that future.

—Gifford Pinchot

Nobody can do it for you.

—Ralph Cordiner

There was a student I once had—we'll call him Jason—who was an intelligent kid with great potential, but who achieved lower than average grades and never put forth his strongest effort. He also had a lot of trouble keeping track of homework assignments and class materials.

In one particular instance, Jason forgot to return a failed test that was required to be looked over and signed by a parent. Can you guess what he said the next morning as he approached my desk empty-handed?

"Mr. G, it's my mom's fault—she forgot to sign it."

My response to Jason was one many young people would benefit from hearing: "You have to look inward rather than blame others for your lapses; it wasn't your mother's responsibility, it was yours. If you had walked up to her with pen in hand and said you were expected to return this test tomorrow, I guarantee she would have taken a second and remembered to sign it."

Now in high school, this same student continues to deny all responsibility. In fact, I've recently learned that upon forgetting his band instrument—five times in one month—and being assigned a detention for it, he was actually angry with the teacher, claiming to anyone who would listen, "I got in trouble because she (the teacher) doesn't like me." Clearly, the irresponsible habit of looking outward has become a part of this young person's makeup, and as such, will likely persist for life. It's too bad, for not only will he the individual suffer, but so too will the society in which we all live.

Indeed, my student, our world is a place where drivers who have caused car accidents actually drive away; where fathers choose to play no role in raising the very children they fathered; and where workers I myself have hired show up late—or not at all—for appointments or work. Every one of them is an adult Jason.

The fact is learning personal responsibility isn't easy, especially when it's not being reinforced at home. My most responsible students come from homes where predetermined consequences are in place, where everyone is expected to do their part with regard to chores (in other words, no family members are waited on hand and foot), and where words of encouragement are utilized to point out and reinforce responsible behaviors.

On the opposite end, my most irresponsible students typically come from homes in which little, if any, consistency exists with the doling out of consequences and sharing of household duties. In addition, their parents tend to convey the message that the way their own lives turned out had more to do with outside factors than with personal choices they themselves controlled.

Such circumstances should never be used as an excuse, though. Regardless of what your own home life is like, *you* are ultimately the one in control. Here's a true-to-life account of somebody who did take control.

During the first month of the school year, this young student promptly developed a pattern of forgetful behavior. Things at home weren't going well either, as her parents were close to giving away the dog she was failing to care for.

In spite of such lapses I felt confident about her potential to become responsible. She was the rare type of individual who, each and every time she slipped up, would look me straight in the eye and admit she was at fault, then accept her consequence and vow to learn from the experience.

The consequence of losing her beloved pet, though, was just too much to bear. The following day she came to me very upset—and intent on permanently reversing her irresponsible tendencies. That's right, having recognized the solution to her problems as indeed being within her own control, she asked for specific strategies as to how to make things better.

I responded by telling her that since responsibility is a habit that's developed over time, she would have to—beginning now and continuing on a daily basis—take care of business both in school and at home. Specifically, I suggested the basic strategy of using pen and pad to jot down everything she had to get done on a given day. To hammer the point home, I asked her how she thought I could remember to mail bills, pick up milk, send a birthday card to my aunt, and make the annual vet appointment—not to mention, meet thousands of other obligations—without writing some of it down.

The second key to becoming personally responsible involves a mental reflex she had already proven capable of. When faced with a problem or unwelcome circumstance, the words we should all have pop into our heads are, *I am responsible. How can* I *change this?* Again, it all goes back to the fundamental concept of looking inward.

Putting these basic bits of advice into practice made all the difference in this young girl's development, and it can do the same for you.

Remember then, my student, you and you alone are responsible for creating your personal life circumstances...*so challenge yourself to look inward.* You can do this.

LIFE APP

THIS WEEK, PAY PARTICULAR ATTENTION TO EXAMPLES OF IRRESPONSIBLE BEHAVIOR—IN CLASS, ON TELEVISION, IN THE NEWSPAPER, ON THE PLAYING FIELD, ETC. (IT SHOULDN'T BE TOO LONG A WAIT BEFORE YOU COME ACROSS ONE.) THEN REFLECT ON EACH SITUATION, USING OTHERS' IGNORANCE AND PROCLIVITY TO LOOK OUTWARD TO REINFORCE YOUR OWN COMMITMENT TO BECOMING A MORE RESPONSIBLE, INNER-GUIDED INDIVIDUAL.

LASTLY, CONSIDER HOW YOU CAN APPLY THIS MIND-SET TO REAL LIFE SITUATIONS, AND THEN FOLLOW THROUGH. FOR EXAMPLE, IF YOU ARE NOT HAPPY WITH YOUR GRADES IN SCHOOL, LOOKING INWARD TRANSLATES TO BRAINSTORMING WAYS IN WHICH *YOU* CAN IMPROVE UPON THEM—AS OPPOSED TO USING EXCUSES LIKE THE TEACHER IS TOO TOUGH OR THE SUBJECT MATTER TOO BORING. SIMILARLY, IF A TEAM YOU'RE PLAYING FOR IS NOT ENJOYING MUCH SUCCESS, LEAD BY EXAMPLE, WORKING HARDER TO IMPROVE ASPECTS OF YOUR OWN GAME—RATHER THAN BY BLAMING LOSSES ON TEAMMATES AND COACHES.

WEEK 5

Delaying Gratification

*In reading the lives of great men, I found that the first victory they won was over themselves...*self-discipline *with all of them came first.*
—Harry S. Truman

Delaying gratification is a process of scheduling the pain and pleasure of life in such a way to enhance the pleasure by meeting and experiencing the pain first...It is the only decent way to live.
—M. Scott Peck

Putting off an easy thing makes it hard, and putting off a hard one makes it impossible.
—George H. Lonmer

Procrastination is like a credit card: it's a lot of fun until you get the bill.
—Christopher Parker

As a young kid, my primary chore was to mow the lawn. It was a tough job by kids' standards, and frankly, one I despised. Perhaps it had something to do with the fact my yard was laden with rocks and trees (not to mention, the occasional canine landmine), all of which forced me to employ expert mowing maneuvers for up to two hours or more. And then there were the 95 degree temperatures, those hated horseflies, and...well, you get the point: it was one of the more unpleasant—painful even—parts of my young life.

During the school year, my parents expected me to complete this job-from-you-know-where at some point over the weekend. They suggested I get it done on Saturday mornings, but made it clear it was ultimately my choice. They knew I eventually would do it rather than face the consequences of being grounded and earning no allowance.

What transpired every Saturday morning, however, had little to do with yard work. Instead, my brain would always end up rationalizing, *Now's a great time to go to the beach or to the batting cages. I'll just do the lawn later on.*

But when "later on" came around, there was, of course, some other pleasure to be had. Again, I would justify my choice by thinking something to the effect of, *No big deal, I'll get it done tomorrow morning, right now I'm going to relish in the freedom of doing what I please.*

The funny thing was, my student, as I'd be trying to enjoy my so-called freedom, the thought of having to mow nagged in the back of my mind. It wasn't even my mom or dad doing the nagging, it was my own conscience.

So guess when I ended up doing the job? As darkness crept in...on Sunday night! I hated everything about the situation I had created. I suppose it was this deep-seated negative emotion that finally prompted the proverbial lightbulb to go on overhead.

Understanding the notion that if you don't like the way something is going, then you yourself must do something differently, I tried a new approach. Contrary to what you might be thinking, though, I did not follow my parents' Saturday morning suggestion. I took it one step further—deciding to instead do the lawn when I got home from school on Fridays.

I cannot tell you how incredibly gratifying it was each time I finished the job, knowing I now had almost an entire weekend of extra free time before me. And yes, while there were still moments when I hated the actual mowing aspects, the thought of getting it over with made things far more bearable, even enjoyable at times. This really did mark the point in my life when I became a self-disciplined individual, one who was finally capable of delaying gratification—in all areas of life—and as such, one who was finally capable of fostering true and lasting fulfillment.

When I tell this story in class, I'm regularly amazed and encouraged by how a handful of my young students respond. Right away they want to try the technique themselves. In the cafeteria, for instance, they make a point of no longer partaking in the now common behavior of eating dessert first. At home, they get everything expected of them done prior to heading out. And in the classroom, they ask if it would be possible to do some of the weekly homework assignments in advance.

On the other hand, a large number of students choose not to use this tool in their lives. (Or if they attempt to change, they end up reverting back to old ways soon after.) Why so many young people lack the self-discipline to delay gratification is a compelling question, one we need to examine.

First and most obviously, we live in a world where instant gratification has become the norm. We've got microwaves, computers, fax machines, slot machines, steroids, etc. Wait for something? What's the point? We're now accustomed to getting what we want *fast*. Growing up in this type of drive-thru culture can obviously influence a young person's willingness to sacrifice and show restraint, especially when it's for the sake of some far-off good.

In addition, many parents—also impacted by the ways of the world—have themselves dismissed or never learned the value of delaying gratification. Clearly, this makes it difficult for them to teach and model such a technique at home.

Then there's the matter of so many adolescents blindly embracing the *live for today* mind-set. In an attempt to make their teen years a time to remember, they casually disregard any impact their actions may have on the rest of their lives. (Now don't get me wrong, I'm all for having fun and enjoying our present moments—but our future moments will belong to us as well.) Those lacking in such long-term perspective either don't understand or just don't trust that opportunities for good times will also be present later in life. Consequently, they refuse to put off any pleasure, often developing self-destructive rather than self-disciplined habits.

Having taken a look at some of the reasons why so many do not delay gratification, let's get back to the relative few who do. Uniquely, such individuals refuse to shy away from hard work or suffering, and as a result, create the likelihood they'll someday reap life's biggest rewards.

Case in point: Starting up a personal business can be as fulfilling a work experience as there is, yet it's just too much of an undertaking for some to handle. Most businesses require time and tremendous effort to grow, which translates into long hours and lean times for the risk taker. However, those who are familiar with the concept of delaying gratification are much more apt to remain motivated and continue sacrificing. Because of this, they are also much more likely to make possible, and someday reap, the many benefits of a thriving enterprise.

Another challenge such individuals have been known to take on is medical school. Again, this isn't even an option for the majority of people, since it's extraordinarily demanding and the rewards so far off. Those who do decide to go for it anyway know full well they'll have to work harder than ever before. They accept that there will be limited occasions in which to go out on the town, attend parties, or to catch movies. Yet they *still* take on the challenge because they understand it will all pay off...down the road.

And indeed it will, for not only will they have created the opportunity to earn big salaries, but they'll also be far stronger and wiser human beings for having persevered in the face of rigorous circumstances. Moreover, they will have forged the type of career that provides chance after chance to make a difference touching others' lives. How does "Doctor" sound before your last name?

Remember then, my student, being strong-willed enough to put off pleasure and get the tough part over with first is one of the key qualities of those who create truly rich, rewarding lives...*so challenge yourself to delay gratification.* You can do this.

LIFE APP

FOR ALL THOSE INTERESTED IN DEVELOPING THE CAPACITY TO DELAY GRATIFICATION, I'VE PROVIDED SOME SPECIFIC STRATEGIES HERE. (I'M CERTAIN YOU'LL FIND YOU'RE ALREADY DOING AT LEAST ONE OF THE FOLLOWING, WHICH MEANS YOU'VE ALREADY GOT A JUMP-START ON THE PROCESS.)

1. GET HOUSE/HOMEWORK DONE PRIOR TO ENJOYING ANY LEISURE TIME.
2. GET STARTED—IN EVEN THE SMALLEST WAY—ON A REPORT OR PROJECT THE VERY DAY IT IS ASSIGNED.
3. JOG OR WORK OUT BEFORE SCHOOL IN ORDER TO FREE UP TIME IN THE AFTERNOON AND EVENING.
4. SAVE A PORTION OF EVERYTHING YOU EARN.
5. STUDY LITTLE BY LITTLE, WELL IN ADVANCE OF AN EXAM.
6. MAKE MODERATION A RULE OF THUMB SO AS TO ENSURE OPPORTUNITIES FOR MORE GOOD TIMES IN THE FUTURE.
7. GIVE YOUR BEST EFFORT IN SCHOOL NOW, KNOWING IT WILL ALL PAY OFF FOR YOU DOWN THE ROAD.
8. GET YOUR WEEKEND CHORES DONE EARLY ON.
9. AND PLEASE, SAVE DESSERT FOR LAST. :-)

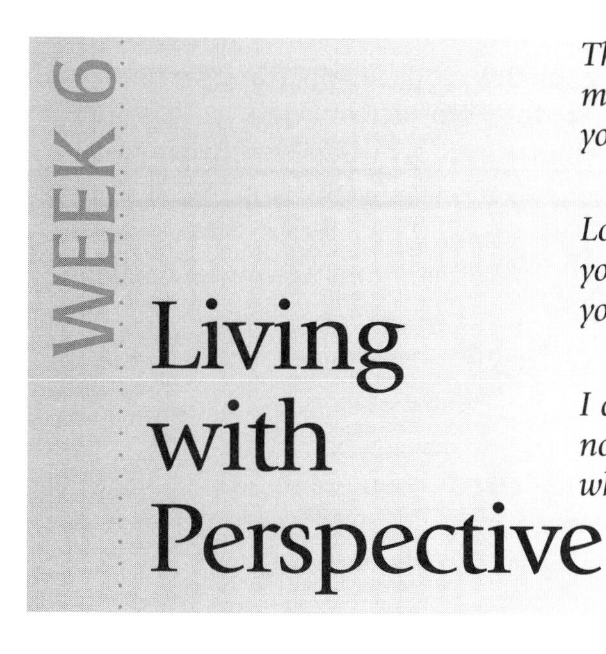

Living with Perspective

The difference between a mountain and a molehill is your perspective.
—Al Neuharth

Look at every situation as if you were in the future and you were looking back on it.
—General Peter Schoomaker

I complained because I had no shoes until I met a man who had no feet.
—Arabic Proverb

Hey, sometimes things in life just don't go the way we'd like. Unforeseeable problems, minor hassles, serious setbacks, and occasional bouts with bad luck are indeed part of the package.

It stands to reason then, my student, that how we respond to unfavorable circumstances will have a whole lot to do with how successful and fulfilling a life we come to create. In spite of all that's at stake, though, the vast majority of us seem intent on responding in self-defeating ways—you know, by complaining, feeling sorry for ourselves, blowing things out of proportion, perseverating, etc. What we need here is a reality check. Or put another way, we need to start approaching life from a more perspective-filled vantage point.

The following insights are intended to foster just such an outlook. We should each work to keep them in mind, especially when the world dares ignore our personal wishes and expectations.

1. The earth itself is over 4 billion years old. If you were to condense all of this time into a 24-hour period, it could be said the human race has been around for a mere 3 seconds. Think about that—3 seconds.

2. In excess of 6 billion individuals call this planet home. Included among this number are people from 7 different continents and 200 or so different countries.

3. There exist among the earth's population, thousands upon thousands of children in third world countries—your age and younger—who work over 100 hours per week. They live in squalor and have no opportunity whatsoever to advance and improve upon their lives.
4. Each and every year, over 7 million children worldwide die before their first birthday.
5. On any given day, a war is actually taking place in some part of the world.
6. In a mere century, each of us will have been replaced. Yes, planet earth will be home to an entirely different 6 billion-plus worth of individuals. (Actually, world population projections have the number of billions tabbed at 9 and higher.)

While insights such as these won't eliminate all pain and stress from our lives, you can certainly see how they can help put our struggles into context—and provide us some comfort. Indeed, the students I know who have adopted this big-picture outlook now view things in a very different light and have benefited tremendously because of it.

Most notably, their shift in focus has enabled them to cut down on the intensity and frequency of self-defeating emotions—and in the process, helped them to become more pleasant, peaceful, happy-go-lucky people. Now things like getting sick, getting dissed, losing a big game, developing a big zit, making a dumb mistake, etc., don't feel like nearly as big a deal.

More than anything, though, living with perspective can lead us to see what's truly important in our lives.

Coincidentally, just as I began work on this advisement, I caught a postgame interview on television that illustrated this very point. A professional basketball player was saying something to the effect that, "Yeah, it was a tough way to end the season—as tough and bitter a loss as there is—but you know what, I'm okay with it; I've come to know what's truly important in life."

He went on to share how in the past he would have reacted much differently, but his experiences traveling the globe—visiting impoverished areas, touching starving children, and walking through disease-ravaged villages—had served to radically change his vision and outlook.

Since then I've heard very few athletes echo the same sentiments. But interestingly enough, every single one of these rare individuals—whether a pro, college, or high school player—was the type who goes all out, who does anything and everything to help their team succeed. It's just that when they do happen to lose, they're able to keep it in proper focus. Even as the sharp sting of defeat remains fresh, they take comfort in the knowledge 100 percent effort was put forth in pursuit of their goals. They also manage to remain grateful—for the opportunities they have to pursue new goals and for the many blessings in their lives.

The biggest challenge I've found, my student, is to hold on to this special feeling, and to live each subsequent day with the same clarity, the same inspiration. Day-to-day life is notorious for weighing us down and shifting our focus away from the big picture, is it not?

Well, you'll be glad to know, a strategy exists that can keep us more in touch with what's truly important.

Whenever I find myself getting bogged down by life's little hassles and losing sight of the big picture, I now stop to reflect on how I want to be remembered. Yes, I actually stop to think about my own funeral. This can lead any individual to ask some all-important questions: *Do I want to be remembered as one who was able to see humor and laugh things off or as a cynic who allowed life to beat me down? As a whiner and complainer or as one who took setbacks and misfortune in stride? As a winner who learned something from problems and mistakes or as one who continuously put himself behind the eight ball? As a person who gratefully lived each day to the fullest or as one who took life for granted and let the wonder of it all pass him by?*

By working such thoughts into your own mind-set, you too can start seeing the big picture with greater clarity and consistency. For example, learning in school may take on greater meaning because you'll now see it as your personal ticket to future success. When you hear others gossiping about someone, you'll see through to the personal insecurities that lie at the root of their behavior. Or perhaps visions of adulthood for you will now involve more than getting a good job and buying a nice house; making the world a better place will also be viewed as a top priority.

On top of all this, the "end in mind" strategy can inspire you to take fewer days and moments for granted. Heck, we may even come to approach life as my close friend—who faced and beat cancer twice—does. He tells me that while it shouldn't have taken a life-threatening disease to open his eyes, he nevertheless lives with ultimate perspective now. Every waking day is perceived as a gift, with even the smallest details of day-to-day life taking on special significance, e.g., eating breakfast with his mom, listening to music on his headphones, sharing a laugh with a buddy, or enjoying a quiet moment staring at the birds outside his window. For him, the picture is now oh-so clear.

Just as this good friend embodies, for me, the ideal of living with perspective, so did the late great Princess Di for the rest of the planet. Here was an individual of great wealth and power who could have easily chosen a life of total leisure. But instead, she insisted on using her position to better the lives of the less privileged. She fought passionately for those who couldn't fight for themselves, and in so doing, made our world a more safe, caring, and compassionate place.

What's more, as a mother she lived every moment spent with her children to the absolute fullest. By all accounts, Diana was a loving, nurturing parent intent on preparing her boys to create full, rewarding lives. To this end, she dedicated herself to passing on a similarly broad and clear perspective. In fact, Prince William often accompanied his mom to poverty-stricken areas within the very borders of the country he is to someday rule.

Certainly, Diana wanted young William to see firsthand just how fortunate and blessed he was. But she also knew with royalty comes tremendous responsibility, and that all these perspective-building experiences would serve to enlarge his mind—as well as his heart. If for no other reason, it's safe to say William, like his mom, will someday make the world a better place for all.

Remember then, my student, those rare individuals who see the big picture are destined to create special lives—lives defined by gratitude, passion, and true fulfillment...*so challenge yourself to live with perspective*. You can do this.

LIFE APP

LEARN "THE LANGUAGE OF" PERSPECTIVE AND BECOME THE RARE TYPE OF PERSON WHO'S ALWAYS READY TO LEND A PERSPECTIVE-PROVIDING QUOTE. BY DOING SO, YOU'LL NOT ONLY ENABLE YOURSELF TO SEE MORE SITUATIONS FROM A MORE WORLDLY VANTAGE POINT, BUT YOU'LL ALSO BECOME A PERSON OTHERS ENJOY AND TAKE COMFORT IN BEING AROUND.

TO THIS END, FAMILIARIZE YOURSELF WITH THE FOLLOWING LIST OF PERSPECTIVE-RELATED SAYINGS, AND BE ON THE LOOKOUT FOR OPPORTUNE TIMES TO SHARE THEM.

1. LIVE EACH DAY TO THE FULLEST.
2. IT IS WHAT IT IS—NO MORE, NO LESS.
3. THINGS HAPPEN.
4. JUST LET IT GO.
5. DON'T SWEAT THE SMALL STUFF.
6. KEEP YOUR PRIORITIES IN ORDER.
7. THAT'S WHAT LIFE'S ALL ABOUT.
8. THIS TOO SHALL PASS.
9. GO WITH THE FLOW.
10. DID YOU LEARN ANYTHING FROM IT?
11. LIGHTEN UP.
12. *QUE SERA, SERA.*
13. MY MOTHER TOLD ME THERE'D BE DAYS LIKE THIS.
14. HERE TODAY, GONE TOMORROW.
15. NO BIGGIE.
16. WHO SAID LIFE'S SUPPOSED TO BE FAIR?
17. WHO SAID LIFE'S SUPPOSED TO BE EASY?
18. IT'S NOT THE END OF THE WORLD.
19. THERE'S ALWAYS TOMORROW.
20. WILL IT MEAN ANYTHING A MONTH FROM NOW?
21. THE SILVER LINING IS...
22. CARPE DIEM.
23. IT COULD BE WORSE.
24. YOU GOTTA DO WHAT YOU GOTTA DO.
25. LIFE GOES ON.

WEEK 7

Thinking of Others, Too

No act of kindness, however small, is ever wasted.

—Aesop

If you do good, people may accuse you of selfish motives. Do good anyway.

—Mother Teresa

In the end, only kindness matters.

—Old Saying

Believe it or not, my student, when it comes to surviving and thriving as a species, ants and bees—yes, ants and bees—have always been two of our planet's premiere performers. Any idea as to why?

Well, it has much to do with the fact that they instinctively form "insect communities." Within such domains, an individual member does not function and work only for itself, but for the good of the entire group. Simply stated, each makes its own contribution to the benefit of all.

In the not-as-different-as-you-might-think people world, it's also vital that each of us play a role in making our community a better place for all. Are we not all connected?

Thinking of others too—on a human level—is not, however, as uncomplicated as it may sound. Especially when you take into account that both the "looking out for number one" and "looking down your nose at others" mind-sets enjoy a growing hold on our society. (For proof, just consider the proliferation of hate crimes, frivolous lawsuits, rampant rudeness, disrespect, and declining charitable contributions.) Indeed, it has become all too easy—almost instinctive—for us humans to get caught up in our individual lives, concentrating solely on personal problems and pursuits.

An all-too-common side effect of growing up in such a culture is something you are likely to be quite familiar with: young people's blatant mistreatment of other young people. For far too long, far too many individuals have deemed it acceptable to be ignorant and cruel. Consider the well-being of others? Yeah, right. In essence, their actions say to the people they choose as targets, "You're not as worthy or important as we are; you and your feelings don't count; we are not connected in any way." I call this "false empowerment"—making oneself feel superior by putting others down.

I've seen this kind of thing firsthand, too. Back when I was in middle school, there was this kid—I'll refer to him as Artie—who, year after year, ended up in the same homeroom as me. Artie was from the wrong part of town, wore the wrong kind of clothes, was in special ed classes, talked kinda funny, and had no friends.

Well, one day in seventh grade, four of my buddies—who routinely teased Artie and others—were back at it again. And as usual, I was laughing along...with the intent of acting like one of the guys. No big deal, I thought. Heck, it didn't even seem to be bothering the kid as he too was laughing.

But this one particular time, Artie happened to tilt his head my way and I happened to catch a glimpse of something that haunts me to this day. There was an entire boatload of tears welled up in his eyes.

Somehow, though, Artie bravely managed to hold them back as not one drop made it down his cheek—and nobody else ever saw.

That night as I lay in bed, I vowed to myself I'd never again be party to picking on or putting down another person—*ever*. Truth be told, I had never allowed myself to think about what it must really feel like to be on the receiving end.

In time, I began standing up for Artie and others like him who were picked on for being different. My plea to the perpetrators evolved into the following: "If you would take just one minute to think of the other person, you'd be able to see they didn't choose to be born with problems. Besides, life can be tough enough for all of us, so what's the point in tearing people down further? What kind of person would want to cause even more pain and difficulty?"

For what it's worth, my personal relationship with Artie was also transformed. I can't say we became best friends or anything, but throughout our high school years whenever we crossed paths, I'd smile and we'd high-five one another. There were even some times when we ate together in the cafeteria.

Many years later, I met Artie again as I was driving through my hometown. And let me tell you, the once young and awkward kid had changed considerably. He looked physically stronger, was far more self-assured in conversation, and had a certain glow about him—an undeniably positive one. You would never have known that this was the same once-miserable teenager. What's more, I learned he was now an effective and highly regarded volunteer at a local camp for kids with emotional problems. *How incredibly admirable,* I thought to myself.

I also discovered something else of great value that day. Right there on the side of the road, Artie admitted that my smiles and high-fives were the only ones he'd ever received from a peer. And that our exchanges had provided him with initial doses of encouragement and self-confidence—enough of a foundation for him to build upon as he battled to make something more of his life. (The funny thing is, I felt—and still feel—our interactions ended up empowering me as much as they did him.)

I guess it's fair to say then, my student, one can never know just how far-reaching an impact even the simplest acts of kindness can have on another's life.

You would have to agree now that treating others with thoughtfulness and respect is perhaps the easiest and most influential way for any of us humans to contribute to the benefit of all, would you not? Excellent, because it just so happens that there are an unlimited number of kind acts just waiting to be discovered and implemented.

With this thought in mind, I often advise my students in class that on the nights they cannot fall asleep, to make the most of the time by thinking up simple ways in which they can touch another person's life. To assist yourself in the process, simply reflect on questions like: *Who do I know in need of a boost? What specific compliments can I give tomorrow? How would I feel if* I *were the kid in class who just moved here? How can I spread, and at the same time, experience what Mr. G calls "real empowerment"?* Not only will you generate a positive plan of action, but before you know it, you'll be waking up—refreshed and inspired—to a new day. Try it.

A couple of my former students who did try it, capitalized on their productive nights of unrest and admirably followed through on their ideas. One ended up collecting over 140 pairs of shoes for the homeless of a nearby city, while his counterpart managed to raise thousands of pennies to donate to a children-with-cancer organization. Talk about individuals making a difference in the lives of others.

Other young people have chosen to carry out less visible but just as meaningful acts. Things like smiling at those who rarely get smiled at, sitting next to that person nobody sits next to, and complimenting the kids nobody seems to compliment. Again, you should try doing one, for you'll soon discover that both the giver and receiver experience "real empowerment"—the kind that can, as it did with Artie, change the entire course of a life.

Remember then, my student, in order to survive and thrive as a species we must fight the instinctive tendency to become self-absorbed, and work to contribute to the benefit of all...*so challenge yourself to think of others, too.* You can do this.

LIFE APP

IF YOU ARE SERIOUS ABOUT MAKING THE WORLD A BETTER PLACE FOR OTHERS—AND WANT TO HAVE FUN WHILE DOING IT—BEGIN TO PERFORM MORE RANDOM ACTS OF KINDNESS. THAT'S RIGHT, ONCE A DAY, ONCE A WEEK, OR EVEN JUST ONCE A YEAR, SECRETLY DO SOMETHING NICE FOR ANOTHER PERSON.

YOU MIGHT WANT TO LEAVE A QUARTER FOR THE NEXT CALLER AT A PAYPHONE, CLEAN UP A NEIGHBOR'S SIDEWALK WHEN AN ANIMAL GETS INTO HIS GARBAGE, OR SOLICIT DONATIONS FOR A LOCAL FAMILY IN NEED. TRULY, YOUR OPTIONS CAN BE LIMITED ONLY BY A LACK OF SPONTANEITY AND/OR IMAGINATION.

AND REST ASSURED, THE "REAL EMPOWERMENT" RESULTING FROM YOUR HEARTFELT ACTS WILL ENRICH THE LIVES OF *ALL* INVOLVED.

WEEK 8

Knowing What You Stand For

The outer conditions of a person's life will always be found to reflect their inner beliefs.
—James Lane Allen

What lies behind us and what lies before us are small matters compared to what lies within us.
— Ralph Waldo Emerson

As you live your values, your sense of identity, integrity, control, and inner directedness will infuse you with both exhilaration and peace. You will define yourself from within, rather than by people's opinions or by comparisons to others.
—Stephen Covey

Live your beliefs and you can turn the world around.
—Henry David Thoreau

Take some time, my student, to reflect on what exactly it is you value, e.g., kindness, courage, loyalty, discipline, originality. It's crucial you do so, considering that your values impact nothing less than how you think and how you act. Indeed, your values lie at the root of who you are and what you're all about as an individual!

In spite of the high stakes, though, would you believe that most kids, and many adults, travel through life without ever stopping to consider what they believe in? Yes, and as a result, their potential for personal growth and happiness often ends up—you guessed it—wasted.

Do you think, for example, that your peers who get into more than their fair share of trouble ever take the time to reflect on what they stand for? Their actions say: "We believe in doing just about anything to be accepted or thought of as cool" and "We value lying to avoid consequences; sacrificing our education and future to be class clowns; stealing on a whim; and letting others make our choices for us." "We even go so far as to believe in using violence to solve problems and making the world a worse place to live."

Think about what your actions say about your values. Have you reflected on what's truly important in life lately? The big-time benefits include:

1. You make better choices.
2. You're far more apt to continue growing and evolving into a confident, sure-minded individual.
3. You're much more likely to succeed at creating a rich and rewarding life.
4. Your self-image and levels of self-confidence rise.
5. Others are more likely to respect, admire, and look to you for leadership.
6. And most powerfully, when you know who you are, you have all it takes to become who you want to be.

With all this in mind, let's do some reflecting of our own. The following are examples of basic values. See whether any of them are worthy of becoming part of (or continuing as part of) your own life.

- *Being kind and friendly*. There's no question if everyone treated others the way they like to be treated—certainly sounds simple enough—the world would be a better place for all. But even if it's naive to believe 100 percent of the population will ever live according to the Golden Rule, why shouldn't we as individuals attempt to make our own small corners of the world more neighborly and pleasant places?

- *Being honest and trustworthy*. Many of us have learned the hard way that friends and parents get much less disappointed and angry when a mistake is owned up to. What's more, in the long run, lying just leads to more lies, more distrust, and more trouble for you.

- *Having courage and taking risks*. Let it be clear that when you try something new and unfamiliar, it's completely normal to feel nervous or fearful. The essence of courage lies in acknowledging such feelings and then *doing it anyway*. And each time you do manage to follow through, you'll find yourself filled with growth-inducing levels of pride, inspiration, and confidence.

- *Respecting elders*. We've all learned firsthand that life can be quite difficult at times. It stands to reason, then, those who've lived longest have usually had to endure and battle through more

> adversity and suffering than the rest of us. If for no other reason, they deserve our sincere respect. Growing up, I for one lived by this belief, and as a result, enjoyed interactions and relationships many of my peers did not—and I wouldn't trade even one of these unique experiences for anything.

Good stuff, eh? It's not enough, however, to merely reflect on or pay lip service to sound values—actions must, of course, accompany every one.

Let's assume you've come to the realization that *keeping your family unit peaceful and strong* is a value you wish to prioritize. In order to make it come alive, you would need to take specific action. You could start by saying "I love you" more frequently. You can be more generous with the doling out of smiles and hugs. Maybe you could do an extra weekly chore (one you're not already responsible for) without even being asked. When a younger sibling is doing his or her best to get on your nerves, simply get yourself out of the house for a while instead of unleashing a physical or verbal assault. Or finally, you can make a point of just sitting and hanging out more often with individual family members.

If, as another example, you possess a heightened sense of justice and believe in *standing up for others,* your actions again need to be properly aligned. For instance, on the occasions you see some friends harassing another individual, you might say something to the effect of, "Knock it off. You certainly wouldn't appreciate it if you were the ones being targeted by a group of older guys." (Perhaps you've taken a stand like this before.)

Or, if you recognize the value of *having good manners* and of *being polite,* your actions may include something as basic as holding a door open for the person walking behind you. Even the simple gesture of saying "please" or "thank you" can serve to brighten another's day, and on a grander scale, spread a sense of hope and optimism for the future among older people.

The neat thing about acting in accordance with your values, my student, is that eventually it becomes second nature, instinctual behavior. This means all that you stand for becomes the biggest, most undeniable part of who you are. And once this change takes place, watch out. For it will mark the time in your life when you transform into an even more secure, an even more grounded, an even more unstoppable individual.

Following is a true account of how strong, ingrained values transformed and served me in the past—and can serve you now.

One afternoon, as I walked home from the practice field, a group of older guys—none of whom I knew very well—called out my name. Upon exchanging a "what's up" with them, they proceeded to try to pressure me into getting high. It was, to say the least, the type of situation no kid in middle school wants to find him- or herself in.

But in all honesty, knowing what I stood for (*following my heart* and *making my own choices*), what I believed in (*being health conscious* and *treating my body as a temple*), and what I prioritized *(keeping my family unit peaceful and strong)*, empowered me to promptly walk away, with head held high. That's right, in what was a particularly tough spot, I was able to fall back on established values and say no. My choice was made easy by the fact I'd previously gotten in touch with, and acted according to, what I valued.

Imagine, again, those young people who never bother to do this—those who unwittingly stand for *doing anything to be accepted, letting others make their choices for them,* etc. You know they would have caved to the pressure and said yes.

Remember then, my student, in order to be true to your beliefs and values, one must first take the time to get in touch with them...*so challenge yourself to know what you stand for*. You can do this.

THIS WEEK, SIMPLY GENERATE A LIST OF WHAT IT IS YOU VALUE. HAVING TO GET IT ALL DOWN ON PAPER WILL FORCE YOU TO DIG DEEP AND REFLECT, WHILE PROMPTING YOU TO START ACTING ACCORDINGLY.

(AS AN OPEN-MINDED INDIVIDUAL COMMITTED TO PERSONAL GROWTH, YOU MAY NEED TO UPDATE THIS LIST PERIODICALLY.)

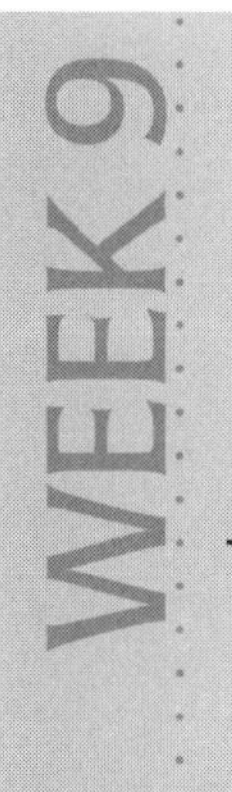

Valuing Mistakes

Remember, even monkeys fall out of trees.
—Korean Proverb

Whenever you fall, pick something up.
—Oswald Avery

Good judgment comes from experience. Experience comes from bad judgment.
—Evan Hardin

Think back to the last time you made a mistake. Did you react negatively, perhaps even muttering something sarcastic like, "Smooth move, stupid" under your breath? If so, you're not seeing mistake making as the valuable—yes, I said valuable—aspect of life that it is.

It's perplexing to me how mistakes ever came to earn such a bad rap. After all, my student, at one point or another, we all mess up. This statement alone should cast a more positive light on mistakes, yet the majority of young people still seem intent on beating themselves up whenever they make one. Maybe it has something to do with our not wanting to come across as fallible or inadequate, even though we're human. Well, whatever the reason, it's finally time to refocus the lenses through which we see mistakes.

To this end, I'm going to go so far as to encourage you to actually feel proud of your blundering ways. That's right, because the people making the most mistakes are quite frequently the ones living life to the fullest, the ones who are completely open to new experiences and routinely take positive risks—all for the sake of personal growth. Conversely, those individuals who mess up on a less frequent basis are likely to be playing things too safe—afraid to fail and afraid to look bad.

You've probably seen examples of this play out in class. Students who are passionate about learning and growing may, on occasion, ask questions that seem obvious to others, or even offer inaccurate answers now and then. But they refuse to change their ways, recognizing that gaining knowledge in the end is more important than any goof-up along the way.

Then there are those individuals you know who don't say much of anything in class. They are hesitant to speak up, partly because they are afraid of being wrong. And due to this fear of sounding stupid or inadequate, they instead choose to take on the powerless role of bystander. If only such students could see things through different lenses; they'd come to recognize that in learning—and living—mistakes are normal, not to mention necessary…something to learn from, not something to beat yourself up over.

Of course, there are other kinds of mistakes, too. I'm talking about the ones that are precipitated by poor choices. Ugh. Contrary to what you may be thinking, though, these aren't necessarily the type you should beat yourself up over, either. A "poor-choice mistake" is usually symptomatic of a lack of life experience and the ignorance that goes along with it. Put another way, you're making a reasonable choice based on what you know and what you've been exposed to up to that particular point in your life.

Case in point: Sticking to the school-example theme, a friend of mine in high school was once caught cheating on a major exam. It was clearly the wrong choice to make, but at that time in his life, he didn't perceive it to be such a big deal. Sure, he, like so many of us who have messed up, should have known better and should have been able to anticipate the results of his actions. But he didn't.

Here was an all-around great kid who had never cheated before, let alone been caught. He hadn't even been exposed to someone else being caught and punished. It wasn't until his own experience began to unfold—complete with very real emotions and consequences—that he grasped just how serious an infraction it was. His parents were called in to meet with the principal and teacher; the person he cheated off of was also given a grade of zero; and his good reputation among both students and teachers was permanently tarnished.

As you would expect, all of this made an overwhelming impression on my friend. He could not believe how shortsighted and naive he had been—and he proceeded to beat himself up pretty badly over it. I wish I had known enough back then to say something supportive like,

"Hey, we all make bad choices. And now that you have a more complete awareness, you know you're the type of person who will never do it again. Besides, you should consider yourself fortunate for having learned so much from a mistake that didn't cost you or anyone else life or limb."

(For what it's worth, this friend never did make the same mistake again. And to this day, he claims the experience prompted him to become an overall more responsible person, someone who considers the issue of right versus wrong *before* acting, as well as someone who now uses others' mistakes and awareness to fill the gaps in his own life experiences.)

All of what we've covered up to this point should have you rethinking how you'll respond to mistakes. Ideally, "live and learn" will now become your personal motto so as to avoid repeating any poor-choice blunders. And certainly, when it comes to mistakes of the more well-intentioned variety, you will no longer be the type of person who wastes time wishing she hadn't even tried in the first place—just because things didn't go according to plan. Rather than be upset about faltering, you'll just learn from it and move forward, secure in the knowledge that mistakes are a necessary byproduct of taking risks and evolving as a human being.

And one last change: You should never again beat yourself up, nor obsess, over past failures or lapses in judgment—even when certain adults seem to insist on it. Comments you may have already faced, like "How could you?" and "You should feel ashamed of yourself," will now serve only as fuel to move forward. And when your peers laugh at or judge you for messing up, you'll recognize that they're still viewing mistakes with clouded lenses. You can assume that either they've never been exposed to the insights we're discussing here, or that they are simply in denial about their own capacity to commit errors.

The bottom line regarding how you should now respond to mistakes is reflected in a piece of frank advice I often share with young people: *Winners, with heads held high, make a point of learning from mistakes…while losers, with heads hanging low, continue making the same ones over and over again.*

Which path you'll take is, of course, entirely your choice.

One might think every individual on the planet would make a point of adhering to the winner's blueprint. But as you've likely picked up on, it's a case of easier-said-than-done for many.

Consider, if you will, the number of families who pass down self-defeating behaviors—sometimes for generations on end. For example, alcoholic and/or abusive parents who raise children that grow up to be veritable carbon copies; teenaged moms and dads whose children eventually become young, unwed parents themselves; and children of parents who suffered from health problems due to smoking or horrendous eating habits, who eventually decide to light up or consume the same diet.

Granted, complex factors are at work in such scenarios, but until an individual learns enough from the dysfunction—and many have—to say, "Hey, things don't have to be this way for me too," the vicious cycle will continue on unbroken. I know the mistakes passed down in my own family will end with me—period. How about yours?

Consider also what we can learn from our peers.

When I was in high school, my senior class was addressed by a 20-year-old girl who had tragically been paralyzed from the neck down. With incredible courage, she spoke of the night she had consumed a few beers and got behind the wheel of her new car. Although her voice began to tremble, she continued on, sharing every detail leading up to the terrible accident that she had caused.

This one graphic account imparted enough in the way of experience and awareness to deter two of my close friends and me from ever considering drinking and driving—we certainly didn't need to experience the horrible consequences firsthand in order to learn the lesson. For several others, however—who had witnessed the exact same speech (but through obviously different lenses)—it wasn't even enough to stop them from doing it again that weekend. Go figure.

Remember then, my student, when on the path to personal growth, properly focused lenses can transform any kind of human error into the most powerful and effective of teachers...*so challenge yourself to value mistakes*. You can do this.

LIFE APP

THE NEXT TIME YOU MAKE A MISTAKE, SIMPLY STATE, "I MESSED UP," AND THEN LEARN SOMETHING FROM IT.

TRY IT. NO EXPLANATIONS, NO EXCUSES, NO MITIGATING CIRCUMSTANCES—JUST AN OPEN MIND AND TOTAL RESPONSIBILITY.

SOUNDS SIMPLE ENOUGH, BUT CARRYING OUT THIS ADVICE WILL REQUIRE THE RARE COMBINATION OF GUTS AND WISDOM. INDEED, ADMITTING YOU'RE WRONG AND THEN LEARNING FROM IT IS A MARK OF TRUE MATURITY, THE MARK OF A SPECIAL INDIVIDUAL DEDICATED TO ACHIEVING HIS OR HER FULL POTENTIAL.

FOR COUNTER EVIDENCE OF THIS POINT, TAKE NOTICE OF THOSE AROUND YOU WHO SEEM INCAPABLE OF ADMITTING ERROR, WHO INSTEAD REACT TO SLIP-UPS BY OFFERING UP EXCUSE AFTER EXCUSE—FAILING TO LEARN ANYTHING AT ALL FROM THEM. ADULT OR YOUNG PERSON, I BET THEY CAN BE DESCRIBED AS IRRESPONSIBLE, IMMATURE INDIVIDUALS WITH LIMITED PROSPECTS FOR PERSONAL GROWTH, HAPPINESS, AND SUCCESS.

WEEK 10

Choosing Enthusiasm

There is real magic in enthusiasm. It spells the difference between mediocrity and accomplishment.
— Norman Vincent Peale

Enthusiasm is the greatest asset in the world. It beats money, power, and influence.
—Henry Chester

...As long as enthusiasm holds out, so will new opportunities.
—Norman Vincent Peale

Have you ever attended a sporting event and witnessed enthusiasm in action? Consider the rare kind of player you've known who cheers his teammates on, who encourages them even when they screw up, who, although he doesn't even get a lot of playing time, can be seen as a leader. How so? Because he is putting his enthusiasm to work in the best possible way. He's making the game more exciting and fun for himself and his teammates, and quite likely influencing its outcome.

Well, my student, despite what you may have always assumed about this person and others like him, the quality of enthusiasm has not been magically bestowed. No, it is—like any other trait, positive or negative—a direct product of individual choice. That's right, when the choice is consistently made over time, enthusiasm can eventually become part of who you are—a personal habit. And, man, what an empowering habit it is.

Have you ever gotten totally enthused about something you were partaking in? I bet it was a time in your life when you felt completely alive, inspired, engrossed, and content. And I bet you did one helluva job. Enthusiasm, after all, has always produced such powerful results.

Without enthusiasm, for example, I myself could never have planned, written, rewritten (several times over), and had this book published—not in a million years. As a teacher, there is no other type of student who I'll so gladly go the extra mile for than the one who, on a day-to-day basis, asks questions, listens intently, gives 100 percent effort, and energetically participates in class discussions. In the world of work, there's not a boss out there who doesn't weigh heavily an individual's levels of enthusiasm before choosing from a pool of potential employees. And in the world of relationships, there's no other personal quality more responsible for sparking connections with good people and enabling you to keep them in your life.

With all this in mind, reflect now for a moment on those people you know to be winners, those who have emerged from the pack and stand out in life. It can either be someone you know personally like a friend, teacher, doctor, or coach; or it can be someone more renowned like a movie star, musician, athlete, or politician. I guarantee you'll be able to say the same thing about each individual on your list: *They approach each new day and each new challenge with renewed levels of enthusiasm.*

Indeed, choosing enthusiasm has always been a character trait of winners. And it's not difficult to understand why when you consider the long list of payoffs.

1. Anything and everything becomes possible.
2. You become a more fun and interesting person, thus allowing you to connect with others on a deeper, more meaningful level.
3. It keeps you on track, motivating you to work harder to get things done.
4. Because it adds spice and substance to everything you do, you come to better appreciate the process of getting things done.
5. With it, you can overcome personal shortcomings and do great things; without it, even the most gifted and talented individuals won't achieve their dreams.
6. Your levels of both optimism and gratefulness increase.
7. You become a tougher, more resilient and self-reliant person.
8. It inspires you to take your personal abilities to the next level.
9. You inspire others around you to work harder at increasing their own levels of enthusiasm.
10. It fills your mind and heart with good ideas and good intentions.

11. Because it empowers you in such a profound way, you're more apt to endure and rise above mistakes, problems, setbacks, etc.
12. You start to notice and appreciate "the little things," thus greatly enhancing the overall quality of your life.
13. Doors that otherwise would have remained closed suddenly start to open wide.
14. It enables *you yourself* to emerge from the pack and stand out as a rare winner in life.

On the flip side, my student, are those who by failing to choose enthusiasm, unwittingly develop opposing habits—habits of the negative, self-defeating variety. And just like before, I'm sure you know the type: someone who goes through the motions and tends to carry himself in a down-and-out sort of way; someone who takes a lot for granted and tends to complain about even trivial matters; someone who acts as though he doesn't care much about anything in or out of school, and won't even try, much less get excited about new experiences.

Of course, it can be said that we've all been guilty of such behaviors at one time or another. The difference, though, is some people—those who fail to recognize that individual choice dictates behavior—allow non-enthusiasm to become a daily habit . . . a part of who they are. And as you also know, being in the presence of such people can be a serious drag.

Clearly, you have an important choice to make as to which path you'll travel down. If you're intent on emerging from the pack, I've included some specific examples of what choosing enthusiasm can translate to:

1. While non-enthusiasts tend to drag themselves out of bed in the morning—and choose to mull over in a negative, pessimistic kind of way all they must do that day—enthusiasts first give thanks for their blessings and then pop up, thinking instead about the many opportunities the day holds.
2. Non-enthusiasts may summon the occasional strength to lift their heads to offer a halfhearted greeting, but enthusiasts will look you in the eye, smile, shake your hand with conviction, and say something to the effect of, "Hey, it's great to see you."

3. In a similar context, when someone asks in passing, "How are you," a non-enthusiast may mumble a reply without looking up. While, on the other hand, someone who is choosing enthusiasm would again look the other person in the eye and say, "Excellent, couldn't be better," and reciprocate by asking the same question. (Try it, even when you're not feeling so excellent. You'll find by spreading an appreciation and zest for simply being alive, your own levels of enthusiasm will rise. In addition, your chosen response will likely deter others from responding with their usual list of gripes.)
4. A non-enthusiast in, say, an art museum tends to walk through mindlessly gazing at each exhibit, while an enthusiast would manage to squeeze every ounce of good from the unique experience. Specifically, she may make a point of staring purposefully, of asking questions, of noticing the little details, of oohing and aahing, and of gleaning a measure of personal inspiration.
5. Non-enthusiastic students may show up for class and go through the motions, but enthusiasts put their whole heart and soul into it. Specifically, they make a point of listening intently to both teachers and classmates, of getting involved by raising their hands and speaking their minds, of concentrating fully on any task before them, and of putting in the time and effort required outside the classroom as well.
6. Non-enthusiastic athletes may show up to play and go through the motions, but enthusiasts put their whole heart and soul into it. Specifically, they make a point of working extra hard in practice, of cheering on teammates in good times and in bad, of hustling and leaving everything they have on the field, and in the end—win or lose—of looking their opponents in the eye and congratulating them.

Certainly, further examples of choosing enthusiasm can be applied to just about any life situation—to things like playing a musical instrument, conversing with a friend, reading a book, learning a new game such as chess, shopping for oneself or others, looking through a telescope, eating a meal, doing chores, listening to the radio...and on and on. But the bottom line remains the same: *Get into whatever it is you're doing,* for this one simple choice—made consistently over time—can empower anyone to create a rich, extraordinary life.

Remember then, my student, when aspiring to emerge from the pack and stand out as a true winner in life, there's one habit you must be able to call your own...*so challenge yourself to choose enthusiasm.* You can do this.

LIFE APP

THIS WEEK, LEAD BY EXAMPLE AND START BRINGING TO LIFE ANY OR ALL OF THE EXAMPLES OF ENTHUSIASM WE'VE COVERED. THEN AS TIME GOES ON, WORK TO APPLY THE HABIT OF CHOOSING ENTHUSIASM TO ALL SORTS OF SITUATIONS.

REST ASSURED YOUR EFFORTS WILL NOT ONLY EMPOWER YOU, BUT ALSO ALL THOSE WHO HAPPEN TO BE IN YOUR PRESENCE. (AND BELIEVE ME WHEN I TELL YOU, THIS IS A VERY GOOD THING CONSIDERING THE NUMBER OF NON-ENTHUSIASTIC PEOPLE IN THE WORLD.)

WEEK 11

Searching for the Bright Side

It is important to live each day with a positive perspective. It is not wise to pretend problems don't exist, but it is wise to look beyond the problem to the possibilities that are in it. When Goliath came against the Israelites, the soldiers all thought, "He's so big, we can never kill him." But David looked at the same giant and thought, "He's so big, I can't miss him."

—Dr. Dale E. Turner

A person's mental health is determined by his propensity to see the good in every situation.

– Ralph Waldo Emerson

A pessimist sees the difficulty in every opportunity; an optimist sees the opportunity in every difficulty.

—Sir Winston Churchill

Because life is far from being perfect, finding the bright side isn't always easy advice to carry out. But it's exactly because life is so far from perfect, my student, that we need to.

Consider as your motivation those who do not: Day after day, their minds focus in on all that goes badly in their lives and the world itself, e.g., "Great, I've got so much to do already, and now this," "Surprise, surprise, more reports of corruption and pollution in the news," and "What *else* could possibly go wrong for me today?"

It's only a matter of time before negativity and cynicism permanently course through their veins. Thus, their hearts, along with any hope of creating a rich, fulfilling life, end up turning to stone. They have come to see the proverbial cup of life as half empty—and there's nothing anyone else can do to change it.

Now consider those who instead consciously focus their minds on the positive and good, e.g., "Hey, I've handled challenges like this before so I know I can get it all done," "I'm going to continue doing what *I* can to make my small corner of the world a better place," and "Things are *bound* to start turning around for me now."

For these people, it's only a matter of time before hopefulness and gratitude build up to such empowering levels that the ideals of doing good in the world, and of being happy and personally fulfilled become realities. Indeed, they've unlocked the secret to developing the most powerful of all traits—optimism.

It's just not possible for me to overstate the value of developing optimism. Not when you realize all the other things we "hopeful spirits" or "half fullers" prove capable of, e.g., being grateful, valuing mistakes, keeping the faith, following dreams, seeing the wonder of it all, building up self-esteem, minimizing stress, maximizing present moments, viewing problems as challenges, taking positive risks, maintaining perspective, connecting with positive people, living with enthusiasm, expecting to succeed, doing our part, learning something from everyone, bringing into being promising opportunities, reacting to setbacks with even higher levels of determination.

Am I saying that those with a pessimistic attitude aren't apt to do these same things? You bet I am. So let them continue labeling us as naive and unrealistic—whatever; we'll just continue to grow and get things done with our positive attitudes guiding the way.

If you are concerned about not yet being an optimistic person, take heart. You see, most adults who aren't, turned out this way simply because they were never advised to think or act otherwise. As a result, negativity was allowed to slowly build up over the years and become a bigger and bigger part of who they are.

But now that you've been made aware of the far-reaching value of searching for the bright side, you can get started right away on changing your personal habits of thought. What's more, there's an old Spanish proverb that essentially says when you're young, bad habits are like cobwebs, because they can be broken with a simple swipe of the hands, or a small amount of effort. As you grow older, though, these habits become more like steel cables which, as you know, are almost impossible to break—regardless of how hard you try.

With this thought in mind, think long and hard about how to react the next time life doesn't go your way. It could, after all, mark the moment you clear some cobwebs of your own and start on the less traveled path toward optimism and fulfillment.

As you strive to become more positive, you should also know there are other circumstances working in your favor. Despite what some would have you believe, a bright side can almost always be uncovered—even when it comes to life's problems and hassles.

Cases in point:

1. It's the weekend and you're broke...*Here's a chance to spend some time with family doing the simple things you used to love to do together.*
2. Your team suffers a season-ending loss...*You're inspired to come back next year stronger and hungrier than ever. (Besides, you finally get a break from those early-morning and/or late-day practices.)*
3. You're stuck at home sick...*It's not life-threatening. (Plus, you have someone there who cares enough to pamper and wait on you.)*
4. Your girl/boyfriend breaks up with you...*It's an opportunity to spend more time with friends—and perhaps meet someone even more special.*
5. You fail a test...*It's a wake-up call to become more serious about asking questions, taking notes, studying in advance, etc. (And at least it wasn't a final exam.)*

With regard to this last example, many young people I work alongside tend to respond with a much different attitude, oblivious to the notion that there could even exist an upside. You probably know a student or two like this yourself. They're the ones who react to failure by avoiding the subject even more, and don't try at all the next time around. They can then rationalize that it's now due to the fact no effort was put forth. You can see how their negative take on things protects them for the time being, but will certainly hurt them in the long run.

By now you may be thinking to yourself, *Okay, Mr.G, I can see the value of searching for the bright side; I'll work at it. But what about when something more serious goes down—am I to truly expect that I'll find something positive then?*

It's a point well taken. First let me say, though, it's the attempt that matters most. Remember, you're working to forge new, more empowering habits of thought—and this act of consistently looking for positives is the key to doing so!

However, I will grant you that it won't always be easy. There will indeed be lots of times when you have to search for even the semblance of a bright side. Furthermore, it's normal to not always want to. I know, for example, when my adored dog died, I needed time to cry and grieve and be angry; the notion of becoming optimistic couldn't have been further from my mind.

But with time, I was able to finally start thinking in a more positive, hopeful way, e.g., *I have so many special memories of her that will never die; she's no longer in any pain; we were both blessed in that she lived a long, happy life.*

Even the most senseless and tragic of all life events, when given more thought and time, can offer us something positive...something hopeful. No one will ever forget the terrorist attacks on the World Trade Center and the Pentagon; a more horrific and evil plot you will not encounter. Well, understandably, many of my students in class back then were perplexed and shaken by this man-made disaster—as was I, of course. It was a traumatizing time for all.

But what finally did provide some measure of comfort was the positive, hopeful observation many made. It was pointed out that while only a relative few evil individuals had caused the tragedy, millions upon millions of good people united and responded to it.

A massive outpouring of concern and compassion did indeed emanate from every pocket of the globe—in the form of grief, prayers, flowers, messages of solidarity, food, blood, and fiscal donations. And more locally, armies of firefighters, police, rescue teams, doctors, nurses, construction workers, National Guard members, Red Cross/Salvation Army/United Way volunteers, iron cutters, and EMTs selflessly worked and searched for months on end. These members of the human race came together—risking their own lives in order to save the lives of others—and in so doing, reaffirmed for all of us that in a world capable of anything, there will always be far more positive and good.

Remember then, my student, choosing an optimistic attitude makes all good things possible—including the productive, fulfilling life so few pessimists ever attain...*so challenge yourself to search for the bright side.* You can do this.

LIFE APP

AT SOME POINT THIS WEEK, YOU WILL HAVE TO CHOOSE YOUR RESPONSE TO A LIFE EVENT. WHETHER IT TURNS OUT TO BE SOMETHING AS SIGNIFICANT AS A SEASON-ENDING SPORTS INJURY OR AS MINOR AS A RAIN-DOMINATED FORECAST, BEGIN WORK ON THE CRITICAL HABIT OF FINDING A BRIGHT SIDE. JUST KEEP IN MIND THAT AN UPSIDE WON'T ALWAYS REVEAL ITSELF—THAT YOU MAY HAVE TO GIVE IT MORE THOUGHT AND TIME.

WEEK 12

Dealing with Emotions

"I lose my temper, but it's all over in a minute," said the student. "So is the hydrogen bomb," I replied, "but think of the damage it produces."
—George Sweeting

Consider how much more you often suffer from your anger and grief, than from those very things for which you are angry and grieved.
—Marcus Antonius

Anger is never without reason, but seldom a good one.
—Benjamin Franklin

First let me say, my student, that it's entirely normal to experience such powerful emotions as anger and frustration; what's not normal, however—or healthy—is how some people choose to deal with them.

Now, let me be as clear as I've ever been: If you as an individual do not learn to control these emotions, *they will end up controlling you.*

Sadly enough, this latter scenario can lead to frequent episodes of intense—and unnecessary—grief for both you and those most important to you. I know, because it's an issue that hits close to my own home.

The mother of my best friend, you see, was notorious for "losing it." For as long as I can remember, she would scream and yell and rage without thinking twice. It was almost unbearable to witness, let alone be on the receiving end. This otherwise "normal" person had obviously never learned how to control her feelings. In fact, what disturbed me most about the long line of blowups was my awareness that all the misery could have been avoided, if only....If only someone had taught her alternative ways to deal with negative emotion.

Well, at least you'll never be able to say that no one provided you alternatives. That's because I've devoted the remainder of this advisement to making you aware of both the constructive and destructive ways in which to deal with negative emotions. Refer to these lists whenever you feel the need!

Let's begin by considering what not to do:

1. Don't take out your frustrations on others. We certainly don't like being on the receiving end of such behavior, so it makes total sense to not put others in that spot. Besides, think about who usually sustains the brunt of our frustration. That's right, the very people most important to us—our family members and closest friends. To add insult to injury, they often have little or nothing to do with what we're feeling—their only offense is being in our presence (the wrong place) at the wrong time. Not much of a reason, now is it?
2. Resist the temptation to blow up, during which you yell and scream whatever pops into your head. Those who do give in to this grossly immature response fail to recognize two critical points. First, whether they're capable of seeing the reality of the situation or not, those they are lashing out at and hurting do not deserve it. That's right, no matter how it's rationalized or justified, the fact remains: *no one* deserves to be attacked and disrespected in this manner. Secondly, blowing up is as selfish an act as there is. I say this because individuals who fly off the handle, totally disregard anyone else's feelings but their own—specifically, those of their victims and any other people who happen to be present. What's more, when all is said and done, guess who's feeling relieved and pacified, having been able to discharge so much negative emotion? Right. And guess who, having been subjected to someone else's wrath, is left feeling distraught, tense, and abused? Like I said, as selfish as it gets.
3. Lastly, my student, avoid making choices of import when caught up in a highly charged emotional state; it's simply not a wise thing to do. Case in point: The very week I began writing to this topic, a young person I know well—we'll call him Todd—made just such a choice. Todd was competing in a tightly contested basketball game during which the opposing team, in an attempt to get the ball back, intentionally fouled him. Granted, it was a hard foul but nothing that warranted what would take place next.

Upon completion of the game, as the two teams exchanged handshakes, the still-agitated Todd made the choice to exact revenge. The ensuing punch set into motion a series of equally unfortunate events. While his victim suffered through a broken jaw and the arduous recovery that follows, Todd himself was physically injured in the altercation, arrested, and suspended from school. On top of all this, his family received notice of an impending lawsuit. They were being sued for the physical and mental distress he had unnecessarily—and unwisely—caused.

Clearly, Todd could have, and should have, handled things differently; his story serves to illustrate just how essential it is to learn to control one's emotions.

Let's now examine how to go about accomplishing this elusive end:

1. Without question, self-awareness is the most critical component. When piqued it is imperative you step back to reflect on what exactly it is you're feeling, and why exactly you're feeling it.

   This may sound self-evident to some, but the reality is that many fail to put an ounce of thought into such matters. They simply react without thinking, and thus surrender complete control to their emotions. So be sure to ask yourself such questions as: *What emotion(s) is trying to take over? Why am I feeling this way—is it a result of being rejected, hurt, or disrespected? Why would this bother me so much; could it have something to do with what I've gone through in the past; might it be I'm just overtired or stressed out? Why, why, why?*

2. When negative emotions persist, it is equally as crucial to talk about them. Work to put into words all that you're feeling and then verbalize it. You can do this in house or over the phone with a friend or relative; you can also meet with a teacher or guidance counselor at school; you can even express your feelings to a loving pet, or by screaming into a pillow in the privacy of your own room. Whomever, wherever, whatever—just be sure to attach words to your feelings.

3. When possible, remove yourself from the situation causing you distress. If your little brother, for example, is doing a good job of getting on your nerves, get out of the house and away from him before your emotions even begin to snowball.

4. Allow yourself time to get over negative emotions. In other words, go ahead and accept whatever it is you're feeling as normal—cry and punch your pillow even—just trust in the knowledge you will

not feel this way forever. For reassurance, simply think back to those occasions when you felt similarly and recall that, in time, the hurt always faded and you were able to move on...even stronger than before.

5. You can choose to do something that makes you feel good—even if you don't particularly want to. I actually have my students in class write out a list of all the things they enjoy doing, e.g., ordering out for pizza, blasting music, biking, going to the movies. You can call it a "what I enjoy list," a "feel good list"—or anything you'd like. The point is, when you're caught up in negative emotion, you simply select something from your list and do it.

   Many times, you may have to force yourself to follow through because of the strong feelings you're experiencing, but once you do act, I can almost guarantee your negative emotions will begin to subside.

6. Recognize the importance of maintaining your sense of humor. Sure, it's a challenge to not take yourself, your problems, and your emotions too seriously, but it can be done. Just once, my student, when ready to scream in frustration, try instead to laugh out loud. I can tell you from experience that when you're finally able to accomplish this, a feeling of rare empowerment will rush through you. After all, your unique display of self-discipline indicates that you are gaining more control of your emotions—rather than the other way around.

7. Understand that powerful emotions like anger can serve positive purposes, too. For one thing, anger clearly communicates to another that you won't stand for being treated unjustly; that you have far too much dignity and self-respect to allow anyone to use you as a doormat.

8. And finally, when your emotions do get the best of you, reflect on the experience so as to learn something from it. The key question being: "How could I have handled things differently?"

Remember then, my student, learning to handle strong feelings is a requirement for those who want to avoid unnecessary grief and create a truly rich, rewarding life...*so challenge yourself to deal with emotions.* You can do this.

LIFE APP

BECAUSE THIS ENTIRE CHAPTER IS ESSENTIALLY A HOW-TO LIST, REFER BACK TO IT OFTEN AND INCORPORATE THE MANY STRATEGIES INTO YOUR DAY-TO-DAY LIFE.

FOR STARTERS, YOU CAN GENERATE THE "FEEL GOOD LIST" WE TALKED ABOUT. KEEP IT ACCESSIBLE AND FORCE YOURSELF TO FOLLOW THROUGH WHEN OR IF YOU GET UPSET THIS WEEK.

TAKE COMFORT IN THE KNOWLEDGE THAT STARTING YOUNG IS KEY TO LEARNING HOW TO EFFECTIVELY HANDLE ONE'S EMOTIONS. INDEED, AS TIME PASSES, YOU CAN EXPECT YOUR POSITIVE, CONSTRUCTIVE RESPONSES TO BECOME AS NATURAL FOR YOU AS OTHERS' NEGATIVE, DESTRUCTIVE REACTIONS HAVE BECOME FOR THEM.

WEEK 13

Appreciating Family

Call it a clan, call it a network, call it a tribe, call it a family. Whatever you call it, whoever you are, you need one.
—Jane Howard

Treat your friends like family and your family like friends.
—Mother's advice quoted by Michele Slung

Happy families are all alike. Every unhappy family is unhappy in its own way.
—Count Leo Tolstoy

Who are the people we most often take for granted yet are least deserving of such a fate? The answer to this life riddle, in far too many instances, is family. Isn't it ironic, my student, that those in the world we are most connected to are the very ones we are most apt to underappreciate and detach from? Well, maybe it's time we (re)gained some perspective.

To begin, let me say there was a time in my own life when I didn't appreciate family. Instead, my mind was always focused in on the little hassles that you can likely relate to. Things like having to share a bunk bed with my brother; my parents saying no (to what seemed like every request); vying for time in our only bathroom; having an earlier curfew than my friends; my mother and father being overzealous and overprotective…you get the point.

At the time it didn't even occur to me to consider my parents' point of view. If I had, perhaps I would have seen how difficult it can be to go to work all day, maintain a house and yard, prepare meal after meal, and pay the bills—all while carrying out the most demanding, albeit sacred, job on the planet: the raising of children.

Well, because I chose to fixate on all the negatives, I was often guilty of acting out in ignorant ways. And as you would predict, this led to lots of fighting in our home. For whatever reason, though, I did nothing to try to help change the tense, combative atmosphere that had taken hold. I guess you could say that when it came to appreciating family, I was failing miserably.

My home-life circumstances, along with my rotten attitude, remained this way for quite awhile, too—that is until one fateful winter day.

It was ice hockey season, and as usual my buddies and I were out skating at the local pond. We were having so much fun, the hours flew by without our even noticing. But as darkness settled in, we decided to play for one final goal.

All I can remember after the ensuing face-off was my friend attempting to clear the puck. I never saw it hit me.

An hour later I woke up in the hospital. There were 12 stitches around my lip, 2 tubes in my arm, and 4 fewer teeth in my mouth. But what made the most profound impression on me were the three people sitting at my bedside—my mom, my dad, and my brother. It was at that second, feeling vulnerable and afraid, that I realized of all the people in the world, these were the ones who cared most—and who mattered most. This marked the moment in my life when I first appreciated, *truly appreciated*, family.

Back on the homefront, I began to put forth greater effort and things began to greatly improve. In fact, in time the improvements were so significant that I discovered something many never do: Being part of a happy family makes for a slice of heaven to be enjoyed here on earth. (To be clear, I'm not claiming everything suddenly became perfect. But armed with my new perspective, I never again permitted myself to act selfishly…nor to ignorantly throw fuel on any family fires.)

Now, to this day, whenever I hear a young person around me speak negatively of loved ones, I instinctively react by asking, "Who would be the first people at your side if you were to wind up in the hospital?" We should each reflect on this question.

While it certainly makes a powerful point, I realize it's not enough to boost levels of peace and harmony in every home. That's why I've provided you with some additional tips.

One, in particular, is almost guaranteed to work. It involves doing more to help out around the house. Specifically, you can make it a goal to do one extra chore per day—without even being asked. (Following my accident, I carried out this exact goal as a tangible way to show my appreciation—and it worked magic.) With life being so hectic, *any* extra help you give will elicit more goodwill and smiles from your parents.

In addition to smiling a lot more, my own parents saw this daily effort as a sign that I was becoming more responsible and dependable. Consequently, I ended up earning extra privileges, two of which were big ones that you, too, would likely welcome: a later curfew and more privacy.

Another more direct way of expressing your appreciation for family is to display affection. Think about it. Early on in life, most kids give out an abundance of hugs, kisses, and "I love you's." But as they grow older, these simple acts get carried out less and less often. Isn't it ironic that just when parents and their kids are most in need of sharing such gestures, they both tend to hold back? Well, it doesn't have to be this way.

Even if you haven't shown affection for a long while, try doing so today. It may feel awkward at first, but in time it can become just as natural as it once was. (If you feel too uncomfortable to even attempt this, there are other ways to communicate your feelings. For example, try expressing a measure of excitement whenever a family member comes home. If the way we feel when a dog does this is any indication, the recipient of your greeting will certainly feel more valued.)

The next tip can also have a positive impact on any family. When you are faced with a problem, who do you typically turn to? A friend, a teacher, a pet, or maybe no one at all? For some reason, many young people fail to utilize their greatest resource: family members.

Whether you can fathom it or not, older siblings and parents have previously been through just about everything you're presently experiencing. You'll be shocked by how much they understand and can relate to; surprised by how clear-sighted and helpful they can be; and encouraged by how much this can serve to strengthen your family bonds. After all, communication is precisely what brings—and keeps—people close.

Last, but not least, you need to recognize that no matter how hard you work to bring your family closer, disagreements are bound to arise. When they do, my student, you must work to remain calm and keep an open mind. Allow me to elaborate.

An age-old precursor to trouble has involved parents rejecting their kids' heartfelt requests. I myself can recall just how frustrating it was to want something so badly, only to have an adult dispassionately say no. The only positive that resulted from my own experiences was it compelled me to search out solutions.

The one I found to be most effective involved taking into consideration where my parents were coming from—their side of the story. Try doing this; it's not as tough as you may think. You'll soon discover that there's more behind your parents' decisions than the common "they're just worry warts" deduction.

Once you're done reflecting in this rare way, you'll be ready to re-present your case—minus any screaming. Start off by revealing that you've been considering their point of view. Then throw them off even further by listing their own possible reasons for saying no. Next, disclose your line of thinking, your position. And finally, ask that they reexamine your request.

It's entirely possible your parents, seeing the amount of time and thought you have put into the issue at hand, will now say yes, or at least offer some type of compromise. And even if they say no again, I guarantee they'll respect your mature actions, which will only lead them to more seriously contemplate future requests.

Remember then, my student, of the billions of people in the world, a precious few care most—and matter most…*so challenge yourself to appreciate family*. You can do this.

LIFE APP

ALTHOUGH THERE ARE SURE TO BE THINGS THAT BOTHER YOU ABOUT HOW YOUR PARENTS PARENT AND YOUR SIBLINGS SIB, THIS WEEK MAKE A POINT OF SEARCHING OUT SOME POSITIVES. REFLECT ON HOW EACH OF YOUR FAMILY MEMBERS MANAGES TO SHOW RESPECT FOR YOU. THEN TAKE THE OPPORTUNITY TO COMMUNICATE YOUR OBSERVATIONS.

FOR EXAMPLE:

1. "MOM, I'VE ALWAYS APPRECIATED YOUR CAPACITY TO LISTEN—REALLY LISTEN—TO ME."
2. "DAD, NO MATTER HOW STRESSED OUT AND FRUSTRATED YOU GET WITH WORK, YOU NEVER TAKE IT OUT ON ME."
3. "SIS, THANKS FOR ALWAYS KNOWING WHEN TO GIVE ME MY SPACE."
4. "BRO, YOU'VE STUCK UP FOR ME MORE TIMES THAN I CAN COUNT."

BELIEVE IT OR NOT, BY PRAISING AND POINTING OUT THE GOOD, YOU ARE NOT ONLY STRENGTHENING FAMILY BONDS, BUT ALSO INCREASING THE LIKELIHOOD THEY'LL CONTINUE TO ACT IN POSITIVE WAYS.

WEEK 14

Appreciating Your Pet

Until one has loved an animal, a part of one's soul remains unawakened.
—Anatole France

A faithful friend is the medicine of life.
—Ancient Proverb

When you rise in the morning, form a resolution to make the day a happy one for a fellow creature.
—Sydney Smith

First off, I have to come clean: I'm a big-time dog lover. It's not that I'm averse to other types of pets—well, reptiles really don't do much for me—it's just that dogs like my golden retriever absolutely melt my heart. But while much of what I've written about in this advisement does stem from a love of dogs, my messages, as you will soon see, can be applied to any kind of beloved pet—your cat, your horse, your bird, your ferret, and yes, even your iguana.

It's often said, my student, that relationships—more than anything else—are what make life special and meaningful. Well, for literally millions of us this would have to include relationships with our pets. They are simply part of the family, devoted contributors of time, patience, love, and support.

Truth be told, they are often the ones we feel most comfortable turning to in trying times. Their warm fur, wet tongues, and deep, sincere eyes are almost always enough to make things right again. When I was growing up, my family's dogs actually knew which bedroom to sleep in each night—based on an uncanny knack of sensing who was in most need of their presence.

Of course, being able to enjoy an animal's companionship does require a certain amount of responsibility and devotion on our part. I've heard many parents who double as pet owners, liken the demands of raising an animal to the constant care required of a newborn baby.

The most successful families recognize just how much work it is, and thus, divvy up everyday duties such as feeding, playing, walking, pooper-scooping, and brushing. Everyone pitches in in some way. Even responsibilities like renewing the town license, keeping the animal on your property, and grooming can be assigned to individual family members.

The beauty of this set-up is that the more you each put into pet ownership, the more you each get out. As an example, my own wife and I have given maximum time, energy, and affection to our newest pup, Summer, and she has turned out to be the most loyal, loving dog—even by golden standards—to have ever roamed a backyard. I really do attribute her unbridled generosity of spirit to our having met her every basic need.

Interestingly, my wife, who spends the greatest amount of time with Summer and is in charge of her daily feedings, shares the most extraordinary bond of all with her. Bearing witness to their loving interactions would prompt even an ardent animal avoider to conclude pet ownership done right can make for a slice of heaven to be enjoyed here on earth. Can you relate?

Sadly, special bonds like this do not exist in every pet owner's home. No, despite the fact dogs, along with other animals, are true teachers and givers of unconditional love, humans sometimes reciprocate with mean and/or ignorant actions. You've probably seen evidence of it: A neglected pet being left outside 24/7 receiving little, if any, attention. An ailing pet in need of veterinary care never getting it. Or a helpless pet being left inside a car at a store parking lot. (Even with windows cracked, temperatures inside can rise so fast that permanent brain damage or heart failure can result.)

In addition, I have witnessed pets being smacked or screamed at for no other reason than they happened to be nearby. Just thinking about the number of people, both young and old, who act in such ways hurts me deeply—and at the same time leaves me seeing red. I mean, sure, life can be demanding and stressful, but that doesn't give anyone the right to take their frustrations out on a defenseless animal, now does it? In fact, they usually have little if anything to do with what's upsetting us. Nor will they understand why they're being mistreated—especially when the bully is the very person their entire universe revolves around.

Clearly, our pets—while here on earth—deserve and depend on us for a good life. And when we provide this precious gift, my student, it can make even the sad day when they pass more bearable. In my lifetime, I have had to say goodbye to three dogs, all of whom I loved deeply. In each instance, what comforted me most, though, was the heart-held knowledge that I had made a point—a daily point—of not taking my pet for granted, and had therefore been instrumental in providing each of them a happy life.

This allowed me, even before the tears and pangs of loneliness had faded, to focus on the good—on the many special moments we shared: reading a book with her lying across my legs...being welcomed home by a wriggling body and thumping tail...playing with the tennis ball for hours on end...walking in the woods together, etc. I'm sure you can relate.

Such memories of our pets will be held in our hearts forever. As will the *many* lessons they so humbly teach us—of friendship, tolerance, trust, responsibility, forgiveness, resiliency, patience, enthusiasm, soulfulness, and unconditional love.

And who knows, maybe one day, you and I really will get to cross that rainbow bridge with our pets at our sides.

Remember then, my student, relationships with animals are certainly included among those that provide life with so much special meaning...*so challenge yourself to appreciate your pet.* You can do this.

LIFE APP

MAKE A CHART WITH TWO COLUMNS. ON ONE SIDE, LIST EVERYTHING YOU DO FOR YOUR PET DURING THE COURSE OF THIS WEEK, E.G., CHANGED WATER DISH, SCRATCHED BEHIND EARS, TOOK ON A MORNING WALK. THEN ON THE OTHER SIDE, LIST ALL YOUR PET DOES FOR YOU.

REFLECTING IN SUCH A WAY CAN CERTAINLY HELP AVOID TAKING YOUR PETS FOR GRANTED. AND AS YOU STRIVE TO MATCH OR EXCEED THE NUMBER OF ENTRIES ON THEIR SIDE, YOU TOO WILL DEVELOP A MORE GIVING NATURE.

IF YOU DON'T HAVE A PET, TAKE HEART, FOR THERE EXIST OTHER WAYS TO BOND WITH ANIMALS. YOU CAN, FOR EXAMPLE, SPEND MORE TIME WITH A FRIEND'S PET, VOLUNTEER AT A LOCAL ANIMAL SHELTER, GET A JOB AT A GROOMING BUSINESS, OFFER TO PLAY WITH OR WALK A NEIGHBOR'S DOG, OR PUT OUT FOOD FOR THE BIRDS AND SQUIRRELS IN YOUR YARD. AND WHILE YOU'RE DOING ALL OF THESE THINGS, TAKE COMFORT IN THE KNOWLEDGE THAT YOU'LL SOMEDAY BE FREE TO GET A PET OF YOUR OWN!

WEEK 15

Thickening Your Skin

Unhappy is the man whom man can make unhappy.
—Ralph Waldo Emerson

Don't accept that others know you better than yourself.
—Sonja Friedman

No one can make you feel inferior without your consent.
—Eleanor Roosevelt

Let's face cold, hard facts, my student: We live in a society where not everybody is going to like and accept us—where some not only won't like us, but will even go so far as to treat us in mean-spirited and downright crude ways.

I'm sorry I had to be the one to break this news to you…wait, on second thought, I'm not sorry. For I can't tell you just how much I wish someone had clued me in.

You see, I grew up under the rather naive assumption that if I was a good person and treated others with respect, they would respond to me in similarly positive ways. Man, was I wrong. Sure it worked out like this at times but certainly not always. And as a result, I had to deal with a lot of needless hurt, frustration, and disappointment in my teen years.

Come to think of it, even now, with some of these old habits stubbornly entrenched, I have a hard time dealing with the disapproval and lack of acceptance from others. It could be anything from a close acquaintance of mine just shaking her head at me, to someone I hardly know not reciprocating a "Hi, how are you?" I just let it eat away at me—sometimes for hours.

The good news is that I've learned a lot regarding how to better handle my problem. And I will soon share with you some effective ways in which we can all continue the important process of thickening our skin.

First, though, let's delve into the question of why people don't like us and/or treat us badly at times. There are, to say the least, a whole host of reasons:

1. *Human frailty.* Spread the word: If you possess any personality at all; if you stand for anything at all; if you aren't afraid to speak up and state your opinions—then you *will* intimidate, put off, or alienate some sector of the population. That's just the way it is.

   The only chance to avoid such a fate would be to be a bland, keep-your-mouth-shut type of person. This way, you don't draw any attention to yourself—and even if you did on occasion, you wouldn't be worth the effort required to judge and dismiss someone.

2. *Power and control.* I'm constantly informing those students who are treated badly by others that they are not the ones with the problem, that those with a need to tease, insult, and bully are. Almost invariably, there is something about *themselves* that they don't like, something about *their own lives* with which they are not happy and feel powerless to change.

   Perhaps they feel stupid in class or their parents fight all the time. Maybe someone picks on them or they're just jealous of you because you're smarter, better looking, happier, etc.—the possibilities are limitless. The point is that they're attempting to feel power (albeit "false power") and control over you because they feel no power or control over changing their own problems. (This is how it works in the adult world of put-downs, too.)

   Bottom line: The act of treating others badly, at any age, says a lot more about the needs and flaws of the perpetrator than the person who happens to be on the receiving end.

3. *Misery (loves company).* Ask anyone who's ever made it "to the top" and tasted success how he is now treated by others. He'll tell you that more people than you'd think become bitter and envious, and act accordingly. Many even go so far as to root for you to fail and self-destruct, simply so you can be miserable—like them.

4. *Resentment.* Generally speaking, there have always been two kinds of people in the world: those intent on growing—like you—and those seemingly intent on stagnating. While one group is busy doing and achieving, the other sits back on the sidelines of life watching and critiquing everything. (Hey, it's an easy job, but they figure somebody's got to do it.)

   The only problem is somewhere deep down, they know they're not living life the way it's meant to be lived. You can imagine, then, that when your paths happen to cross, they will be more inclined to communicate feelings of envy and resentment toward you than those of respect and approval. Just take it as a sign that you're doing something right.

5. *Personal issues.* It's an undeniable truth that how we treat others is directly linked to how we feel about ourselves. It stands to reason, then, that those who are uncomfortable in their own skin, those with no connection to their own hearts, those who don't like who they're becoming, etc., won't be overly intent on spreading tidings of joy and goodwill among all.

6. *Ignorance.* As you go through life, you'll quickly learn that there exist in society those who "see only what they believe." Regardless of how you act or what you say, they see only their preconceived notions and judgments. The act of thinking about and weighing the personal qualities of each individual would require just way too much effort on their part. Consequently, you will *not* be treated with kindness and respect...indeed, you never stood a chance.

7. *Stress.* Who among us hasn't been rude and inconsiderate to another person simply because we were having a bad day—or even a bad moment? Both can be brought on by any number of a million circumstances: from failing a test to failing to get enough sleep; from having money problems to having a family fight; from dealing with traffic to dealing with a major crisis—and on and on. Whatever the underlying cause, it can have absolutely nothing to do with those we encounter, yet still manage to impact—no, dictate—how we treat them.

With so many reasons behind why others come to dislike us, and/or treat us badly, you really have to wonder why we'd ever allow it to get to us. Indeed, the issue of personal choice does play a major role here. Yes, my student, despite the fact that many young people don't even realize it, we all have two basic choices from which to select when being dissed.

The first is the one we tend to choose instinctively, without even thinking. You know the routine: We let 'em get to us—responding by hunching our shoulders, developing a sinking feeling in our gut (that "pit sensation"), and thinking it's our fault; that there must be something wrong or inadequate about us. On certain occasions, we may even sink to their low level, lashing back with a shove or an insult of our own. Such reactions, however, only prove to the perps they penetrated our skin—that they achieved power and control over us.

Choice number two, on the other hand, is flat-out refusing to allow another to use you as a personal stepping stool. What you do instead is reveal no outer reaction at all while thinking to yourself, "I wonder which of the "why" categories he fits into; regardless, *he's* the one with the problem—not me. There must be something wrong in his life since people who like and respect themselves certainly don't have the need to feel power over others; he's actually revealing a personal weakness of his—without even knowing it. And besides all this, he doesn't know the type of person I am deep down—the kind of heart I have and what I'm all about."

This second option probably has you inspired to *never* again let another person get you down. But be forewarned, there is a catch. The first few times you attempt to rationalize away their crudeness, you may instead instinctively experience the pit sensation and lack of control associated with choice number one. This is how it works with old habits, and nothing other than patience, focus, faith, and repeated effort will fix it.

So just work through, by reminding yourself of all that's at stake, and by continuing to employ choice number two's thoughts. Then one day soon, it'll happen. The moment will come when you find yourself walking away from a dirty look or rude remark thinking, "Wow, that didn't bother me in the least—I feel fine!"

And when your skin does become this thick, watch out. For it will mark the time in your life when you first realize just how strong, resilient, and self-assured you're capable of being; when you take back control of your own life and see that happiness, confidence, and peace of mind can only come from within.

It's now a distinct possibility you'll never again allow someone else's thoughts and actions to affect your feelings. Imagine, no more of those unnecessary emotions—hurt, frustration, and disappointment. Talk about becoming truly free and at peace with yourself. You can finally get on with the business of being a more happy-go-lucky, enthusiastic, genuine, confident, spontaneous—and fulfilled—individual.

Remember then, my student, there will always be those who don't like and accept you—that's just the way it is...*so challenge yourself to thicken your skin*. You can do this.

LIFE APP

THERE'S AN OLD SAYING THAT SUGGESTS WE CORRECT IN OURSELVES WHAT WE DON'T LIKE IN OTHERS. WITH THIS IDEAL IN MIND, LET US EACH COMMIT TO BECOMING THE RARE KIND OF PERSON WHO NOT ONLY REFRAINS FROM PUTTING OTHERS DOWN, BUT TAKES IT ONE STEP FURTHER BY COMMITTING TO BRING OTHERS UP.

WHAT BETTER WAY TO ACCOMPLISH THIS THAN TO BRING MORE COMPLIMENTS INTO THE WORLD? AFTER ALL, WORDS CAN HEAL, TOO. IT DOESN'T MATTER WHO IT IS—FRIEND OR FOE, FAMILY MEMBER OR NEW ACQUAINTANCE—EVERYBODY CAN BENEFIT FROM ONE.

START OFF THIS WEEK BY GIVING AT LEAST ONE PER DAY; JUST BE SURE YOU'RE SINCERE ABOUT WHAT YOU'RE SAYING. SOON, YOU'LL EXPERIENCE FIRSTHAND THE KIND OF LASTING *REAL POWER* THAT RESULTS FROM FILLING OTHERS' NEEDS, AND TOUCHING LIVES IN A PURELY POSITIVE WAY.

WEEK 16

Seeing the Wonder of It All

There is something of the marvelous in all things of nature.
—Aristotle

Youth is happy because it has the ability to see the beauty. Anyone who keeps the ability to see the beauty never grows old.
—Franz Kafka

By having reverence for life, we enter into a spiritual relation with the world.
—Albert Schweitzer

Without question, my student, planet earth provides the ultimate in artistic backdrops. Words simply can't do justice to the natural wonder imprinting every corner of our vast globe.

With so much of this wonder right at our own doorsteps, you'd think we would be in a constant—or at least, frequent—state of wide-eyed amazement. But this is not the case, now is it? Far too many of us are going about our lives rarely stopping to take notice, failing to stop and smell the roses.

Perhaps it's due to the fact that our own human influence—in the form of roadways, homes, skyscrapers, etc.—is so darn capable of numbing the senses. Or maybe it's because we just don't realize how inspirational, how miraculous our natural surroundings truly are. It is, after all, first necessary to get to know something before one can develop a genuine respect and appreciation for it. Whatever the reason, seeing the wonder of it all needs to become a higher priority in all our lives.

With this objective in mind, I have compiled some examples of nature at its most captivating, its most extraordinary. Each one, in and of itself, is enough to prompt *anybody* to stop and take notice—and will hopefully motivate you to see them someday. (Not only have I had my breath taken away by each of the following, but they served as the original inspiration for this advisement.)

Some natural wonders to appreciate: the colossal redwood and sequoia trees of Northern California; the indescribable Crater Lake in Oregon; a multicolored, awe-inspiring Key West sunset; a family of majestic humpback whales using bubble nets to feed in the Alaskan waters; a calving glacier echoing in Glacier Bay; oozing volcanoes in Hawaii's national park; a rainbow emerging over the green-blue hues of the Caribbean Sea; the spectacular varieties of coral and fish in Cozumel's serene Paradise Reef; the three magnificent waterfalls of Yosemite; and from a bird's-eye perspective aboard a plane, the eye-popping, mind-blowing Rocky Mountain Range.

While such examples do well to illustrate just how wondrous the natural world can be, you can find just as much evidence from the vantage point of your own backyard. That's right, although we tend to take what we regularly see for granted, you'll find there exists much magic in the ordinary as well. You just need to open yourself up to it, or in other words, to start seeing with your heart as well as your eyes.

Things like a robin deftly locating a worm below ground; the mesmerizing motions of a fleeting butterfly; ominous storm clouds and lightning approaching from a distance; your pet instinctively watching over its territory; a chipmunk diligently going about its autumn ritual; the countless variations of local trees, shrubs, and flowers; a spider tenaciously weaving its web of sustenance; birds feeding peacefully in the quiet of early morning; a dancing queen bee carrying out her enormous responsibilities; and at any time of any day, the wonder-workings of the ever-enchanting sky above.

Once you start seeing more of the wonder of it all, you can rest assured that you'll begin benefiting in meaningful ways. Apart from all the genuine thrills you are bound to experience, you will, for example, be more motivated to explore and interact with nature. Soul-enriching activities such as hiking, snorkeling, bird watching, mountain biking, cross-country skiing, and scuba diving can help anyone at any age to accomplish this worthwhile end.

In addition, you'll be inspired to learn more about the world you have begun to discover. What's especially nice about this, my student, is as your levels of knowledge and understanding deepen, so too do your feelings of awe and respect for Mother Nature. Many times, in fact, this growth process is exactly what leads to someone assuming a role of environmental leadership. Who better and more willing to make and model the personal sacrifices required to preserve our natural surroundings? Sure, it's an enormous responsibility to take on, but those individuals who come to truly appreciate the glory of our natural world have met with the ultimate in inspirational forces.

Anyone who makes *seeing the wonder* more of a priority will also benefit by becoming a more thoughtful, reflective person. For when so much magic and fascination is being appreciated, you really have no other choice. I for one have mulled over the following thoughts on countless occasions:

1. How is it humpback whales manage to navigate their 3,000-mile journey from Hawaii to Alaska in what amounts to almost a straight-line path?
2. It amazes me that 10 trillion ants exist and can be found on just about every corner of the planet—including barren desert and ice cold arctic regions.
3. Can you believe how most mountain ranges are formed? Enormous pieces of our earth's shell—in constant slowwwww motion atop an ocean of lava—meet head-on, and for literally millions of years, push up, under, and against one another.
4. How astonishing that our moon, of all things, is the controlling force behind the oceans' alternating tides.
5. I never knew seeing a creature, like a bear, swordfish, or even a backyard deer, in its natural environment, could be such a moving experience.
6. Just how advanced are elephants? Herds of them demonstrate humanlike bonds—complete with emotions for and memories of one another.
7. How in the world have so many animals developed the adaptation of giving birth in early spring? For the longer the interval to winter, the better the chances for their babies'—and hence, their species'—survival.

Nothing else in the world, though, prompts me to reflect more—nor feel more alive—than simply staring up at the sky. Have you ever lain in the grass, eyes wide open, and just let your mind go? Besides detecting various images in the passing clouds, thoughts of wonder and amazement also begin to take shape.

For example, on a hot, summer day you may find yourself contemplating our planet's position in the solar system—not too far from the sun to support life, but not too close, either—a divinely perfect

93 million miles away. Or in the peace and quiet of nighttime, while gazing at the stars above, you may end up pondering the possibilities of what exists light years away. Lastly, closer to home while peering at the moon, you can marvel in the knowledge that human beings have actually walked around up there.

It's too bad more people don't take the time to just look up, let go, and enjoy.

Remember then, my student, we are surrounded by a miraculous natural world, one that is—like any majestic work of art—capable of stirring body, mind, and soul...*so challenge yourself to see the wonder of it all.* You can do this.

LIFE APP

THIS WEEK, FIND BOOKS IN A LOCAL LIBRARY OR BOOKSTORE THAT LIST THE NATURAL WONDERS IN YOUR STATE OR REGION, INCLUDING GUIDE BOOKS THAT DESCRIBE STATE PARKS AND OTHER HIKING AREAS. ALSO, CHECK YOUR STATE'S TOURISM WEBSITES FOR PLACES YOU CAN VISIT TO ENJOY THE WONDER OF IT ALL.

IN ADDITION, MAKE IT A LIFELONG GOAL TO SEE IN PERSON AS MANY OF THE NATURAL WONDERS OF THE WORLD AS YOU CAN. I MYSELF HAVE ALREADY TRAVELED TO SEVEN NATIONAL PARKS AND AM PRESENTLY PLANNING AN AFRICAN SAFARI TRIP. SO YOU CAN BELIEVE ME WHEN I TELL YOU, YOU WILL NOT COME BACK THE SAME PERSON.

IT'S FUNNY, TOO, BECAUSE INITIALLY I THOUGHT SEEING SO MUCH OF THE EXTRAORDINARY COULD ONLY SERVE TO DIMINISH ONE'S APPRECIATION FOR THE MORE FAMILIAR AND ROUTINE. TO THE CONTRARY, I'VE FOUND IT SERVES TO FURTHER INGRAIN A SENSE OF AWE AND RESPECT FOR ALL OF NATURE. EACH ONE OF MY VISITS HAS INDEED DEEPENED MY PERSONAL RELATIONSHIP WITH THE NATURAL WORLD—A RELATIONSHIP THAT ENDURES WHETHER TRAVELING IN SOME FAR-OFF PLACE, OR SAFARIING IN MY VERY OWN BACKYARD.

Keeping the Faith

Your faith is what you believe, not what you know.
—John Lancaster Spalding

Life is a wilderness of twists and turns, where faith is your only compass.
—Paul Santaguida

Doubt sees the obstacles. Faith sees the way. Doubt sees the darkest night. Faith sees the day. Doubt dreads to take a step. Faith soars on high. Doubt questions, "Who believes?" Faith answers, "I."
—Author Unknown

Disease. Shootings. Plane crashes. Birth defects. Natural disasters. Bombings. The list can go on and on.

And because so many bad things happen in life—even to the best of people—some of us quickly conclude there can be no God. After all, if an all-powerful entity did exist, it certainly wouldn't permit such circumstances to coexist, right?

Then there are those who, despite all the bad in the world, remain faithful. They are people from any number of religious backgrounds who share the same recognition: that faith comes down to believing in what cannot be known, and trusting there does indeed exist a higher power. They take comfort in the conviction that their God, having accorded human beings free will in a random universe, grieves along with them and is there to provide strength and stability when they are in need.

So yes, my student, bad things do happen. But with faith in hand—and in heart—spiritual beings have exactly what it takes to overcome.

You've probably heard the old expression, "Everything happens for a reason." It's a message of comfort and hope usually uttered by the faithful in the wake of an unfortunate event. My personal feeling, however, is that each human being possesses free will—not to mention the capacity for both good and evil. So it stands to reason that arbitrary, senseless tragedies of the man-made variety are bound to occur. No one can tell me, for example, there was a reason or higher purpose for the Columbine High incident.

That said, I do believe it is in the wake, and midst, of such tragedies that the fruits of faith become invaluable—and most evident. I can't tell you how many times my own belief system has allowed me to come to terms with terrible events. Or how something positive has inexplicably emerged from even my most regrettable experiences—things I would never have been able to predict. Could it be this is where God's influence resides? Could it be that our faith empowers us to both find good in, and make good from, despair and loss? Think about it.

Even the horrible Columbine incident can serve as a case in point. For in the midst and wake of all that chaos, several extraordinary acts were carried out. One victim, in particular, found herself face-to-face with the barrel of a gun. As the shooter prepared to pull the trigger, he taunted her, asking if she now believed in God. With more courage and bravery than most of us could imagine, she looked past the gun barrel into his eyes and responded...yes.

The girl's grieving family, as well as the families of several other victims, later allowed TV crews to broadcast funeral proceedings. This selfless and virtuous gesture resulted in immeasurable good.

During one ceremony, a mime routine was acted out in honor of another girl. It served as a beautiful visual representation of the deep and passionate faith both young ladies possessed. Countless viewers from all over the world—including me—were moved to the point of becoming determined not to let their deaths be in vain. And in addition to providing the impetus to act, these two souls inspired millions to renew or strengthen their own faith. A more powerful legacy you will not encounter.

The kind of deep faith we've touched upon does not just happen, though. Like anything else of great value, my student, it requires lots of individual time and energy to develop. At a point in my own life, I actually had little to no interest in putting in the necessary effort. Perhaps you can relate. Looking back, I believe it was a matter of my not wanting to be told what to think or feel. I needed to forge my own beliefs. And I highly recommend you do the same.

Eventually, I did go to work investigating the roots of religion and faith. This boiled down to reading lots of pertinent articles, asking lots of questions, and doing lots of reflecting. Some of the things that influenced me most were: accounts written by faith-filled POWs and Holocaust survivors claiming that God's *presence* was most responsible for sustaining them through their horrific experience; my dad's belief, based on his own life experiences, that God's presence is most palpable—most undeniable—as people come into or depart this world; my mom's assertion that she sees and feels God in even the ordinary—in things like her backyard garden and the piece of art hanging on her bedroom wall; and my longtime teacher and friend's thought-provoking point that we each have nothing to lose and everything to gain by choosing to be faithful.

While several such opinions and tidbits of information impacted my thinking, my feelings—particularly while praying and attending church—are what influenced me most. Perhaps you'll identify with some.

To this day, each time I pray, feelings of calm and inner peace take over. Even when something big is weighing on my mind, if I choose to get it off my chest through prayer, I immediately sense part of the load being lifted. With years of this type of positive experience under my belt, I have come to love the feeling associated with simply closing my eyes and clasping my hands together. It must be because it signals the second the rest of the world gets shut out, leaving my God and me alone to connect. And like any conversation with a dear friend, there is no fear of being judged or misunderstood; we can just speak openly and get down to the heart of the matter.

If this is sounding to you like each of my prayer sessions is a momentous and empowering experience, it's because each is. No matter how lengthy or brief the session, not a time goes by without feeling that I've been provided with loving support and direction. The perspective-laden answers that have somehow emerged include: *Take a stand; look at things through her eyes; our actions—good and bad—will echo in eternity; this may be your purpose in the world; you have what it takes to bounce back; work to make a difference in his life; just concentrate on what's within your circle of influence.*

I bet you can now guess the first thing I did upon hearing of the situation at Columbine High. Yes, out of faith, habit, and love I immediately began to pray for all involved.

And as specific information came in, I found myself spending extra time focusing on one specific student, a girl who had reportedly been shot in the head and was now in intensive care fighting for her life.

Amazingly, she ended up surviving her ordeal. Of course, my student, I'm not claiming she made it largely, or even partly, because of prayer. But I do believe that when scores of faithful people—who may not even know one another—focus collectively on a specific matter, it fills the spiritual airwaves with positive energy...with the highest, most far-reaching decibels of hope, compassion, and goodwill. And again, whether you're skeptical of this type of thinking or not, you have nothing to lose—and much to gain—by involving yourself.

Because the act of praying packs such an emotional punch, it is certainly instrumental in helping you or anyone else to further develop faith.

Just as instrumental, and emotion-rich, is the attending of church services. At least this is my personal feeling. You see, there are many—including some close friends of mine—who take issue with the role church plays.

These individuals argue that a relationship with their God can be maintained without ever attending, and that most services are too boring to tolerate anyway. To this, I always counter by calling attention to the vital community aspect of church, as well as of religion itself.

Will there not be times in our lives when each of us in genuine need of others—their help, their sympathy, their mere presence? And in a society increasingly marked by competitiveness and division, is there any other place in which we can come together as equals united by a common bond, to worship, rejoice, and perform good? Besides, is it not comforting, as well as reinforcing to one's faith, to stand together and be reminded of the fact we all share the same hopes and the same fears? (Just think back to how much this helped in the aftermath of the World Trade Center and Pentagon attacks.)

As for their other argument, I can agree that, yes, some services can be perceived as boring. But ultimately, does each individual not have the final say as to what he or she will take from the experience? Can it not be considered another case of "what you put in is what you get out"?

My wife and I choose to hold hands during prayers, sing along with the choir, and focus our minds on all readings so as not to miss the underlying messages. Perhaps this is why I can say, in all honesty, that not a service goes by without me experiencing whole-body chills.

And as if this were not motivation enough to attend, each time we as parishioners exchange handshakes and other gestures of goodwill, I am left feeling happy and whole—in closer touch with myself, my community, my faith, and the God who resides in my heart. These feelings can be yours as well.

Remember then, my student, trusting that you're not alone as you walk through life will provide nothing less than perspective, joy, comfort, and strength—including when bad things happen...*so challenge yourself to keep the faith*. You can do this.

LIFE APP

THIS WEEK, IF YOU SO DESIRE, BEGIN TO MAKE PRAYING A PART OF YOUR NIGHTLY ROUTINE. AS YOU GO TO SLEEP, RECITE A FAMILIAR PRAYER, GIVE THANKS, ASK FOR GUIDANCE, AND/OR SIMPLY TALK ONE-ON-ONE.

INITIATING THIS PURE AND PEACEFUL ACT MAY WELL BECOME THE TRIGGER FOR MAKING GOD'S PRESENCE MORE PALPABLE IN YOUR LIFE, TOO.

WEEK 18

Doing Your Part

I am only one, but still, I am one. I cannot do everything but I can do something. And, because I cannot do everything, I will not refuse to do what I can.
—Edward Everett Hale

Never doubt that a small group of thoughtful, committed citizens can change the world. Indeed, it is the only thing that ever has.
—Margaret Mead

We must not, in trying to think about how we can make a big difference, ignore the small daily differences we can make which, over time, add up to big differences that we often cannot foresee.
—Marion Wright Edelman

I bet you don't realize just how little effort is required to make our planet a cleaner, better place.

It's a critical point to examine, my student, considering just how many in the adult world now see our environmental problems as too big, too overwhelming to be tackled. The vast majority have given up, essentially turning their backs on Mother Nature's ills.

With this troubling thought in mind, consider the following hypothesis: What if out of the blue a doctor were to inform you that in order to live any longer, you would have to start following through on some specific suggestions? Wouldn't you try to, even if it required some sacrifice and discipline on your part? Wouldn't anyone? Well, believe it or not, we do know, specifically, what can be done to improve our ailing earth's condition. It's now a matter of getting the word out, and at the same time, reversing the growing attitude of indifference.

While it may be true each of us is limited by being only one person, we all certainly have the option of being one person who does his or her part. Did you know, for example, every time one person simply turns the water off while brushing his teeth, up to five gallons of water is saved? Can you grasp the savings that would result if all 265 million people in our country, on a brush-to-brush basis, decided to do their part? Or even if only the millions in your generation ended up following through? Do the math and you'll see that together we really can make a monumental difference. I'm certainly going to continue doing my part in this simple way—are you with me?

Another fruitful act any able-bodied person could perform would be that of planting a single tree. That's right, for not only does one tree positively impact both earth's atmosphere and climate—it alone can filter up to 60 pounds of pollutants from the air each year—it can also provide you, the sower, with a real emotional reward.

My own experiences serve as a case in point. Back when I was maybe five or six years old, my dad had me plant a white pine seedling in our backyard. As I grew up, I was able to watch it grow and change in truly striking ways. (Even now, whenever I go home for a visit, I find myself staring pridefully at the 50-foot high monument—as if I were responsible for all its magnificence and splendor.) It truly is a work of art. And as corny as it may sound to some, the two of us—boy and seedling, man and tree, spirit and roots—will forever be connected. Not bad for a mere few minutes worth of work, eh?

Yet another basic measure worthy of one's trouble—and within our control—would be to turn off the lights each time we leave a room. Again, if millions of individuals accepted this tiny responsibility, an enormously significant amount of electricity could be saved. Now don't get me wrong, I'm not naive enough to believe this is all that must be done to eliminate the problems associated with mass-produced electricity (e.g., global warming and acid rain) but I do contend it is a small step in a positive direction. And just as importantly, it's an act—a personal choice—inherent to those individuals likely to someday do more.

I also recognize that getting millions of people to carry out even these simple suggestions will not be easy. I am convinced, however—based on my interactions with young people like you—that your generation is as up to the challenge as any before.

Let's assume for a moment I'm right and you all do manage to get others involved. Well, you can all then look forward to someday sitting back and watching your leadership efforts trickle down to even more individuals. That's right, the example you work to set now will have an impact on the mind-sets and actions of an untold number of future citizens!

A present-day case in point would involve recycling. Never before have so many opportunities to recycle been available to us, and it's due directly to the efforts of none other than my generation. Indeed, most municipalities now run roadside collections for aluminum, glass, newspaper, and plastic. And again, my student, it wasn't always this way. The regenerating of such materials saves nothing less than trees, energy, water, and landfill space—*and* creates jobs. I guess it can be said the more prevalent recycling continues to become, the more pride I myself will take, and the more profound the legacy my generation shall have left behind.

Several young people I know have already gotten started on this business of setting a caring example and of forging a legacy. Some have done so by simply taking charge of the recycling efforts in their own schools and homes. One has dedicated herself to stopping junk mail from being delivered day after day to those who don't want it. Another has organized local battery collections arranging for over 1,000 to be disposed of properly. Still others have joined adult groups that intermittently get together to clean up small parks and riverbanks. (The participants have discovered it to be a satisfying, albeit out of the ordinary, way to spend a Saturday morning.)

You can rest assured that even more opportunities to do your part will present themselves in the future. One way, in particular, involves your future right to vote—since all politicians will eventually have to decide where they stand with regard to environmental matters, and since the choices we make in the voting booth are as important to the environment as the choices we make in our homes. Just be informed, and if you so choose, utilize your votes to support those who understand mankind needs to do much more on behalf of our ailing planet.

I for one will support any national candidate who sees the logic in mandating that all oil companies spend the extra money required to build double-hulled ships. I will also support someone who uses his influence to fight for international regulations that impede rainforest decimation.

As a related sidenote, I once heard a politician declare that because so many trees exist in the world's rainforests, and more can be regrown, there is no need to spend time worrying about the deforestation issue. I seriously doubt, however, that he realized 4 *billion* trees are currently used each and every year for paper products alone. Or that it can take hundreds of years for an area of cleared trees to return to its original state—if ever.

While disheartened by his uninformed stance, I did agree with one point he made: the "don't worry" point. In fact, I frequently tell my students in class that there's no sense lamenting over the many environmental challenges facing us; that worry won't change a single thing and serves only to take the place of action. The bottom line remains: All any of us can control is what's within our individual circle of influence. (As you come to accept this reality, you will take more comfort in knowing you're doing your part.)

And who knows, someday your circle of influence may well expand to take on greater dimensions. Perhaps *you'll* be the politician I choose to support, or the next leader of an environmental organization known the world over for challenging the status quo. You may even end up the head of a corporation who's responsible for deciding whether to secretly dump toxic waste into a nearby river, or to part with the extra money required to dispose of it legally.

As a future wage earner, shopper, and investor, you'll also be able to expand your role by casting votes with your dollars. It's not difficult to find out which companies have track records of irresponsible polluting and which are leaders in the area of environmental sensitivity. You, the informed consumer, can then use such information to decide with whom you are most comfortable doing business.

With regard to specific products, you may want to buy tuna only from those distributors who take extensive measures to protect dolphins; or deodorant and makeup from those who refrain from testing their products on animals.

However you choose to contribute, you must in the end trust that even your smallest of actions are part of a greater effort. For imagine if one day people *everywhere* abruptly decided to burn down a tree or start throwing trash out their car windows—it wouldn't take very long to notice the changes, now would it?

Well, fortunately for us, the concept works both ways.

Remember then, my student, the planet—home to all of us—is in dire need of our individual attention and care...*so challenge yourself to do your part*. You can do this.

LIFE APP

LEAD BY EXAMPLE, DEMONSTRATING TO THE HOPELESS AND INDIFFERENT THAT SPECIFIC SUGGESTIONS DO EXIST—ONES THAT WHEN CARRIED OUT REALLY CAN SERVE TO STABILIZE, AND EVEN UPGRADE, THE EARTH'S CONDITION.

DID YOU KNOW, FOR EXAMPLE, THAT A NATURAL ALTERNATIVE FOR JUST ABOUT EVERY HOUSEHOLD CLEANING CHEMICAL IN OUR CLOSETS AND CABINETS HAS ALREADY BEEN DISCOVERED (AND IS NOW BEING PRODUCED AND SOLD BY A CUTTING-EDGE COMPANY CALLED *SEVENTH GENERATION*)? OR THAT JUICE BOXES, MILK CARTONS, AND BIKE TIRES ARE INCLUDED IN THE TYPES OF MATERIALS THAT ARE EASILY RECYCLED?

DID YOU KNOW THERE EVEN EXISTS AN ADDRESS YOU CAN WRITE TO IN ORDER TO REDUCE THE AMOUNT OF YOUR JUNK MAIL? (THE DIRECT MARKETING ASSOCIATION, MAIL PREFERENCE SERVICE, P.O. BOX 9008, FARMINGDALE, NY 11735-9008)

THERE ARE MORE EASY-TO-DO AND EASY-TO-FIND PRESCRIPTIONS FOR HELPING OUT THAN YOU COULD POSSIBLY IMAGINE. AND WHILE THERE MAY ALWAYS BE A SECTOR OF PEOPLE IN SOCIETY WHO DON'T BOTHER TO EVEN TRY, EVENTUALLY—WITH INDIVIDUALS LIKE YOU LEADING THE WAY—THE ACT OF FOLLOWING THROUGH ON THESE AND OTHER PLANET-FRIENDLY IDEAS WILL SIMPLY BECOME A NEW WAY OF LIFE.

IN CLOSING, I'D LIKE YOU TO CONSIDER THE FOLLOWING "RECYCLING REALITIES," WHICH HAMMER HOME JUST HOW MUCH OF A DIFFERENCE IS MADE BY DOING OUR PART:

1. BY RECYCLING ALL THE MORNING NEWSPAPERS READ AROUND THE COUNTRY, 41,000 TREES WOULD BE SAVED DAILY AND 6 MILLION TONS OF WASTE WOULD NEVER END UP IN LANDFILLS.

LIFE APP

2. IF EVERYONE IN THE U.S. WERE TO RECYCLE EVEN 1/10 OF THEIR NEWSPRINT, WE WOULD SAVE THE ESTIMATED EQUIVALENT OF ABOUT 25 MILLION TREES A YEAR.
3. RECYCLABLE PLASTIC GARBAGE THAT INSTEAD ENDS UP IN THE OCEAN KILLS AS MANY AS ONE MILLION SEA CREATURES PER YEAR.
4. A SINGLE QUART OF MOTOR OIL, WHEN DISPOSED OF IMPROPERLY, CAN CONTAMINATE UP TO 2 MILLION GALLONS OF FRESH WATER.
5. THE ENERGY SAVED FROM RECYCLING A SINGLE GLASS BOTTLE WILL LIGHT A 100-WATT LIGHTBULB FOR 4 HOURS.
6. THE ENERGY SAVED FROM RECYCLING A SINGLE ALUMINUM CAN WILL RUN A COMPUTER FOR THREE HOURS.
7. AMERICANS THROW AWAY ENOUGH ALUMINUM EVERY THREE MONTHS TO REBUILD ALL THE PLANES IN THE NATION'S COMMERCIAL AIRLINE FLEET.

POINT MADE.

WEEK 19

Giving Animals a Voice

The greatness of a nation can be judged by the way its animals are treated.
—Gandhi

Humankind has not woven the web of life. We are but one thread within it. Whatever we do to the web, we do to ourselves. All things are bound together. All things connect.
—Chief Seattle

Every time I look into the eyes of an animal I see life; the force of life and the beauty of creation.
—Radar O'Reilly

A severely burned cat repeatedly enters a fire-engulfed building to rescue her kittens. A dog, already shot at close range, continues to attack an intruder, ultimately saving his owner's life but losing his own. The sheer majesty of an eagle in flight, a horse in full stride, or a lone lion on the lookout. Families of apes, whales, and elephants exhibiting advanced capacities—devotion and grief included—providing *us* with actual lessons in humanity. Mass numbers of cows, chickens, pigs, etc. providing life sustenance in the form of their milk, their eggs, and their very flesh.

Examples of such wondrous "animal contributions" abound, as clearly, my student, they represent one of earth's most vital resources...and one of life's most precious gifts.

Considering their undeniably immense value, a visitor to our planet might expect to see animals being respected, revered even, or at the very least watched over by us humans. But as you know, this is not always the case. The reality of the matter is examples of animal abuse and exploitation abound.

The day I vowed to write this advisement was a most disturbing one for me. As I walked through a popular New England fair, I witnessed firsthand just the kind of animal exploitation to which I am referring. It wasn't the first time I had attended this fair, either. Growing up, my family visited on an almost annual basis. It was just the first time I chose to look—really look—at the animals. (I challenge everyone to take this longer, harder look.)

There was a lone giraffe staring motionless into the top of a tattered tent. Three tigers lying separated—and silent—in their undersized cages. And a similarly lethargic elephant providing ride after ride, as if it were more a robot than a living, breathing being. It was by far the most unnatural scene I had ever laid eyes on—one that left me overwhelmed with strong feelings of guilt and obligation.

It was at this moment of emotional upheaval that I realized animals such as these were in dire need of a voice. And I immediately knew that rallying the ranks of young people everywhere—many of whom understand the value of doing good in their world far more than their adult counterparts, and already possess a "what can I do to help" attitude—would provide the most vocal and far-reaching one of all.

Fairs are not the only public attraction with a history of exploiting animals. No, my student, the ever-popular circus has been doing it for quite some time, too.

So long, in fact, each new generation of families rarely thinks twice about paying the price of admission and taking in the show. It's become a rite of passage, something every family gets to do together at least once or twice. But what if "a voice" were to ask these same people—many of whom are uninformed, but nonetheless, well-intentioned and compassionate—to consider the type of circumstances under which circus animals are forced to exist?

Did you know, for instance, circus elephants are usually stolen from their families and, according to testimony of former trainers themselves, subjected to physical abuse and neglect for the purpose of breaking their wild spirit? The remainder of their lives (upwards of 50 years) can be defined by little more than chains, long grueling road trips, confinement to boxcars and cages, stressful training sessions, and, of course, performances that leave families smiling and clapping.

The families of these elephants, on the other hand, are often left devastated by the loss of one of their own. I'm not exaggerating either, as deep, powerful bonds have been shown to exist among the species. Male elephants remain with their mothers for 10 to 15 years, while females stay by their mother's side *for life*. And when other family members are threatened, some within the fiercely loyal herd have even been recorded fighting back in the face of insurmountable odds—swirling helicopter blades and earsplitting gunfire included. Lastly, on top of all this, elephants are known to have specific behavioral rituals related to death—their own way of grieving.

Clearly, these peaceful, intelligent creatures have as much a right as we do to live out their natural lives. But tragically, those in captivity will never again get to experience the sweet realities of family unity and freedom—no, our "amusement" is now their sole destiny.

Make no mistake, though, by providing these animals a voice, we pay deep homage to their struggles as well as to their very being. And the day our society truly moves forward by making animal circuses an event of the past, we will have helped to make certain their suffering did not go in vain. I really do believe your generation's voice can be the one to accomplish this, the one that finally establishes circuses with amazing *human* performers as the family shows-of-choice for the next millennium.

You may be surprised to learn that the common cat and dog are also involved in some heart-wrenching predicaments and also in desperate need of a voice. The following statistics do well to illustrate this point:

1. While approximately 11,000 human babies are delivered each day, more than 70,000 puppies and kittens are born in the same 24-hour time frame, and a mere 1 out of 5 of these animals finds a home.
2. Millions of these "leftover" animals are abandoned and suffer needlessly before perishing, with about 17 million per year actually ending up in animal shelters. But because only 1 out of every 10 gets adopted, over 15 million are left behind to be destroyed.

To be perfectly honest, I don't allow myself to think much about such numbers—they're far too troubling. But let me tell you, on those occasions when I do let them sink in, I'm left feeling both numbed and perplexed. I just cannot believe—nor accept—the reality of it all. This is the 21st century, is it not? What a horrible legacy for our nation to *still* be leaving behind.

Obviously, a great deal more needs to be done to get this situation turned around; and our voices—yes, yours and mine—can be instrumental to the process. Most critically, we need to get the word out about family pets being spayed or neutered. This one simple act could *significantly* reduce the number of unwanted and homeless animals in the world.

Next, families who've decided to get a new pet should be advised to first try their local Humane Society shelter. Even if they're set on acquiring a certain breed of dog, they need to know they still have a legitimate shot of meeting with success there—as one out of every four homeless dogs is, believe it or not, purebred. If things do not work out for them at the shelter, they can simply turn to the Yellow Pages and look under "animal rescue." The organizations listed there take in so many unwanted pets themselves, it's an attempt well worth making.

Lastly, people need to be encouraged to think long and hard about purchasing animals at pet stores. These stores buy predominantly from breeding centers, (a.k.a. mills or factories), which only add to the overpopulation problem by mass-producing babies. What's more, my student, so many of these babies are being born that meeting even their basic needs has become an enormous task. And as a result, some of "the product"—mothers and their helpless offspring, mind you—have been discovered suffering from diseases and severe neglect.

My own wife feels so strongly about this issue that she won't buy anything—not a crate, not food, not even a toy—from any business that chooses to sell animals. Indeed, if more people were to see the big picture, stores such as these would switch their profit focus from mass-produced animals to pet supplies. And then all the activity at breeding centers—not to mention at the shelters and pounds—would finally slow down.

The fact there exist so many battles to be fought on behalf of our animal counterparts (greyhound racing, whale hunting, pollution of natural environments, cockfighting, fur trapping, bull fighting, and poaching, just to name a few more) can leave even the most driven individual feeling deflated or overwhelmed. But take heart, for there exists some encouraging news, too.

In the face of all the planet-wide challenges, more and more people—voices from every generation—are choosing to step up and answer the call to get involved. Some of these individuals help to make up the dedicated animal organizations that have established a strong, far-reaching voice of their own. These groups are renowned for doggedly working to educate the public, while always pushing for more humane animal conditions. And thanks to all the effort, huge success stories have been—and continue to be—written (e.g., the Endangered Species Act, the banning of DDT, the strengthening of animal cruelty penalties), all of which have indeed made a tremendous difference in the world.

Even in my own neck of the woods—New England—some long-awaited signs of change are in the air. In Maine, for example, the Humane Society along with local animal protection groups, have—as of this writing—proposed a bill that would no longer allow steel-jaw leghold traps to be used. Other states have already acted on making this trap device less barbaric—Maine has not. If this issue makes it to the November statewide ballot, however, residents armed with a voice in the form of their right to vote are expected to strike an overdue blow to this clearly inhumane practice. (If the thousands of animals whose fur renders them a target could say thanks for caring and thanks for the voice, no doubt they would.)

And even in Taunton, Massachusetts, where city residents recently voted down a proposal to eliminate dog racing at the local track, a silver lining can be found. At least the opportunity to rescue the greyhounds was finally won. And as more and more voices get involved with spreading awareness, our ranks—along with the opportunities and promise for positive change—will only continue to grow.

Remember then, my student, the living, breathing beings with whom we share this planet have no say whatsoever in how they are treated—or mistreated...*so challenge yourself to give animals a voice*. You can do this.

LIFE APP

YOUR OWN OPTIONS FOR PROVIDING ANIMALS A VOICE—AND THUS, FOR DOING MORE GOOD IN THE WORLD—ARE LIMITLESS. YOU CAN, FOR EXAMPLE, MAKE A PERSONAL POINT OF PURCHASING ONLY THOSE BEAUTY PRODUCTS (E.G., SHAMPOO, LOTION, MAKEUP, AND HAIRSPRAY) MARKED WITH THE "NO ANIMAL TESTING" LABEL. (YES, SOME COMPANIES *STILL* SUBJECT ANIMALS TO PAIN, SUFFERING, AND UNKNOWN SIDE EFFECTS FOR THE SOLE PURPOSE OF EXPANDING THEIR PRODUCT LINES AND PROFITS.)

YOU CAN ALSO HELP TO SPEARHEAD MONEY-RAISING EFFORTS FOR NON-PROFIT ORGANIZATIONS COMMITTED TO HELPING ANIMALS. I MYSELF AM INTENT ON RAISING MORE FOR THE BEST FRIENDS SANCTUARY IN UTAH, AS WELL AS THE YANKEE GOLDEN RETRIEVER RESCUE IN MASSACHUSETTS—BOTH OF WHICH DO A TREMENDOUS AMOUNT OF GOOD IN THEIR SMALL CORNERS OF THE WORLD.

YOU CAN EVEN CHOOSE TO EAT DIFFERENTLY. BUY ONLY KOSHER MEATS, OR IF YOU DESIRE, ADOPT A VEGETARIAN LIFESTYLE.

FINALLY, YOUR LOCAL HUMANE SOCIETY OFFICE CAN HELP GUIDE YOUR PERSONAL EFFORTS. ALL YOU HAVE TO DO IS CALL OR VISIT AND ASK IF THERE'S ANYTHING YOU CAN DO TO HELP. BASED ON THE EXPERIENCES OF THOSE I'VE KNOWN, YOU MAY END UP STARTING A PETITION DRIVE, CLEANING CAGES, ADOPTING AN ANIMAL, LEADING A LOCAL AD CAMPAIGN (E.G., TO GET MORE PEOPLE TO SPAY OR NEUTER THEIR PETS), JOINING A PICKET LINE, EDUCATING FELLOW STUDENTS, OR WRITING STATE LEGISLATORS ON BEHALF OF AN ANIMAL-FRIENDLY LAW. INDEED, IF EVERYONE WHO READS THIS ADVISEMENT ADDS THEIR OWN VOICE TO THE MIX, WE WILL UNDOUBTEDLY SUCCEED AT IMPROVING THE LIVES OF OUR ANIMAL FRIENDS, AND IN THE PROCESS, MAKE THE WORLD A BETTER PLACE *FOR ALL*.

WEEK 20

Being Less Judgmental

We are inclined to judge ourselves by our ideals; others by their acts.
—Sir Harold George Nicolson

If you judge people, you have no time to love them.
—Mother Teresa

Great Spirit, help me never to judge another until I have walked in his moccasins.
—Sioux Indian Prayer

Unless you yourself have been regularly judged, you probably haven't put a whole lot of thought into this particular behavior. I can assure you, however, that the day someone unfairly judges you—based on gossip, hearsay, first impressions, outer appearances, etc.—will come. And when it does, deep-rooted feelings of injustice and frustration will leave you in search of answers.

Let's examine together, then, why it is so many members of our society—people of all ages—feel the need to criticize and/or categorize those who are even remotely different, or those who just happen to rub them the wrong way.

After putting much research and thought into the matter, I've come to the conclusion that specific payoffs are reaped from the act of judging others. Perhaps you've experienced some of them firsthand.

For one, the widespread appeal has much to do with the feelings of superiority that result from "looking down one's nose" at another. Those who judge may not recognize this as a contributing factor, but on some level, they relish in the sensation of power (albeit "false power") that races through them. Secondly, my student, it's a means to simplify things in a complex world. Heck, if someone can manage to label an entire group of people (e.g., jocks, foreigners, lawyers, etc.) as lazy or ignorant or dishonest, for instance, he no longer has to put much if any thought into matters involving them, right? And lastly, being judgmental serves to protect our own bruised and tattered self-images. Let's say, for example, you were to laugh at or be overly critical of a peer's performance in the spotlight. You would then be left feeling—at least for the time being—more capable and talented yourself.

Of course, as it is with any dubious behavior, there are also pitfalls. (Based on personal observations, I've found most people to be far less in tune to these as they are to the so-called payoffs.) For example, with regard to the hypothetical situation that had you picking apart a peer's performance, do you realize while you may have been able to temporarily boost your own ego, you also succeeded at opening yourself up to similar criticisms the next time *you* are in the spotlight? That's right, judging others leaves you more susceptible to your own inner voice, or inner critic, as well as to others' real or imagined critiques. So I guess there is something to the old "what comes around goes around" adage.

Next, being overly judgmental increases your chances of being wrong about others, and consequently, of missing out on positive interactions and relationships. Case in point: I once judged someone based solely on what others had told me. They had proclaimed—at a time when the young lady in question was not around to defend herself—that she was arrogant and self-centered in the most typical of ways. Ignorantly, I deemed it best to keep my distance. As fate would have it, though, the two of us were paired up to work together on an important project, leaving me no other choice but to get to know her.

Well, she turned out to be much different from what I had heard. In fact, we had so good a time working together we struck up a friendship that has lasted to this day. It's unsettling for me to think I could have lost out on a lifetime of camaraderie just because I was once foolish enough to let others' judgments influence my own. The moral of the story is to *form your own opinions* of people no matter what you've heard through the grapevine.

That said, if you ever have trouble following such advice, simply think back to a time when someone who didn't truly know you passed judgment before providing even half a chance. Indeed, your deep sense of injustice and frustration will serve as a powerful motivator to not repeat the mistake yourself—I can again personally attest to it.

Just recently, you see, two women to whom I was introduced treated me in a disrespectful and rude manner. They let it be known that my being a teacher, of all things, did not sit well with them. I believe *overpaid* and *underworked* were the exact terms they used. (For the record, this was far from the first time I'd encountered such prejudice since, according to many outside the classroom, teachers don't work as hard or as often as those in "the real world" do.)

Well, as we abruptly parted ways I was left to wonder, *Did it ever cross their minds, since they've never done my job, that they really have no idea as to how demanding or time-consuming it is, hence no basis whatsoever to judge the profession, let alone me as a person? Did it ever cross their minds that believing teachers only work when students are in the classroom is as narrow-minded as assuming trial attorneys only work when jurors are in the box, or as inaccurate as presuming priests only work when parishioners are in the pews? Did it ever cross their minds to instead judge me in a more positive light as someone who became a teacher to make a difference in young people's lives, who saw the classroom as the place where he could make his greatest contribution?"* Apparently, and sadly, not.

The fact that so many people feel compelled to judge others in overly harsh or cynical ways is unfortunate, but it's a behavior that can be eradicated. For starters, each of us needs to recognize that no matter how confident we are in our opinions of another, we do not truly know the person. Just as there are multiple sides to every story, there are layers to every individual that only those closest to him or her could possibly know. Even in instances when you've judged someone based on factual information (as opposed to impressions, rumors, etc.), you can't be sure your views are, or always will be, entirely accurate.

Let's suppose that someone who really was an arrogant and self-centered person in the past—and deserved to be judged as such—has come to see the error of his ways. Admirably, he has committed to the challenge of changing and growing into a better human being. Should he be labeled for life among those who know, knew, or had heard about him? Or should he be given the chance, free of any judgment, to redefine himself? As you reflect on these questions, keep in mind that each and every one of us is a work in progress.

So really, what on earth is the purpose behind habitually judging others? Do we not all come from different backgrounds? Are we not all at varying stages of our personal development journeys? What's to say that if we had lived through another person's identical life experiences, we wouldn't act in the same ways, value the same things, and even commit the same blunders—the very ones we tend to piously look down upon?

Clearly, the time has come to show the world the next generation is secure and insightful enough to break the trend of judging others in overly harsh and habitual ways—once and for all.

Remember then, my student, there is no redeeming value—for you or for the rest of the world—behind cynically categorizing, criticizing, and casting others in a negative light...*so challenge yourself to be less judgmental.* You can do this.

LIFE APP

MAKE A POINT OF GETTING THROUGH AT LEAST ONE DAY THIS WEEK WITHOUT NEGATIVELY JUDGING ANOTHER. IN FACT, EACH TIME YOU CATCH YOUR MIND GOING IN THE CATEGORIZING OR FAULTFINDING DIRECTION (E.G., HER TASTE IN CLOTHES IS A JOKE, YOU CALL THAT MUSIC, HE CHOKED AGAIN IN A CLUTCH SITUATION, WHAT A TERRIBLE-LOOKING HAIRCUT, THEY WALK AROUND LIKE THEY'RE BETTER THAN THE REST OF US), ACTUALLY TRANSFER YOUR ENERGIES TO FINDING SOMETHING POSITIVE AND REDEEMING ABOUT THE PERSON OR GROUP.

FOR IF JUDGING PEOPLE IN A MORE OPTIMISTIC WAY EVENTUALLY BECOMES A PERSONAL HABIT, YOU CAN REST ASSURED YOUR OPPORTUNITIES TO CONNECT WITH OPEN-MINDED, INTERESTING PEOPLE—AND HENCE, YOUR LIKELIHOOD OF FORGING A TRULY RICH, REWARDING LIFE—WILL BE GREATLY ENHANCED!

WEEK 21

Being a True Friend

Wishing to be friends is quick work, but friendship is slow-ripening fruit.
—Aristotle

Friendship consists in forgetting what one gives and remembering what one receives.
– Alexandre Dumas

A friend is someone who knows all about you, and loves you just the same.
—Author Unknown

Simply put, in order to have good friends you must be a good friend. That's right, my student, it starts with *you*, so look inward for a moment and reflect:

1. Am I a person worth knowing?
2. Do I respect others' feelings?
3. Can I be trusted?
4. Am I a good listener?
5. Have I proven capable of being open and truthful?
6. Do I put an act on around others or am I able to be myself?
7. Do I have the courage to let someone *really* know me?
8. Have I proven capable of being compassionate and supportive?
9. Do I tend to be positive and enthusiastic instead of dull and negative?

Fortunately, these are all aspects of yourself you can work to develop. (And even if you've got a long way to go, take heart, for as long as you're striving toward such ends, the possibility of striking up quality friendships exists.)

Once you do indeed become confident in your own friendship capacities, you'll be far more apt to pass the type of "friendship tests" with which life is known to challenge us.

Let's assume, for example, your soccer team is on the verge of winning a state playoff game. Almost inexplicably, the goalie—who happens to be a friend—allows a weak shot to dribble by him into the net. You wind up losing and the season ends abruptly. Most of the team, the fans, and perhaps even the coaches, react instinctively by turning their backs on this individual.

Do you have it in you to be that rare human being who walks right up to him, looks into his eyes, and says, "Keep your head up. I know you were out there giving your best. This kind of fluky thing could have happened to anybody—even a professional."

Certainly, this is the rare mark of someone who's there for others when they're in most need, when it's not easy to be there, or put another way, the mark of a true friend.

Having thought about what's required of you to form special friendships, you're now equipped to more accurately assess the character of others, too. And rest assured, such insights will not only help guide you in determining which individuals are worthy of your loyalty, but also which are not.

Frankly, the plenty who aren't—what my students in class and I refer to as false friends—don't tend to concern themselves with the type of criteria you're now striving to meet. In fact, they seem intent on proving just how unaware and unfit certain individuals are capable of being. Following is a list of attributes that can be associated with these false-friend types. I'm sure many will sound familiar to you.

1. They are notoriously poor listeners.
2. They cannot be trusted with a secret.
3. They talk about others behind their backs.
4. They are unwilling to consider opinions different from their own.
5. They insist that conversations revolve around themselves.
6. They don't care if they hurt others' feelings.
7. They routinely apply negative peer pressure.
8. They pursue friendships for superficial reasons, e.g., the other person is popular, owns a car, has a swimming pool, etc.

On top of all this, there is one more telltale trait for you to consider. If anyone who calls himself a friend ever tries to coerce you into doing wrong, watch out. For a person who truly cares about you would never—under any circumstances—act in such a way.

While this may strike you as an obvious sign of trouble, it is lost on scores of other young people. Many naively continue to hang around with those who continue to show little regard for their well-being. I'm sure you know someone who fits this description, too.

I myself once made this mistake. Looking back, I believe I may have turned a blind eye simply because I wanted to be a part of the group. Besides, I rationalized, there were other times when they seemed to treat me great. Still, my student, I should've known that anybody who tries to talk you into doing wrong—even once—is not a true friend. I guess you can say I learned this life lesson the hard way.

One day after school, the usual group and I gathered at my house. A few of the "leaders" had brought some spray paint along and it was decided—no, declared—that we'd mark up some neighborhood street signs. I didn't have a good feeling about the plan, yet a small dose of pressure from the guys was all it took to get me to go along. Well, to make a long story short, about four signs into the vandalizing spree, a police car approached—and everyone ran except for me. I figured, hey, since I hadn't personally sprayed any signs, there was no reason for me to flee.

What I failed to realize, however, was that in the eyes of the law—and in the eyes of everyone else for that matter—I was guilty for simply being with the perpetrators. (The official term for this is guilt by association.) Even so, the police informed me if those who actually did the painting admitted to it, I would be let off the hook.

So what do you think happened? You got it. Not one of my so-called friends—all of whom had heard about the offer—came forward. My parents were then called in and I lost for what seemed like forever every privilege I'd ever known. (In retrospect, the only thing that really lasted that long was the invaluable lesson I had learned.)

The big payoff for learning from your own false-friendship experiences will come the moment you realize you've finally found a genuine friend. Typically, this happens when you least expect it, and with an individual you would not have predicted. That's right, things like race, religion, and gender are simply nonissues when it comes to true friendship. The bottom line is—as anyone who's ever been a part of a tight bond would attest—you are both fortunate to have found one another.

A true friend, after all, is like adding another member to your family—is it not? And each of you will now have someone to do the kind of things friends have always enjoyed doing: share feelings, advice, laughs, and pizza...blast music...work out...study...shop...catch a movie...talk on the phone...try out new experiences...stick together through tough times...care enough to listen—really listen...do nothing...allow room for change and growth...actually keep a secret... etc. Essentially, a friend is a person you choose to share the good and bad of life with. And what could be more meaningful than that?

As fate would have it, though, even the closest of friends sometimes end up drifting apart. Now I'm not saying this will happen to you, since lifelong friendships do exist, but the possibility does remain. I know I would've never predicted that my best friend from high school and I would end up going our separate ways, but we did. He continued making self-destructive choices I just couldn't support any longer. And while I did my best to help him through, it eventually led to a breakdown in communication, respect, and trust. We still tried to hang out and act as though nothing had changed, but things just never felt the same. It's funny how gut feelings can clue us in to when it's time to allow a friendship to end, to when it's time to move on.

Remember then, my student, forming the special bonds that add so much special meaning to life starts with *you...so challenge yourself to be a true friend*. You can do this.

LIFE APP

AT SOME POINT THIS WEEK, REFLECT ON THE FOLLOWING QUESTIONS:

1. WHO AM I FRIENDS WITH AND WHY?
2. WHO DO I WANT TO BE FRIENDS WITH AND WHY?
3. IN WHAT CIRCUMSTANCES HAVE FRIENDS LET ME DOWN?
4. IN WHAT CIRCUMSTANCES HAVE I LET MY FRIENDS DOWN?
5. IS THERE A FRIENDSHIP I SHOULD HAVE ALREADY ENDED?
6. AM I OPEN TO THE POSSIBILITY OF STRIKING UP NEW FRIENDSHIPS?

WEEK 22

Avoiding Gossip

Whoever gossips to you will gossip about you.
—Spanish Proverb

What you don't see with your eyes, don't witness with your mouth.
—Jewish Proverb

A rumor is the one thing that gets thicker instead of thinner as it spreads.
—Richard Willard Armour

The jealous are troublesome to others, but torment to themselves.
—William Penn

"Can you believe what so and so is up to?" "What do you know about her?" "I've heard he's always been that way." "The word around town is..."

Ughhhh. Let me go on record, my student, as saying I can no longer stomach this kind of petty blather. Perhaps you can already relate.

To me, the act of gossiping as much as any other dysfunctional behavior is symptomatic of the most common human ailment: *ineffective living*. Life is simply too miraculous and far too short to waste even a single moment pointlessly digging up and spreading dirt on others. I mean it. In fact, when in the presence of any rumormonger—and believe me, they're well represented in every age group—I invariably find myself wanting to scream, *"Would you please get a life!"*

In all seriousness, though, I don't believe such individuals ever stop to consider just how senseless and unredeeming an act gossiping really is. First off, gossip is a notoriously unreliable source of information, is it not? There are no judge and jury in need of convincing, nor is the person "on trial" around to present the ever-elusive but all-important other side of the story. Consequently, important details, and yes, even a few cold, hard facts end up taking a backseat to a shallow person's need to feel worthy or superior.

Second, you can literally spend a lifetime doing it. That's right. Because no human being is without faults, those who actively search out negatives in others are guaranteed to succeed. In other words, there exists an endless supply of fuel for the fire. (Perhaps this has something to do with why so many succumb to the habit.) If only more of us realized that searching out the positives in others is just as much a sure bet.

Lastly, there's good reason for gossip to be routinely referred to as "backstabbing." You should therefore remain wary if the group you hang with is prone to digging up and spreading dirt on others. I mean what's to say they're not doing the same thing to you when your back is turned? Have they not shown their stripes? Do you think busybodies have any other loyalty but to themselves? Unfortunately, most of us end up learning these answers the hard way.

On a personal note, being around people who have given in to the gossip lure leaves me feeling remarkably similar to how I once did when in the presence of those who gave in to alcohol and other such drugs. It just feels wrong; there's this deep sensation within that says things are not supposed to be this way—that our time on earth is meant to be so much more.

Because of my strong sentiments pertaining to gossip, I've actually begun to let people know—in a rather blunt way—that I'm not at all interested in talking or hearing about others who aren't around to defend themselves. Usually my position on the matter is respected, or at least accepted, but I've also encountered more than a few who snap back with, "Oh, what do you think, you're above it all and those who do it?"

To this I now reply (and feel free to use my words if ever in a similar spot), "I certainly aspire to break free from and rise above the false allure of gossiping; I try to remind myself that life is way too short, and each one of its moments far too precious, *to waste* being petty. Besides, what do you think you're all doing when you gossip? Essentially, each of you is saying, 'I'm better, or above, another person.'"

If you are not comfortable speaking out, my student, simply try an alternative approach. Refuse to participate by sitting silently, or by attempting to change the topic of conversation. A strong message can also be delivered by saying something positive about the individual(s) being dissed. And if all else fails, walk away, as even this simple, quiet act will speak volumes.

If you do summon the strength to take a personal stand against gossip, you should also take great pride in the knowledge you are on the less traveled path to living *effectively*. Oh yes, such people do not have the need or desire to faultfind and backstab—nor do they have the time. They're too busy living with perspective, purpose, and passion; too busy appreciating and enjoying their present moments; and too busy growing and evolving into a person they can be proud of!

In spite of what my strong feelings may be conveying, I harbor no ill will or contempt for those who insist on sticking their noses in other people's business. More than anything, I feel sorry for them. In fact, I often wonder if they realize just how wasteful and damaging the habit is, since ultimately, our lives are defined by how we choose to live moment to moment.

I also wonder if they ever stop to reflect on why it is they feel the need to partake. Based on my own observations and reflections, I've concluded it has much to do with personal insecurities—a vulnerable self-image, if you will. They use this type of behavior as a means of keeping their focus off themselves and their deep-rooted frailties, while attracting the surface attention of others. Essentially, what they're saying is: "Hey, look at me...listen to me...I've got some juicy news...I'm worthy and important."

Whatever the individual reasons, I root for every gossip to eventually rise above the pettiness.

Remember then, my student, just because people from every walk of life and every age group choose to engage in a particular behavior doesn't make it any more sensible—nor any less a waste of precious time...*so challenge yourself to avoid gossip*. You can do this.

LIFE APP

IT'S NOT A GOOD SIGN THAT OUR SOCIETY SEEMS TO LITERALLY THRIVE ON CONTROVERSY AND SCANDAL. IF YOU EVER GET DRAWN IN, VIEW IT AS A CRYSTAL-CLEAR SIGN YOU NEED TO ADD MORE PURPOSE AND MEANING TO YOUR LIFE. (AND TAKE COMFORT IN THE KNOWLEDGE THERE ARE MULTIPLE WAYS TO GO ABOUT DOING THIS—WITH THE TOPICS IN THIS BOOK PROVIDING PLENTY OF SUPPORT AND DIRECTION.)

NEXT, WHEN WONDERING IF YOUR OWN WORDS ABOUT ANOTHER CAN BE CONSIDERED GOSSIP, ASK THE SIMPLE QUESTION, "WILL THOSE I'M TALKING TO WALK AWAY FROM THIS CONVERSATION THINKING ANY LESS OF THE PERSON?"

AND LASTLY, ANY TIME YOU PERSONALLY ENCOUNTER GOSSIP, BE READY TO TAKE A STAND BY IMPLEMENTING THE STRATEGIES WE'VE COVERED. WE CAN, AFTER ALL, CHANGE THE WAY OUR SOCIETY FUNCTIONS—OR DYSFUNCTIONS—ONE INDIVIDUAL AT A TIME.

WEEK 23

Being More Assertive

Learn to value yourself, which means: to fight for your happiness.

—Ayn Rand

It's important to let people know what you stand for. It's equally important that they know what you won't stand for.

—B. Bader

Promote yourself but do not demote another.

—Israel Salanter

Have you ever responded "yes" when you really wanted to say "no"? Can you recall a time when you stayed silent as someone proceeded to put you down? Have you ever, while in the presence of others, held back a question or opinion you desperately wanted to voice?

It's safe to say, my student, you've been there, done that with one or even all of these examples. The good news is you don't have to continue behaving in such ways. In fact, you owe it to yourself to become a more assertive individual now.

Let's begin by exploring the reasons why so many choose to be passive. For example, nodding your head in agreement, even when you disagree, is a way to evade tense and uneasy situations. Backing down, even when you're being put down, is a way to steer clear of confrontation or further abuse. And lastly, not speaking up, even when you desperately want to, is a way to avoid the risk of sounding dumb, or dare I say, different.

In all three instances, you've succeeded at avoiding something else as well: the disapproval of others. That's right, for some of us approval is being attained at any and all cost.

Make no mistake about it, though, at some point the cost must be weighed, for there is a steep price paid by those who fail to act assertively. Psychologists report that such individuals are generally self-critical and often unhappy with themselves—and it's certainly not hard to understand why. Just how many times can a person sit by silently while others take advantage of him? Nothing less than his dignity, mind you, is being compromised.

And then there's the looming long-range consequence. Imagine someday looking back on life only to realize you never developed the ability to speak your mind and stand up for yourself, that you instead spent much of your time bowing to the whims of others—many of whom could care less about you! It really is no wonder passivity, alone, can destroy one's deepest sense of self-respect.

Thankfully, it's never too late for a young person to change. If the idea of becoming more assertive appeals to you, a change in underlying attitude is where your focus should lie. Yes, my student, you need to start seeing yourself in a totally new light. Specifically, as someone who deserves and expects to be treated with the same level of respect you afford others, and as someone who's now intent on acting confidently—from a position of strength. Also understand that no one can ever take advantage of you without your permission.

Such a commitment can translate into something as basic as walking into a room with more pride and purpose; or as clear-cut as now looking people straight in the eyes when you respond to them. It also requires, on those occasions when you're not feeling particularly confident, that you make a point of *acting* as though you are.

For example, the next time anxiety over being wrong and sounding dumb is keeping you out of a class discussion, raise your hand into the air anyway, take a breath to suspend the butterflies, and proceed to state what's on your mind. (Do it in your firm, clear voice, similar to the one you use when interacting with friends and family.) You'll soon discover that each time you battle through passiveness, it becomes less and less an act, and more and more a natural outflow of the new individual you're becoming.

For me, personally, there was once a time when I had to summon every ounce of courage just to say the simple word "no." And even then, because others knew me as someone who had always "given them permission" to take advantage of me, I was often prodded to change my mind. Well, after coming to the harsh realization I was not living life on my own terms, and certainly not acting from a position of strength, I challenged myself to respond to requests of my time with more assertiveness. It took some acting, much practice, and even more persistence, but I'm now at the point where I can actually look someone in the eyes and say, "No, I'm not interested in doing that"—without offering a single reason why.

While this certainly rates as a significant personal accomplishment, it tends to open up a whole 'nother can of worms...one that you, too, need to be prepared for. You see, despite the fact that I make a point of responding to people in polite and respectful ways—and still say yes at times—I have on more than one occasion been painted as selfish, even arrogant, for saying no. Some people, for obvious reasons, just prefer the pushover type.

Amazingly, though, this type of disapproval no longer fazes me. That's right, with all the newfound pride and self-respect I've reaped from being more assertive, I can actually handle it. And besides, attempts to guilt us into reverting back to old ways are known to come with the assertiveness territory. I mean what else do you expect when those accustomed to using/abusing you suddenly realize their personal well has run dry?

As you can see, I speak from experience when I claim assertiveness can grant a whole new lease on life. Indeed, as you gradually develop this habit you'll find your own levels of self-respect surging. You'll start feeling more relaxed, more in control, and more secure in all types of interactions. The likelihood of being used and taken advantage of by others will be greatly reduced. As will the days of being disappointed in yourself for shying away from confrontation and not speaking your mind.

Moreover, living assertively earns the respect and admiration of others. Those who share your outlook will naturally attract to you, thus increasing the number of quality relationships in your life. Those who are put off or intimidated by your self-assured ways will have to at least give you credit for being honest and forthright. And those impacted most directly, while certainly inconvenienced by the change, will often come to think most highly of all about you. As strange as it may sound, standing up for yourself earns the most respect from the very people most accustomed to holding you down.

Remember then, my student, respect should belong to everyone in equal measure—you included...*so challenge yourself to be more assertive.* You can do this.

LIFE APP

THERE WILL BE PLENTY OF OPPORTUNITIES FOR YOU TO DEVELOP THIS MIND-SET/HABIT. FOR EXAMPLE, ARE THERE ONE OR TWO FRIENDS OF YOURS WHO ALWAYS DECIDE WHAT THE GROUP DOES, WHICH MOVIE TO SEE, ETC.? DO YOU LET YOUR OLDER BROTHER OR SISTER BOSS YOU AROUND? IS THERE A CERTAIN CLASSMATE WHO REGULARLY INTERRUPTS AND SPEAKS OVER YOU? WELL, NOW IS THE TIME IN YOUR LIFE TO START MAKING CHANGES.

ANOTHER OPPORTUNITY WILL PRESENT ITSELF THE NEXT TIME YOU'RE DINING AT A RESTAURANT AND YOUR FOOD IS NOT TO YOUR LIKING, E.G., YOUR STEAK IS OVERCOOKED OR YOUR SOUP IS NOT HOT. DO WHAT SOME PEOPLE—MORE THAN YOU'D THINK—ARE INCAPABLE OF, AND SPEAK UP. JUST REMEMBER THAT WHILE YOU ARE PAYING FOR THE SERVICE, THERE IS NO REASON TO BE RUDE—YOUR SERVER IS A REAL PERSON WHO DESERVES TO BE TREATED AS SUCH. SIMPLY STATE THE REQUEST IN A POLITE, RESPECTFUL WAY…AND ALLOW ASSERTIVENESS TO SERVE YOU.

WEEK 24

Learning Something from Everyone

What we have learned from others becomes our own by reflection.

—Ralph Waldo Emerson

No one lives long enough to learn everything they need to learn starting from scratch. To be successful, we absolutely, positively have to find people who have already paid the price to learn the things that we need to learn to achieve our goals.

—Brian Tracy

Try the following experiment in school: The next few times a teacher calls on another student during class, pay close attention to how you react.

Do you tend to tune in or tune out to the ensuing exchange? Does it have anything to do with the judgments you harbor for the other person, e.g., "He just likes to hear himself talk" or "She thinks she knows it all"? I can tell you from experience, my student, many young people instinctively choose to tune out. They haven't recognized yet just how much there is to learn from others' viewpoints and questions—yes, even those of individuals they may not particularly like.

Unfortunately, if they continue to disregard the input of others they will not only miss out on a ton of valuable knowledge in school, but will also set themselves up for future failures in life. In many careers, for instance, you *must* remain open to learning from others—bosses, co-workers, customers, and competitors, alike—in order to stay on and eventually get ahead.

That being said, now is the ideal time for you to adopt a new mindset. Please tune in, then, to this statement: *You can learn something of value from every single person you encounter—irrespective of their age, race, personality, social class, etc.*

Clearly, this is a powerful, life-altering message, especially since we live in a world where many tune out—or look to judge and tear down—others who are somehow different. Indeed, it's a message capable of refocusing the lenses through which we all see the world. For, now, instead of entering into personal interactions with a negative or ignorant attitude—which literally makes it impossible to learn anything—we can view each as a golden opportunity.

Just consider the possibilities: every classmate, every coach, every relative, every new acquaintance, every person interviewed on TV—even those who rub you the wrong way or hold opinions dissimilar to your own—can now be seen as someone with something of value to offer.

As an individual devoted to personal growth, I myself am constantly on the lookout for such lessons. And it entails far more than just focusing on what others are saying. I also take notice of things like their physical mannerisms, their attitude, their ability to articulate thoughts, their sense of humor, even their fashion choices.

Because this outlook prompts me to suspend negative judgment while I search for *something* valuable, it really has helped me to become a better person, as well as to see more people in a positive light. In fact, my student, some of the advisement ideas I've chosen to write about, and take the most pride in, originated after interacting with individuals I ordinarily would have judged or simply not noticed.

Case in point: Just last week while waiting for my car to be repaired, I decided to try to strike up a conversation with an older woman who was sitting with her daughter. As we began to connect, she got to talking about their recent journey to America—and let me tell you, I got far more in terms of insight and inspiration than I ever bargained for. It was eye-opening to hear about the extensive struggles and personal hardships she had overcome in order to attain her lifelong goal of moving her family to our country.

Just as inspirational, though, was the conviction and passion in her daughter's voice as she spoke of the dreams she was now determined to make come true. You just knew, since she'd been tuned in to her mom's empowering example for so long, that nothing was going to stand in her way.

As I drove home that day, it struck me that my own feelings regarding the value of *not giving up*—even in the face of adversity or overwhelming odds—had deepened considerably. I also found myself reflecting on other ideals (all are now advisement topics, mind you), e.g., *setting a strong example, being more patriotic, believing in yourself, living with a grateful heart, and having goals and dreams.*

Approaching life with this new kind of outlook is also beneficial in that it enables you and me to turn negative situations or encounters into positive ones. Allow me to explain.

Despite being young, I'm sure you've already picked up on the fact there exists in our world those who are unpleasant, even annoying, to be around. This segment of the population includes—among others—the trash talkers, the complainers, the long-winded, and the spewers of absolute ignorance. Well, on the next occasion you find yourself in the company of such a person, you will have a choice as to how to respond. While many will continue to suffer through these experiences, viewing them as nothing other than a waste of time and energy, you can now view it as yet another opportunity for reflection and personal growth.

The next time you're face-to-face with a rabid complainer, for example, first allow all their negativity and all their cynicism to seep into your veins. Then make a mental note of just how uncomfortable being on the receiving end of such a transfusion can leave you feeling. Next, examine the content of what the person is saying for clues into what lies at the root of his complaining ways. Maybe he's acting according to his parents' example, possesses a need to bring others down, or is just having a bad day. Regardless, you will learn something of value from your encounter.

An identical approach can be utilized when you meet up with the arrogant, bragging types. As you again begin to examine what lies at the root of their self-absorbed behavior—as well as experience the discomfort that comes from being on the receiving end—one thing will become crystal clear: you will never allow yourself to develop these types of negative personality traits. Lesson learned.

Imagine that. We can actually glean valuable insight and awareness from those who would ordinarily do nothing more than annoy and offend.

Remember then, my student, approaching life with this outlook ensures you will continue to grow and evolve into a positive, reflective, open-minded individual...*so challenge yourself to learn something from everyone*. You can do this.

LIFE APP

AS YOU WORK TO ESTABLISH THIS NEW LIFE HABIT, BE SURE TO TAKE ADVANTAGE OF THE OPPORTUNITIES THAT PRESENT THEMSELVES THIS WEEK—WHETHER IT BE WHILE SITTING IN CLASS, SITTING IN A WAITING AREA, LISTENING TO A CYNIC, TALKING WITH A FAMILY MEMBER, READING AN ARTICLE OR BOOK, WATCHING TELEVISION, ETC.

BEFORE LONG, YOU'LL FIND THAT *LEARNING SOMETHING FROM EVERYONE* COMES AS NATURALLY TO YOU AS *FINDING SOMETHING NEGATIVE* DOES FOR SO MANY OTHERS.

WEEK 25

Being More Patriotic

...Our heroes are those among us who, in putting aside all regard for themselves, act above and beyond the call of duty and in so doing give definition to patriotism and elevate all of us. Ideals such as peace, freedom, justice, opportunity and individualism are just dreams without someone to turn those ideals into reality. Let's never forget the debt we owe to our fellow citizens. America is the land of the free because we are the home of the brave.

—David Mahoney

I hope you will serve your country. The nation as a whole will profit from your private careers, but please give something of yourself back, something more than just tax dollars.

—Donald T. Regan

For as long as I can remember, I've experienced both butterflies and chills when listening to our national anthem being performed. Perhaps you can relate, my student.

These deep-rooted feelings were fostered by my parents and grandparents, all of whom felt a deep obligation to love and support their country. And because a patriotic attitude was such an ingrained part of their makeup, it has naturally become a big part of who I am today. My wish now is for all my students to feel that same sense of obligation...as well as those same butterflies and chills.

Within my own extended family, there are exactly 12 veterans—an even dozen. Each one of them chose to serve in our country's armed forces, and did so with a tremendous amount of pride, honor, and humility. (Most recently, my brother Jeff, a member of the Army's 101st Airborne Division, spent nine months in the deserts of the Middle East.) Many young people, though, do not personally know even a single vet, and hence, are often less aware of just how much these individuals have sacrificed so as to provide and protect the fruits of freedom.

Case in point: One evening during World War II, General Dwight Eisenhower made a special visit to members of the 101st Airborne Division. Why did he do this? To say thank-you and good-bye to the expected *80 percent* of them who would die the next day. That's right, and the next day—June 6, 1944—over 9,000 American men did pay the ultimate price on the beaches of Normandy. Of those who did not perish, a significant number were left to deal with horrific memories and debilitating injuries. Why did they do this? To keep the rest of America (and the world) safe—our people and our nation—from Nazi Germany. So, if you ever wondered whether a total stranger would really give his life for you, the answer is a resounding yes...many have and many continue to. *Do we not owe them something in return?*

Well, befitting such heroism, several holidays do exist to pay tribute to vets—both the living and deceased—along with the ideals of liberty for which they so selflessly fought.

It is all too apparent, however, that many Americans have forgotten all we are deeply obligated to remember. Indeed, they have come to see these holidays as a mere break from work or school—another opportunity to hit some big storewide sale. Again, perhaps it has something to do with the fact that they do not personally know a vet. Regardless, it would be ignorant for anyone to not stop and reflect on the true intentions of the day.

For those of you who also decry this state of circumstances, who want to prove some people still are grateful, and who do care about honoring our vets, I've compiled the following list of ideas:

1. On Flag Day (June 14th), start developing the habit of saying the Pledge of Allegiance more thoughtfully. Instead of simply parroting the words like so many do, actually think about what each line means as you, along with your peers, pay real tribute—not mere lip service.

   Another point that should go without saying involves behaving respectfully while "The Star Spangled Banner" is being performed. At any public event, however, you're likely to see some kids, and even a few adults, talking or leaving their hats on during the anthem. Rather than let their ignorance eat at you, simply lead by example with an even greater sense of pride. In the process, you'll also be doing your part to model respect and patriotism for any younger children in attendance who—believe me when I say it—are likely to be watching you.

2. On Memorial Day (May 31st), offer a special prayer or if you prefer, plant a tree in honor of those who made the ultimate sacrifice while serving our country. Personally, I also include in my thoughts and actions any POWs who may still be imprisoned—since they too have sacrificed their lives for us—as well as any civilians who have tragically become casualties of war.
3. On Independence Day (July 4th), give thanks for living in a great country where we are free to, yes, enjoy backyard barbecues and public fireworks displays, but also to vote, speak our minds, and choose our religion.
4. On Veteran's Day (November 11th), consider writing a letter to a vet. Communicate to them you care…you remember. Many feel they have been forgotten and that young people of today are not being made aware of all they sacrificed. Prove to them otherwise. Students of mine actually write on Valentine's Day, as part of Dear Abby's Valentines for Vets program. So I speak from experience when I say your gesture will warm a deserving person's heart—as well as evoke a tear or two of pride.

Finally, there exists one more special day that provides the opportunity to proudly express patriotism. When you turn 18 years of age, you too will inherit the right and privilege to vote—on Election Day. (Yet another monumental right secured by veterans.)

Make no mistake, though, in a free country founded on democracy, voting is more than a right or privilege—it is an obligation. Why is it then that an increasing number of people are failing to follow through on this, their most important civic duty? Good question. I myself have heard a multitude of excuses—from "no good candidates" to a lack of time—but my answer remains the same: plain old ignorance. (Such individuals don't realize, for example, that those in third-world countries would literally die to earn their future generations the right to vote.)

The good news is your own generation represents the future. And my impression based on personal experiences is that you already see such matters of patriotism far more clearly than many adults do. When it comes time, whether it be to vote for president, governor, mayor, or even a seat on the local board of education, make yourself aware of the issues and candidates, and then make the time to get to the polls.

Lastly, realize that on top of all we've discussed, there are a variety of other ways for you to be more patriotic. For example, paying taxes without cheating or complaining; picking up litter and in general trying to live in an environmentally friendly manner; showing respect for police, firefighters, civil servants, etc.; being patient with airport security; appreciating diversity—*all things* that are good for America and respectful of it.

Remember then, my student, we are privileged to be living in this great country—truly the land of the free and home of the brave...*so challenge yourself to be more patriotic*. You can do this.

LIFE APP

FOLLOW THROUGH ON THE SPECIFIC HOLIDAY SUGGESTIONS MENTIONED IN THIS ADVISEMENT. YOU'LL FIND THAT THE REWARDS OF BEING MORE PATRIOTIC FAR OUTWEIGH ANY EFFORT REQUIRED OF YOU.

IN ADDITION, YOU CAN KEEP A RECORD OF THE WAYS IN WHICH YOU DEMONSTRATE PATRIOTISM—WHETHER IT BE A SIMPLE GESTURE (E.G., HONORING A PARADE PARTICIPANT WITH A SALUTE OR PLACING FLOWERS AT THE BASE OF THE VIETNAM WALL) OR A MORE SIGNIFICANT ACT (E.G., VOLUNTEERING AT A NEARBY VETERAN'S HOSPITAL OR GIVING BLOOD IN A TIME OF NATIONAL CRISIS).

IT WILL EVOLVE INTO QUITE A LENGTHY AND INSPIRATIONAL LIST, ONE THAT CAN SOMEDAY BE SHARED AS YOU ATTEMPT TO PASS ON THIS VERY SPECIAL VALUE.

WEEK 26

Using Your Sense of Humor

The human race has one really effective weapon, and that is laughter.
—Mark Twain

...Your ability to go through life successfully will depend largely upon your traveling with courage and a good sense of humor, for both are conditions of survival...
—John R. Silber, President of Boston University

You grow up on the day you have your first real laugh at yourself.
—Ethel Barrymore

Among those whom I like or admire, I can find no common denominator, but among those whom I love, I can: all of them make me laugh.
—W. H. Auden

It's safe to say you appreciate a good, hard laugh now and again. Who doesn't? But I bet you weren't aware that a sense of humor is required for more than just enjoying laughs—that of all things, my student, it is instrumental in succeeding and even surviving in life.

My own former boss, for example, told me once that he hired me because, yes, I was qualified (as were other candidates) but really because I smiled more than the others and made him laugh.

Also consider that every thriving, successful adult I've ever asked has been emphatic about the importance of using one's sense of humor in life. If you were to inquire into the experiences of those you know to be old and wise, you'd likely hear some of the same claims I did: "Without my sense of humor I would have gone crazy long ago," "If it weren't for a finely tuned sense of humor, I could never have achieved so much, let alone lasted 40 years in my profession—never," "My sense of humor, more than any other quality, was what sustained me through 83 years of life's little, and big, hassles—as a matter of fact, it's still getting me by now."

Well, now is the time for you to discover your own sense of humor and to make using it a habit for life. To be perfectly clear, this is not something you should expect to just happen on its own. A conscious, persistent effort is required on your part, and it shouldn't be hard to understand why. Do we not tend to get caught up in the small, insignificant stuff of day-to-day living? Do we not tend to be lured into taking our own problems too seriously at times? And are there not entire days that tend to go by without a single laugh flowing from our mouths? It's apparent the world does have a not-so-funny tendency of trying to thwart one's sense of humor.

Because life can be so challenging, it is critical we commit to changing the most basic ways in which we see and interpret the world. This requires that we take a step back in order to first detect, and then to see more clearly, the outlandish and comical sides of situations—rather than continue to focus solely on the negatives.

Consider, for example, the possibilities associated with the following life events, the kind of unexpected events some have actually come to expect: having a bad hair day; having the teacher call on you at the only moment your attention happens to wander; spraining your ankle during the first practice session of the season; seeing the girl who you thought liked you, at the movies with someone else; stuttering on the first few words of your speech; dropping your tray of food in the jam-packed cafeteria.

While some may view these experiences as sense-of-humor destroyers, I say, "When better to put one's sense of humor into practice?" Think about it; there's a clear choice here as to how someone can respond. Do you want to be the person who becomes mortified, crushed, or angered—and acts like it's the end of the world (as some dramatic people you know would)? Or would you be better served by simply throwing your arms in the air, shaking your head in amazement, and chuckling to yourself, "Can you believe this one?"

It's easy to see how the latter reaction—a prime example of stepping back to view things in a different light—can serve to short-circuit negative emotion, helping to keep you more positive and hang-up free as you go through life.

Truth be told, there was a period in my own life—prior to the successful job interview—when I would not have made the more empowering choice. In fact, my student, some of these events did happen to me while growing up and my response to them always involved getting quite upset. It would even be fair to say that during my adolescent years I was way too uptight, took way too much personally, and was not too much fun at all to be around.

Well, as you're already aware, there exist lots of people in the world who think like the old me. These are individuals who, having not yet learned the value of a sense of humor, are lacking in such critical areas as lightheartedness, perspective, and spontaneity. Herein lies your opportunity: Take it upon yourself to become a leader in the area. The world is certainly in need of more such people, and hey, it's got to involve having some fun, right?

For example: It's the day of a big geometry exam and everyone is tense and uptight. You walk into class wearing a pair of your mother's 1980s-style sunglasses, and suddenly everyone is cracking up, feeling less stressed about the test. It's that easy.

Without question, spreading the sense-of-humor bug in such a manner can make for having good times. Plus, the world suddenly becomes more interesting to you than ever.

Acting like this also serves to make you the kind of person that others enjoy being around. Just think about some of the people you love to hang with—they are likely those in the world with whom you can laugh most openly and freely.

Lastly, as you help others to laugh more and find humor even in the most unlikely of places, an amazing discovery will take place. This involves the realization that you now possess the most powerful weapon of all, a weapon that when used correctly allows you to carry out much good in the world.

Specifically, you can use humor to:

1. Relieve tension in the air—helping others to keep it real.
2. Break down barriers and connect with all kinds of people.
3. Fill others' hearts with happiness—helping you to deepen the quality of relationships in your own life.
4. Ward off negativity and cynicism—helping to keep your spirit in good health.
5. Create emotional releases that leave you feeling so good—helping to keep you at peace with yourself and the world.
6. Teach others the considerable difference between laughing with, and laughing at, someone.

7. And while you may not be able to eliminate life's minor irritations or major ordeals, you can also use it to spread sunshine and hope in their aftermath.

Hey, you should've known by making something so positive a bigger part of your life, there would be many significant payoffs involved. Payoffs that benefit not only you, but the entire world!

Remember then, my student, laughter, an eye for the comical, and a little lightheartedness are life companions no one should choose to travel without...*so challenge yourself to use your sense of humor*. You can do this.

DURING THE COURSE OF THIS WEEK, MAKE A CONSCIOUS EFFORT TO LAUGH LONGER...TO LAUGH HARDER...AND TO LAUGH MORE OFTEN. YOU—AS WELL AS THOSE AROUND YOU—WILL BE GLAD YOU DID.

WEEK 27

Harnessing the Power of Goals

Obstacles are things a person sees when he takes his eyes off his goal.
—E. Joseph Cossman

The victory of success is half won when one gains the habit of setting goals and achieving them. Even the most tedious chore will become endurable as you parade through each day convinced that every task, no matter how menial or boring, brings you closer to fulfilling your dreams.
– Og Mandino (The Greatest Salesman in the World)

Do you know what it feels like to wake up with purpose? It's truly an extraordinary experience. Before you can even open your eyes, a surge of excitement sweeps through body and soul, as your mind begins to anticipate the possibilities of the day ahead. Indeed, something has you so revved up that even the drab morning routine gets carried out with positive energy. Unfortunately, things don't work this way for most. No, in reality, as the relative few are buzzing around their homes, millions of others—young and old alike—are stuck in an all-too-familiar rut. Day after day, they struggle to get out of bed because no such inner spark exists. In other words, there exists in their lives no purpose…no new challenge…no goals.

Let me be perfectly clear, my student: Writing goals is a power *anyone* can choose to tap into. And it's a simple act well worth anyone's time and effort.

Goals infuse life with meaning. They serve as your ticket to making positive personal changes, and ultimately, to evolving into the best person you can possibly be. Each time you take a step toward achieving one, your self-esteem levels, as well as your personal sense of efficacy, develop further. What's more, scientific research has revealed time and time again that those who regularly write goals lead far more prosperous lives than those who don't.

When taking all of the evidence into consideration, you really do have to wonder why everyone's not doing it.

To get started on the goal-setting process, you simply need to generate ideas. With regard to long-term goals, look to your own dreams, e.g., *I want to dance professionally, I will work for NASA, I will own my own business*. For goals of the more short-term variety, just think about those things in your life with which you're not currently happy or satisfied, things you'd like to change, e.g., *I will improve upon my algebra grade, I want to become more confident in social situations*. (When helping my own students in class to generate ideas, I encourage them to look at six critical areas: nutrition, school, family, exercise, friendships, and personality. This way, they become rare well-rounded individuals.)

Following are two student examples of short-term goal ideas—one on family, and one on nutrition—that will be referenced throughout this advisement.

A. Goal: *I will* (not "I will try" or "I should"—"*I will*") *get along better with my brother.*
B. Goal: *I will eat junk food on a once-a-week-only basis.*

Keep in mind that many young people think, upon generating an idea and writing a goal, that things magically start falling into place. Obviously, this is not how it works; just as it is with one's values, actions are required to bring goals to life. Therefore, it's critical to also include *how* you will go about accomplishing each one.

A. How: *by walking away rather than exchanging insults; by letting the little things he does slide; by giving him space when he needs it.*
B. How: *by asking my parents to buy healthier snacks; by resisting the temptation to indulge; by treating myself on the same one night of each week.*

When done brainstorming "the hows," you can count on feeling even more inspired and motivated to work toward your goals. However, my student, with human nature being what it is, you can also count on some of this same motivation fading over time. In order to prevail, you must ask yourself—and then write out—*why* it is you want to go after each goal.

A. Why: *so we can have more fun and enjoy more good times together; to make things at home more peaceful; because he's my brother.*
B. Why: *to be fit and healthy; because too much of anything is not good; to avoid health problems down the road.*

Reading and rereading these types of "why lists" is like taking a dose of preventative medicine, in that you're not allowing a lack of motivation to materialize in the first place.

I would advise you, however, to go even one step further. That's right, I've discovered that accounting for, and then writing out, what would result from *not* achieving a goal to be the most inspirational technique of all.

A. *If I Don't:* *We'll continue to build a wall between us. Mom and Dad will continue to be upset and hurt. Day-to-day life won't ever be what it should.*
B. *If I Don't:* *I may very well become unfit and overweight. I will have failed to develop self-discipline in this area of life. I'll form poor eating habits that can realistically persist through adulthood.*

Every single time I read over my "If I Don't" lists, I end up pushing harder than ever to make my goals happen. (I guess pressure and dissatisfaction also have an upside to them.)

Writing out your goals in such a detailed manner can certainly pay big dividends. But before you start thinking you have this goal thing all figured out, it's important we also examine why some people still fail.

First, when you set your sights on something, it helps to have the support of those close to you. Don't make the mistake of always trying to go it alone. Besides, telling others about your goals makes them more real in your own mind and puts additional "good pressure" on you to follow through.

By far the most common error, though, is made by those who write goals without including the aforementioned, "hows," "whys," and "if I don'ts." Little do they know, this small amount of extra effort can—and often does—mean the ultimate difference between success and failure.

But even when each of these categories is included, the ever-present threat of forgetting remains. This is why you cannot neglect to read your goals over on a regular basis. The expression "out of sight, out of mind" definitely applies here, so keep them handy!

And there is yet one more caveat to consider. You must realize no matter how frequently you remind yourself of your goals, it's still going to take major doses of persistence and hard work to attain them.

Many people don't realize just how much tenacity is required. When they experience failure, or merely a temporary setback, for example, frustration often sets in and the decision to give up on their goals soon follows. So let's be clear on this matter: Roadblocks, or setbacks, will occur. It's a normal part of the process...which means everyone will experience them at one point or another. The determining factor will be how you choose to handle the inevitable bumps in the road. I tend to use setbacks as motivation, my mind-set being, *I may have stumbled this time but now I'm coming back stronger, wiser, and more determined than ever!*

Lastly, make it a point to not get caught up in the habit of writing unrealistic goals. Lots of people become turned off to goal setting simply because poor goal selection leaves them relying on chance rather than concrete action. *I will attend an Ivy League college someday* is a perfectly legitimate long-term goal because there are specific steps ("hows") you can take in order to succeed. *I will grow to be over 6 feet tall,* on the other hand, is nothing more than a pipedream since there are no concrete ways for you to actually make it happen.

Remember then, my student, creating a sense of purpose—that all-important inner spark—is essential to growing as an individual and creating a truly rich, inspired life...*so challenge yourself to harness the power of goals.* You can do this.

LIFE APP

THREE TIMES A YEAR (E.G., NEW YEAR'S, THE BEGINNING OF SUMMER, AND THE BEGINNING OF THE SCHOOL YEAR), CONSIDER WRITING OUT YOUR OWN SHORT- AND LONG-TERM GOALS.

TRY TO COVER ALL IMPORTANT AREAS, E.G., NUTRITION, SCHOOL, EXERCISE, FRIENDSHIPS, FAMILY, AND PERSONALITY. AND BE SURE TO INCLUDE THE "HOWS," "WHYS," AND "IF I DON'TS," AS THIS YOUNG STUDENT MODELS BELOW:

GOAL: *I WILL DEVELOP INTO A MORE SKILLED FISHERMAN.*

HOW: *I WILL OBSERVE MY DAD, ASK LOTS OF QUESTIONS, AND PRACTICE MY TECHNIQUES EVERY WEEKEND.*

WHY: *I WANT TO MAKE MY DAD PROUD, NOT TO MENTION, CATCH MORE BIG FISH.*

IF I DON'T: *I WON'T REACH MY POTENTIAL IN A SPORT THAT I ABSOLUTELY LOVE.*

WEEK 28

Taking It One Step at a Time

It's the constant and determined effort that breaks down all resistance, sweeps away all obstacles.
—Claude M. Bristol

Patience and perseverance have a magical effect before which difficulties disappear and obstacles vanish.
—John Quincy Adams

There is no sudden leap into the stratosphere...There is only advancing step by step, slowly and tortuously, up the pyramid toward your goals...
—Ben Stein

Have you ever looked at an ultra-thick book and wondered how on earth any one individual could've written it? After all, to generate that much information would require a superhuman effort—or one that very, very few are capable of—would it not?

But what about looking at it this way, my student: If a writer were to complete a mere single page a day, he or she would have compiled—yes—365 pages in a single year. Now the accomplishment appears attainable. Yet, doing something day after day (a.k.a. persistence), is much easier said than done, and actually *is* something of which few prove capable.

To truly appreciate the value of developing persistence, consider those who have suffered through a serious injury and the grueling therapy that follows. Many must start off by relearning the things the rest of us most take for granted: how to sit up, how to grip an object, how to walk, how to talk. Day after day, they push themselves to the point of extreme fatigue and excruciating pain just to make some tiny, almost imperceptible gain.

I personally know an individual who, after being involved in a car crash, was told he'd be lucky to regain any movement at all in his legs. He was devastated...for about three days. Then all he wanted to hear about was what he could do to improve his chances.

Today, with the support of leg braces, he is now walking! That's right, it took six years of relentless effort, but he eventually accomplished something that supposedly couldn't be done—and he's not satisfied yet. When asked how he beat the odds, he replies matter-of-factly: "When faced with a long, uphill road, what else can you do but persistently place one foot in front of the other?" Think about it.

I now share this tale of inspiration each school year—especially with the struggling readers in my classes. They know firsthand what it's like to work hard and still feel like progress is barely being made. In fact, it often feels to them like *no* progress is taking place, which can obviously lead to intense feelings of frustration and the eventual decision to quit. But when these same young people come to understand that persistent effort spawns tiny, almost imperceptible gains that add up over time, they become far less likely to give in to their feelings of futility.

Consider the ideal of becoming physically fit as another real life example. As someone who has been working out for quite a while now, I can honestly say that day-to-day changes are not detectable—at all. Indeed, my student, there were many times when I was ready to throw in the towel because it appeared my efforts were not producing results. These feelings vanished, however, the moment I came across some old pictures of myself. I could barely believe my eyes—the differences in muscle mass, definition, body fat, etc. So the moral of the story remains: Stick with whatever it is you're working at—even when it *seems* like you're not making headway; positive results do accumulate over time and will ultimately prove that persistence pays.

If you're intent on applying this rare trait to your own goals in life, there's one last pitfall of which you need to be aware. Lots of people start off strong and determined when working toward a goal, but as days and weeks go by, they often get lazy and decide, "Why bother anymore?"

Well, because the tendency for laziness lurks within every one of us, we must anticipate that in time it will rear its ugly head. Just remember that, while many do fall prey—day after day—to its deceptive allure, laziness has been conquered countless times before.

Doing so demands you "take a step"—even when you don't feel like it. And no, this is not an easy feat, but each time you do manage to rise above the temptation, your ability to resist laziness on future occasions will improve as well. Then, in less time than you'd imagine, this reaction will become ingrained...and others will begin describing you in such non-lazy terms as "ambitious," "energetic," "driven," and "persistent." Has a nice ring to it, eh?

Truly, taking one step at a time is the type of advice that can be applied to any area of life. School-related challenges, for one, present the perfect opportunity to put your newfound knowledge to the test.

If you have a month to complete an eight-page report, for example, set a goal to finish two pages per weekend. (Now that's doable.) Or when you have two weeks to prepare for a big test, spend a mere half hour a night studying. It's such a simple, effective technique, yet so few people take advantage of it. Instead, they become overwhelmed by the task at hand and give up without even trying, or attempt to do everything last second, which can lead to even more stress and frustration. It's just not a logical approach.

Remember then, my student, persistently placing one foot in front of the other is *the* secret to gaining ground on any goal...*so challenge yourself to take it one step at a time*. You can do this.

LIFE APP

LIST EXAMPLES OF WHEN YOU WERE WORKING TOWARD A GOAL BUT ENDED UP GIVING IN TO LAZINESS OR AN APPARENT LACK OF PROGRESS. THEN, JOT DOWN THE TIMES YOU PERSONALLY PROVED PERSISTENCE DOES PAY OFF.

AS YOU GROW OLDER, YOU WILL NOTICE ONLY ONE OF THE TWO LISTS GROWING ALONG WITH YOU—IT'S ENTIRELY YOUR CHOICE AS TO WHICH IT'LL BE.

WEEK 29

Succeeding In—and Through—Sports

The spirit, the will to win, and the will to excel are the two things that endure. These qualities are so much more important than the events that occur.

—Vince Lombardi

Your opponent, in the end, is never really the player on the other side of the net, or the swimmer in the next lane, or the team on the other side of the field, or even the bar you must high-jump. Your opponent is yourself, your negative voices, your level of determination.

—Grace Lichtenstein

I once heard of a Special Olympics competition in which an extraordinary thing happened. It was a short race, no longer than 100 yards, and as the runners lined up at the start, each was thrilled with the anticipation of the challenge and the prospect of even winning the event. Every face reflected absolute determination.

But as fate would have it, just as the contenders began to emerge from the pack, a lone runner fell hard and began to cry. Upon hearing the commotion, each of the other athletes slowed down to look back. And then something took place that those in attendance will never forget: Every single one of the runners stopped and ran back to the fallen competitor's side...and as if that were not inspiring enough, each and every one of them then interlocked arms and proceeded toward the finish line—which they crossed together.

I tell you this story, my student, because it illustrates a number of wonderful things about participating in sports. It also reminds us that sports are not just for high-caliber athletes—sports are for everyone. Any person from age 5 to 105, no matter his or her ability level, will reap several benefits from simply participating. And these benefits go well beyond the playing fields, carrying over to positively influence the way we live our lives.

All participants:

1. Are provided a positive, challenging outlet—often for a lifetime—through which they can direct their energies and release their pressures.
2. Enjoy higher levels of physical fitness, e.g., increased strength, flexibility, and coordination.
3. Learn firsthand about the concepts of sacrifice, self-discipline, and self-improvement.
4. Gain experiences pertaining to being a leader and a team player.
5. Are able to fend off apathy and boredom because there's always something fun for them to be doing.
6. Discover the power of setting both individual and team goals.
7. Experience a strong sense of accomplishment, as well as feelings of pride, friendship, and camaraderie while working toward their goals.
8. Build both the physical and mental strength required to consistently outwork and outperform others.
9. Develop time-management skills as they find ways to juggle and work in all their activities.
10. Learn what is required to overcome adversity as a team, and then get to reap the exhilarating rewards.
11. Learn what it takes to achieve, and to then maintain, excellence in performance.
12. Are able to compete alongside, and/or against, people of widely diverse backgrounds.
13. Discover that when they dig deep within themselves, both their skill level and level of intestinal fortitude can develop beyond even their own expectations.
14. Come to learn how to deal with the ups and downs inherent to sports—and life itself.
15. Discover that each game, just like each day, represents nothing less than a new beginning!

Now that we've detailed just how profound and beneficial sports participation can be, it's time to focus on how to go about fulfilling your individual potential as an athlete.

In athletics, physical attributes like power, speed, and agility are important, but *mental* prowess above all else is what distinguishes someone as truly extraordinary.

As any athlete knows, mental pressure is something that simply comes with the competitive territory. You can rest assured that at some point in a contest you will find yourself smack in the middle of a tense situation. How you come to respond in such times of challenge will go a long way in determining whether or not you ever perform to your potential.

Consider those individuals who, even at elite levels, have allowed the pressure of the moment to impact their thinking, and subsequently, their performance. Whether it was a basketball player missing a game-tying free throw with seconds remaining or a golfer blowing a short putt that would've put him over the top, the common thread in their demise was their very own thoughts.

Let me be crystal clear about this: If you are afraid of looking bad, if you allow thoughts of how important the game is, of how many eyes are watching, or of how others will judge you if you don't come through, you too will choke and fail.

You should also recognize, my student, that any team or person can play up to their potential when all the bounces are going their way. But only a relative few can sustain a positive mind-set and high skill level when adverse circumstances take shape, e.g., in the form of a raucous crowd, a bad call, an overtime deficit, a costly turnover, a key injury. A rare dose of mental toughness is the only known cure.

Developing such mental toughness takes practice and includes techniques like deep breathing, focusing your mind on the task at hand so as to block out both internal and external noise, trusting in prior preparation so as to free your mind from worrying about technique, and visualizing the exact scenarios you want to have play out.

With regard to visualization, you should know that the more detail and the more senses you incorporate into your thoughts, the more dramatic the results. If, for example, you are visualizing coming through with a game-winning hit, you will need to take it frame by frame. Imagine yourself in the on-deck circle taking a few relaxed swings. See yourself walking toward the plate. Feel the calmness within as you gaze at the pitcher. Hear the pitch cracking against your bat. See, hear, and feel your teammates, coaches, and friends mobbing you in jubilation. Make it all so real in your mind that you can even *taste* sweet success!

It is important to note that these mental strengths will also help you in any tough or stressful situation in life.

Another way to improve your athletic performance is to raise the level of intensity with which you play. Indeed, in any game I've ever been a part of, there are only a select few players who make a point of going all out, or full throttle. These are the rare individuals who play like they actually love to play. You'll see them diving for the loose ball, hustling on and off the field, pumping up their teammates and themselves, sliding headfirst into third base, etc.

Playing in such a way is uncommon, in part, because of the sheer amount of physical conditioning it requires. But going all out also demands an enormous amount of mental resolve. After all, in any contest there will be good enough reason to lose focus and ease up. (Remember the examples of adversity from the previous page?) So prior to each season, to each game, and even to each big play, these rare individuals make a point of reminding themselves that in order to be their best they must put forth their best—no excuses. Accordingly, they hold themselves accountable for giving everything they have to give whether it be while practicing, working out, or actually playing a game.

Believe me, my student, if you commit to meeting similar standards, you too will stand out as extraordinary—on the playing field and in life. Partly because you'll be performing to your utmost potential and partly because you'll be demonstrating a great deal of what can be referred to as "sports perspective." Sports perspective is understanding that winning isn't everything.

Not everybody understands this concept, though. I'm referring to the growing number of parents who choose to berate officials, coaches, and even the players themselves. This is especially damaging because such behavior serves to negate so much of the good that sports are capable of fostering in young people. Perhaps if these individuals looked at things through the eyes of the Special Olympians mentioned earlier, their own capacity to see and understand the big picture would evolve.

Finally, I'd be remiss if I were not to share another example of what it means to possess sports perspective.

Whether you are ready to accept it yet or not, the vast majority of players your age will never grow up to play for pay. (The statistics you've heard about are all true.) Accordingly, academics need to be placed first in your life; and the sooner you choose to make your education priority number one, the better. Even those of you good enough to someday play on the collegiate level will be required to pull your weight in the classroom. If you cannot, there will be plenty of other student athletes waiting in the wings to fill your spikes.

Consider yourself extraordinary—a true winner—not for striving to be a superstar, but for simply taking the initiative to get involved in sports, placing academics first, working to improve your skills—both physical and mental, playing hard and clean, and applying lessons learned to the most important game of all: the game of life.

Remember then, my student, participation in sports inspires greatness well beyond the playing field...*so challenge yourself to succeed in, and through, sports*. You can do this.

LIFE APP

AFTER EVERY GAME (OR PRACTICE) YOU PARTICIPATE IN—WIN OR LOSE—TAKE SOME TIME TO REFLECT:

1. WHAT DID I DO WELL?
2. WHAT ASPECTS OF MY PERFORMANCE DO I NEED TO WORK HARDER AT IMPROVING?
3. IF I COULD GO BACK AND REPLAY THE GAME (OR PRACTICE), WOULD I DO OR THINK ANYTHING DIFFERENTLY?
4. AND LASTLY, BUT MOST IMPORTANTLY, ARE THERE LESSONS (E.G., *PERTAINING TO LEADERSHIP, DETERMINATION, HUMILITY, ENJOYING THE MOMENT, RESPECT, RESILIENCY, RELAXED CONCENTRATION, COMMITMENT, UNITY, HONOR, GRATITUDE, ALL-OUT EFFORT, ACHIEVEMENT, OR PERSPECTIVE*) THAT I CAN CARRY OVER AND APPLY IN MY LIFE?

IF YOU HAVE NEVER PARTICIPATED IN SPORTS OUTSIDE OF REQUIRED PE CLASSES, MAKE A LIST OF THE DIFFERENT SPORTS ACTIVITIES AVAILABLE TO YOU, FROM TEAM SPORTS AT SCHOOL TO LOCAL BOWLING LEAGUES AND KARATE CLASSES, AND CONSIDER TRYING ONE OR MORE.

WEEK 30

Respecting Your Money

Whatever you have spend less.

—Samuel Johnson

A person's treatment of money is the most decisive test of his character, how they make it and how they spend it.

—James Moffatt

Success produces success, just as money produces money.

—Diane Ackerman

A young person I know recently received a $500 cash gift at her graduation party. Not bad for a kid from a middle-class background. Rather than saving some of it, though, she spent every last dime (at the mall, of course) within the very same weekend.

I'm sure she, as well as anyone else who is partial to splurging, has a great time doing so, but trust me, it's not the type of habit any young person wants to be developing. You see, the key to achieving financial success in the future is developing respect for your money now.

The way to do it, my student, is to develop such habits as creatively earning money, thinking before you spend, utilizing a budget, setting financial goals, and most importantly, being self-disciplined enough to save some portion of everything you receive.

One might think parents everywhere are already promoting habits like these, but the reality of the matter is, with family life pulling them in so many different directions, many aren't. That's why I'm advising *you* to take personal control of the situation.

With this objective in mind, try approaching Mom or Dad with any number of the following financial proposals:

1. Suggest you'll work to earn a weekly allowance by helping with routine chores like emptying the garbage and dishwasher.

2. If you want to earn extra money, ask if there are bigger, more demanding and time-consuming jobs you can take on (like raking leaves, vacuuming, or weeding the garden).
3. When asked what gifts you prefer, suggest stock shares in your favorite companies (e.g., Nike, Target, American Eagle, McDonald's) or shares in mutual funds. (There are actually funds offered exclusively to young investors that teach about investing and interest earning.)
4. Propose a family version of the powerful 401(k) savings plan. This way your parents, just like a corporation, would be obligated to match some of what you manage to sock away each month. For instance, if you saved $50 one month, your mom and dad may kick in an additional $25, or 50 percent more.

Believe it or not, you have an excellent chance of getting ideas such as these approved. In all likelihood, your parents will view them as preparation for the ways of the real world. Most parents also understand that working to earn money and then saving/investing a portion of it, fosters nothing less than creativity, responsibility, vision, self-restraint, and an empowering sense of accomplishment.

Another big perk will come once you've proven you are indeed capable of showing restraint and saving. You may want to sit down for this one. You see, my student, you will have earned the privilege to splurge—at least on occasion. It is, after all, a lot of fun to reap the rewards sown by personal sacrifice and discipline.

While enjoying yourself, just remember to still think before you spend. I'm not trying to take the spontaneity out of splurging, it's just that this habit is valuable and effective under any circumstance. Ask such questions as "Do I really need this, or will it end up sitting in the back of my closet a month from now?" and "Can I find it on sale or at a better price elsewhere?"

I myself go even one step further by figuring the number of hours I need to work in order to pay for an item. Since I currently make about $25 an hour, a $400 mountain bike, for instance, would equate to 16 hours of work. I know full well just how much I do in that amount of time so it really makes me think twice before forking over the cash. As a matter of fact, I often decide to hold off, or to select a cheaper model. And even when I do choose to go ahead and splurge (as I did with the mountain bike), I tend to appreciate the product that much more.

In a society increasingly marked by materialism and greed, I'd be remiss not mentioning that, while money is obviously important and worthy of our attention, we must work to not lose sight of what's truly valuable in life. *Being true to one's self, standing for something, building close relationships with family and friends, being compassionate, etc.*—things no one can assign a dollar amount to—should always be prioritized accordingly.

With that said, it's still important—as well as intelligent and shrewd—to learn how to put your money to work for you. To give you a basic idea of the power of investing and interest earning, try the following activity on a calculator: Take one penny and double it, and keep doubling your total sum every day for 31 days.

Amazingly, the number you arrive at is no mistake. In one month that penny grew to almost 11 *million* dollars.

Granted, this is an extraordinary—unrealistic, even—example of compounding interest, but rest assured you'll be pleasantly surprised by what time and interest can do to any nest egg.

Consider, if you will, the well-known Rule of 72. It states that you divide 72 by the amount of interest your money is earning in order to determine the number of years it will take for your sum to double. For example, those who invest in the stock market have historically earned about 9 percent interest. Using the rule, you would divide 72 by 9—sooo, your money will double every 8 years. If, however, your selected companies outperform the standard and earn, say, 12 percent, it will be a mere 6-year wait. (Money may not grow on trees, but you can certainly see how it can grow in the stock market.)

Conversely, in a year 2004 bank savings account, you'd be earning in the range of 3 percent interest. As you can quickly figure, it will be quite some time before any sum of money doubles here. Seventy-two divided by three equals...yes, *twenty-four years*. Keep the Rule of 72 in mind—now and in the future—as you make your own investment decisions.

Finally, you can rest assured that any cash you manage to cultivate will someday come in handy—whether it be used for helping others, for college, a car, or even a down payment on your own future home!

Remember then, my student, forging strong financial habits at your young age will pay off in far more ways than one...*so challenge yourself to respect your money*. You can do this.

LIFE APP

THIS WEEK, GENERATE SOME IDEAS AS TO HOW YOU CAN EARN EXTRA INCOME. FIRST, CONSIDER WHAT IT IS YOU'RE GOOD AT (OR WHAT YOU WOULD LIKE TO BE GOOD AT) AND THEN THE TYPES OF SERVICES THAT ARE IN DEMAND, E.G., LANDSCAPING, SNOWPLOWING, TUTORING. THIS WAY, YOU'LL HAVE AMPLE OPPORTUNITY TO KEEP BUSY, DEVELOP YOUR SKILLS, AND, OF COURSE, MAKE MONEY—ALL WHILE ENJOYING YOURSELF.

IN ADDITION, BEGIN UTILIZING WHAT I CALL A BUDGET BOOK—A REGULAR OL' NOTEBOOK IN WHICH YOU WRITE DOWN EVERYTHING YOU SPEND EACH WEEK. I KNOW IT SOUNDS DIFFICULT, BUT IN REALITY, IT REQUIRES ONLY A SMALL AMOUNT OF EFFORT. AND ONCE YOU DO GET IN THE HABIT, YOU'LL FIND THE INFORMATION TO BE QUITE VALUABLE.

IT WILL SHED LIGHT ON JUST HOW MUCH OF YOUR HARD-EARNED CASH IS BEING POURED INTO PIZZA, CDS, AND OTHER SMALL STUFF...HELPING YOU TO SEE JUST HOW MUCH YOU HAVE LEFT OVER FOR BIGGER AND BETTER THINGS. IDEALLY, THIS WILL LEAD YOU TO BECOME MORE MINDFUL OF WHAT YOU SPEND, WHICH WILL RESULT IN AN INCREASE IN THE AMOUNT YOU CAN ACTUALLY SAVE AND INVEST.

WEEK 31

Taking Risks

There is no nobility in being superior to others; true nobility is in being superior to your previous self.

—Hindu Proverb

It's better to be 0-for-20 than 0-for-0.

—Michael Levine

For all sad words of tongue and pen, the saddest are those "It might have been."

—John Greenleaf Whittier

Lay it on the line...stick your neck out...go for it...push past your comfort zone...throw caution to the wind...blow through the wall...take a chance...bite the bullet...

No matter how you phrase it, my student, taking risks has always been a requisite for one of life's ultimate pursuits: *discovering the greatest within.*

To begin, let's be clear that a big risk can range anywhere from raising one's hand in class to going after the lead role in a play—it depends entirely on the individual. But regardless of the circumstances, when one does manage to follow through in the face of fear and uncertainty, one does automatically grow and evolve as a person.

Case in point: I'll never forget this one "jittery" student named Kelly who, after delivering a speech to the entire school, triumphantly declared to her friends, "Of course it was intimidating to get up there; my heart was pounding. But doing something in spite of all the apprehension can lead you to see yourself in a whole new light. And I can't tell you how exhilarating it is to have shocked myself and those who know me best. I now feel unstoppable. As a matter of fact, I know I could get up there and do it again and again—and be even better than the first time!"

I'm not sure if I can convey to you the magnitude of this student's statement, but I'll try: From her experience, Kelly had evolved as a person. She managed to literally transform herself into a more confident and competent individual by putting her feelings of stress and discomfort aside and taking a risk.

I'm not exaggerating when I say it doesn't get any more momentous than this. Life at its essence is about changing and growing and pushing yourself beyond the familiar, beyond the comfortable, all for the sake of becoming a more complete and fulfilled human being. Indeed, it can be said that *life is growth*. Kelly, for one, had managed to learn this powerful truth firsthand—and early on.

Unfortunately, many others—young and old alike—never put themselves in a position to discover what she did. Instead, they travel through life purposefully avoiding any kind of risk. And whether they realize it or not, my student, they're doing it because of fear—fear of failure as well as fear of criticism.

These individuals are choosing the safe and ordinary so as to not subject themselves to the natural outgrowths of the risky unknown. But can you see the great irony in this line of thinking? By avoiding risk, they are taking the greatest risk of all: that they'll never unlock their personal potential and know what could have been.

I wish I could explain to each of these individuals that, even if they did encounter failure, they'd survive. There'd be no wilting, no falling apart, no disintegrating. You just learn something from the experience and move on. We do actually learn more from failure than success, do we not? Besides, trying and failing is far more noble than not trying at all, is it not? And as for any criticism, should others' opinions of you ever be allowed to matter more than your own? I think not.

Well, at least the rest of us can learn from passive people's mistakes. They are, after all, living, breathing proof of the reality that in order to unlock one's potential and live life to the fullest, one *must* step out of his or her comfort zone.

In fact, I actually tell my students in class that they're on the right path if, from time to time, they are being criticized; if they are unsure and nervous; and if they are foundering through new experiences. Consequently, their maxim often develops into, "Let's try it—what's the worst thing that could happen?"

If only more young people would take on this mind-set and recognize that even if things don't work out every time, they are still benefiting and evolving from the attempt. Then we'd have a world teeming with vibrant, developing individuals answering the call...following their destiny...facing their fears...going out on a limb...

Remember then, my student, by avoiding opportunities to grow as a person, you will end up paying the ultimate price: never discovering the greatness within...*so challenge yourself to take risks*. You can do this.

LIFE APP

EXPLORE THE OPPORTUNITIES YOU HAVE TO TAKE RISKS—AND DON'T BACK DOWN FROM THE CHALLENGES THEY PRESENT. FOR EXAMPLE, TRY A NEW SPORT, RUN FOR CLASS OFFICE, GET OUT ON THE DANCE FLOOR, CALL THAT PERSON YOU'D LIKE TO GET TO KNOW BETTER, SPEAK LOUDER, SING LOUDER, LEARN A NEW LANGUAGE, VOLUNTEER IN CLASS, DELIVER A SPEECH, ETC.

FINALLY, TALK TO THOSE ADULTS WHO YOU KNOW AND RESPECT, AND ASK THEM ABOUT THE RISKS THEY HAVE TAKEN (OR HAVE FAILED TO TAKE). TOGETHER, REFLECT ON HOW SUCH CHOICES ULTIMATELY IMPACTED THE OUTCOME OF THEIR LIVES.

WEEK 32

Watching What You Eat

Don't dig your grave with your knife and fork.

—English Proverb

Gluttony is an emotional escape, a sign something is eating us.

—Peter de Vries

What we as a society choose to eat is an issue that now demands attention. Truth be known, my student, a full one-out-of-three Americans is overweight; and next to tobacco, the leading causes of adult deaths are linked to none other than diet and obesity!

At what stage of life would you say the habits responsible for such statistics actually form? That's right; in fact, for the first time in history, obesity reigns as the most common nutritional disease among our country's youth. But take heart, for developing the right habits now can not only prevent you from becoming one of the statistics, but can also lead to a more fulfilling, higher-quality life.

Consider, if you will, only a few of the benefits associated with eating well: having a healthier skin complexion, feeling more energetic, performing better in school, building more muscle, and living long enough to attend your grandchildren's weddings. So much of this really can be determined by our own food-related decisions and behavior.

Now for the advice. Should such grim statistics really come as a surprise to anyone? Do we not, for example, live in a society saturated with junk-food offerings—complete with unlimited flavors of ice cream, cookies, cakes, chips, pies, candy, and doughnuts?

Heck, "junk" could easily be considered our fifth food group. And because such products are literally everywhere, people no longer seem to think twice about indulging in them. The concepts of moderation and balance have definitely been lost on us—young and old alike.

Believe it or not, there was once a time when I actually would have advised young people to go ahead and enjoy the pleasures of junk food while they can. But I now recognize that they, too, should impose limits on themselves. For again, the eating habits formed at your age often endure for a lifetime.

Some of the adverse health effects now showing up more and more in young people include high cholesterol, diabetes, and clogging arteries. Scary but true. So I guess the bottom line is: Feel free to enjoy on occasion, my student, but remember that too much of a good thing is not a good thing.

If we can label "junk" as our unofficial fifth food group, I know what would have to be considered the sixth. Fast food has just as naturally woven itself into the fabric of American culture. In fact, it is now cheaper and more widely available than ever before—and with family life being so hectic, has become a convenient crutch that millions of us lean on.

The problem with this is fast-food selections are generally very high in fat and salt. That's why on the occasions I find myself ordering at the ol' drive-thru, I make it a point to first stipulate "no mayo, no cheese, please." This way, an entirely unhealthy meal—loaded with dangerous saturated fats—is transformed into only a moderately unhealthy one. On many occasions, I also switch from a burger to a grilled chicken sandwich, and from fries to a baked potato, if available. Lastly, to improve on things further, I then request skim milk or water as opposed to liquid sugar.

My somewhat unique approach to ordering fast food is obviously less ideal than not ordering it at all. But let's be realistic—the rat race won't soon be slowing down. Eat on the run when you must, but at least take the small, protective measures we've covered.

The next nugget of nutritional advice should go without saying; however, my experiences with young people have proven otherwise. How many times have you heard that breakfast is *the* most important meal of the day? Yet, countless individuals persist in putting little, if any, time or planning into it. Many are even known to skip it entirely.

To set the record straight, "breakfast" broken down translates into "break the fast." After all, upon waking, your body has just gone about

10 hours without any form of sustenance. Its subsequent condition can be likened to a smoldering fire in desperate need of some fresh kindling. And indeed, a balanced meal *is* necessary to get it back to normal functioning and energy levels. If you don't believe it, check out your classmates who didn't eat before school. The trademark behaviors to look for in breakfast skippers include lethargy, irritability, and an inability to focus.

With all of this information in mind, you may be feeling inspired to consume a more healthy and balanced diet. But perhaps you're thinking that, in the process, you'll be forced to sacrifice taste and pleasure. Well, think again.

Because variety is so essential to eating right, something on your plate is bound to meet with your tastebuds' approval. In fact, there are hosts of healthy, yet palatable, options available. These include carbohydrates like pasta and brown rice, lean proteins like barbecued chicken and seasoned fish, veggies such as fresh carrots and corn on the cob, and fruits like plums and watermelon.

What's more, a funny thing happens when you commit to consuming a healthier diet: your sense of taste actually evolves. You can fully expect that certain foods you once considered bland and flavorless will become better appreciated, e.g., for their unique texture and subtle flavors. And as for sweets, many will actually become *too* stimulating and sweet for your tastebuds. (Who knows; maybe this is our body's way of telling us something.)

Remember then, my student, many will pay a heavy price later for making uninformed, undisciplined nutritional choices now...*so challenge yourself to watch what you eat.* You can do this.

LIFE APP

REFLECT ON YOUR PERSONAL EATING HABITS AND WHERE YOUR WEAKNESSES ARE. THEN COMMIT TO CONSUMING ONLY ONE JUNK-FOOD TREAT OR FAST-FOOD MEAL THIS WEEK. YOU CHOOSE THE DAY TO INDULGE, MAKING SURE TO FIGHT ANY TEMPTATIONS DURING THE REMAINDER OF THE WEEK.

REALISTICALLY, THIS COULD LEAD TO NEW AND IMPROVED EATING HABITS, ESPECIALLY WHEN YOU REALIZE YOU POSSESS THE DISCIPLINE AND WILLPOWER REQUIRED TO FOLLOW THROUGH ON CREATING A HEALTHIER LIFESTYLE. I'M ALSO CONFIDENT YOU'LL NOTICE POSITIVE DIFFERENCES IN HOW YOU FEEL PHYSICALLY—WHICH WILL ONLY PROVIDE FURTHER MOTIVATION.

LASTLY, IF YOUR FAMILY'S KITCHEN IS REGULARLY FILLED WITH UNHEALTHY OPTIONS, YOU NEED TO SPEAK UP. ASK THE GROCERY SHOPPER(S) IN YOUR HOUSEHOLD TO REPLACE THE DOUGHNUTS AND FROZEN PIZZA, FOR EXAMPLE, WITH HEALTHIER ALTERNATIVES SUCH AS YOGURT, FRUIT, SOUPS, AND BAGELS. YOUR REQUESTS WILL BE MET WITH LITTLE RESISTANCE.

WEEK 33

Examining Alcohol Use

Always count the cost.
—American Proverb

Facts don't cease to exist because they are ignored.
—Aldous Huxley

...Truth does not change because it is, or is not, believed by a majority of people.
—Giordano Bruno

Over the years, many, many people your age have remarked to me, "If alcohol is so bad, Mr. G, then why does everyone seem to be drinking it?"

It's a logical question, indeed, my student—especially when you consider annual sales of booze total in the hundreds of millions of dollars, and use among those your age continues to become more and more routine.

Well, in an attempt to shed some light on the matter, the students in my class and I compile an annual list of motives that we feel impact any young person's personal decision to drink. We call it the *Why List.* (Reflect, if you would, on each of our reasons before moving on to the next.)

1. Young people equate drinking with being cool and acting grown up.
2. They think it will help them to fit in with peers.
3. It's available right inside many of their own homes.
4. Many young people do not stop to think about what it is they value and truly believe in.
5. They are curious about how "being drunk" feels.

6. Young people tend to buy in to what TV, movies, and advertisements portray, e.g., that popular, good-looking people drink.
7. They see their own family members doing it.
8. They view it as a problem solver and stress reliever.
9. Drinking is a perfect way to rebel against parents and other authority figures.

While I'm sure you can think of even more reasons why, it's safe to assume that those who choose to drink do so because of one or more of these factors.

Make no mistake, though, also playing a big role is their tendency to ignore the reasons why they should *not* drink—or perhaps, it's that they've never been exposed to all of them in the first place.

To make certain you examine both sides of the alcohol story, I've included our *Why Not List* as well. Again, reflect on each entry before proceeding to the next.

1. Alcohol is damaging to your body, e.g., kills brain cells and hinders liver functioning.
2. It slows down your reflexes—which is especially significant for anyone who plays sports.
3. People from every walk of life make foolish, often regretful choices when under the influence of booze. It actually strips you of your greatest power: the power to make your own choices.
4. What's really scary is there's always the risk of getting hooked. Did you know 1 out of every 10 adult drinkers becomes physically addicted, while the chances are even greater for young people?
5. It only seems like everyone else is drinking alcohol. (Believe me when I tell you, there are lots of individuals who choose not to.)
6. The companies who create those misleading commercials have one goal in mind: to separate you from your cash. Obviously, then, they're not likely to include any of the ill effects involved, e.g., people suffering from liver disease, people causing car accidents, or people throwing up all night.
7. Drinking sets a terrible example for younger kids.

8. Driving while intoxicated causes thousands of car accidents each and every year, many of which kill or paralyze innocent people.
9. Real friends will respect your decision to be your own person.

I know from experience, my student, that this list can be an invaluable addition to any young person's life. Just think about how difficult it is to say no, especially when a group of so-called friends are the ones egging you on. Without these *why not* insights in mind, you would be hard-pressed not to give in to the pressure. But with them, you can generate exact reasons for not wanting to drink, and then commit them to memory.

You may choose a couple of favorites to use, e.g., "Alcohol doesn't allow me to be the best athlete I can be" or "It sets a bad example for those who look up to me."

Clearly, knowing how the *why nots* fit in with your personal values—and preplanning which you'll use—are the keys to handling peer pressure. The problem is far too many young people are failing to stop and think about what they truly believe in or how they'll say no—and consequently, are getting caught off guard. (At least you and the rest of my students will now be ready.)

Still, being bold enough to walk away from the temptation will not be easy. That's why doing it successfully fills you with so much real power—and serves to distinguish you as a true individual. Proof of this will come the first time you fall back on your values and walk away from a pressure-filled situation. You'll feel smarter, stronger, and more in touch with who you are and what you're all about. Plus, it will make saying "no" easier the next time around!

Someday, when you're old enough to drink legally, you may decide to finally say yes. There are, after all, many adults in the world who responsibly and maturely drink in moderation. Such individuals resist the temptation to overindulge and *never* drive while under the influence.

I myself, on the other hand, rarely choose to drink. As an adult, I've just never needed it to relax or celebrate. And even back in college, I can recall attending the ubiquitous keg and frat parties as a nondrinker. There was actually an entire group of us (about five or six guys) who would show up, pay the cover charge, not drink, and proceed to have an absolute blast. We'd just hang out and have fun...as much fun as anyone that got drunk was having. And the next morning, while those who did drink were hungover and regretting things they'd done, my friends and I would be heading to the gym to lift or play hoops.

When in high school or in college, just *try* partying sober. I guarantee you'll have as much fun as those choosing to abuse alcohol—and you, unlike them, will enjoy the added pleasure of actually recalling your good times.

Remember then, my student, the large number of people who do choose to drink choose to consider only one side of the story...*so challenge yourself to fully examine alcohol use.* You can do this.

LIFE APP

ALTHOUGH WE'VE COVERED LOTS OF *WHYS* AND *WHY NOTS* HERE, THERE CERTAINLY EXIST MORE OF EACH. WITH A FRIEND OR ADULT, ADD YOUR OWN THOUGHTS TO THE TWO SIDES. THEN DOUBLE STAR (**) YOUR PREFERRED *WHY NOTS*, COMMIT THEM TO MEMORY, AND USE THEM WHENEVER FEELING PRESSURED.

(KEEP YOUR LISTS HANDY, BECAUSE AS YOUNG PEOPLE GROW OLDER, THEY HAVE A TENDENCY TO RECALL THE *WHYS*—BUT NOT THE *WHY NOTS*.)

WEEK 34
Handling Life's Curveballs

The art of living lies not in eliminating but in growing with troubles.
—Bernard M. Baruch

When things go wrong—don't go with them.
—Anonymous

The bravest sight in the world is to see a great man struggling against adversity.
—Seneca

You gotta play the hand that's dealt you. There may be pain in that hand, but you play it. And I've played it.
—James Brady, Presidential Press Secretary *(who was shot—and paralyzed—while walking alongside President Reagan)*

Have you ever been blindsided or backstabbed by a trusted friend? Ever had to move to a new town and/or new school? Perhaps you've been diagnosed with a health problem of a serious nature. Has the sky-high divorce rate impacted you on a personal level? How about an unexpected death or injury in the family?

These are all ways in which life tests our levels of will and character. Yes, my student, unforeseeable difficulties—commonly referred to as life's curveballs—are simply part of the big game.

But while we may lack control over such curveballs, we *can* control how we perceive and react to them.

Consider this example from my life: When I was in eighth grade, my family moved out of state. To me it seemed like the end of the world, or at least, the end of my world. My response was to rebel in every way imaginable; but regrettably, all my antics accomplished was to make a tough situation even tougher on everyone involved.

Since then, I've been told my reaction was typical, that I was just grasping for control in the midst of a traumatic event. But because I can recall all of the grief that resulted, I now make a point of letting young people know there are other, more redeeming ways to maintain control while battling life's curveballs.

How we react to curveballs will indeed go a long way in determining how productive and rewarding a life we come to create. This certainly renders the following advice of utmost importance: *Even if your life has been adversity-free up till now, you need to accept the imminence of trying circumstances and then commit yourself to not letting such circumstances get the best of you. Put another way, when you get knocked down by a curveball—which is bound to happen—you must be ready to pick yourself up, brush the dirt off, and get back into the batter's box of life with more determination than ever.*

This will not be easy advice to carry out, my student, as certain events are almost guaranteed to cause you great pain. However, there is a big difference between being knocked down or hurt by something, and letting that something defeat you. Plus, there exist several specific thoughts and courses of action to help us get back on our feet.

If you are also faced with a move, for example, let me first say that it is completely normal to feel sad and even ticked off about it. I mean you are being uprooted—involuntarily, mind you—from everything you've ever known. Regardless, though, you will eventually have to face up to and deal with the situation.

Option number one consists of doing what I did: Concentrate your thoughts on the scary, negative aspects of the move. For instance, bitterly brood over how unfair it is, expect the worst about the people you'll meet, and convince yourself you'll never be able to recover from the blow. Going this route will more than likely lead you to rebel and to feel sorry for yourself—neither of which serve much purpose.

Option number two, on the other hand, involves the focusing of your energies on more positive thoughts. Things like being able to finally get your own bedroom; the opportunity to make a fresh start in which new doors open and you meet new people and make new friends; the bonus of experiencing another part of the state, country, or world; knowing that no one can ever take away what you had; and recognizing that even a big change does not change everything.

With regard to this last thought, make the time to actually write down the things that won't change—"the constants" as my students and I refer to them, e.g., your personality, family unit, clothes, furniture, pets, CD collection, unique talents, memories. Doing so will provide comfort and grounding while serving to make you a stronger, more resilient individual.

And one last tip: Prior to your move, make sure to exchange addresses, phone numbers, or e-mails with all those you'll miss. Even if you don't end up staying in touch with everyone, this will provide you with both a tangible and symbolic connection to your past. (Interestingly, only a handful of my students who have moved end up needing to correspond—probably because they discover that they're stronger and more resilient than expected. Of course, some keep in touch simply because they want to.)

If you happen to be wrestling with a life curveball of another sort (e.g., the considerable challenge of a divorce, a death, or a serious illness), my advice remains essentially the same. That's right, as you struggle to come to grips with the situation at hand, you can again make the empowering choice to focus on what will not change. In addition, you can reflect on the sentiments—not to be mistaken with be-all, end-all answers—that I have offered as comfort to the young people in my own life:

1. When it comes to divorce, it's common—even natural—for the kids involved to see themselves as the cause. So let me be as clear and straightforward as possible: Divorces happen because the husband and wife have failed—they are no longer willing or capable of making their marriage work. End of story.

   Once you recognize that you aren't to blame, take some time to reflect on the realistic alternative to your parents' decision. Would you not likely be left to deal with loud, persistent conflicts and all the negative emotions that go along with them? That's not how life's meant to be lived. (In fact, as radical a notion as it may sound, there are untold numbers of young people who grew up wishing their feuding parents would split up, so day-to-day life would be more peaceful and normal.)

   And lastly, you need to know—without a shadow of a doubt—that parents' deep-rooted love for their children will never change, no matter what the living and visiting arrangements happen to be.

2. As for what is perhaps the biggest life challenge of all, death, you need to try to think of it as a passage, not an ending. Yes, I know it does end a life here on earth—but make no mistake, it does *not* end a relationship. Wherever you go, you carry the person—pieces of their love and their influence—in your mind as well as in your

heart. Those who have passed do live on...within all those they loved and influenced while here on earth.

As you struggle to come to grips with a death, it also helps to focus on how much time you did have together. Imagine if you'd only known and been able to connect with the person for a mere 60 seconds. It's safe to say you'd feel lucky for even that brief an encounter. Then consider that you had so much more than a single moment to enjoy, share, and just be with one another.

And finally, ask yourself how the person would want you to respond. Would they want you to yield to the pain or would they want you to struggle through it and get on with your life? I think you know the answer.

3. To those dealing with a serious health condition, first let me say that it's perfectly understandable to ask the question, "Why me?" I mean, so many people in the world are walking around in good health, at times it must seem as though you're the only one who's not. In order to get beyond such feelings and eventually come to accept the reality of your position, you'll need to summon the deep faith required to assume that much good can come from any and all circumstances.

   Also keep in mind that, even when you're feeling weakened and under siege, it is still possible to dig deep and resolve to meet the challenge—the enemy—head-on. This requires the adopting of a tough, defiant attitude in which you actually declare out loud, "It's going to take a lot more than this to beat me"—and then a commitment to act accordingly. In so doing, you will be setting a powerful example for those around you, providing them with hope and inspiration as they tackle their own afflictions. And what's more, my student, by summoning the courage, faith, resiliency, and self-belief required to beat the odds, you ensure yourself of ultimate victory, of having lived life as a winner by any standard.

The fact is that while life's curveballs are certainly hard to take, they do have major-league upsides to them as well. If, for example, you were to ask anyone who's endured even several encounters with adversity, you'd soon learn they have been changed—transformed actually—for the better.

Perhaps you'll hear of how their experiences came to reveal things about themselves—and life itself—they would otherwise never have known; or how looking misfortune straight in the eye and choosing to fight can build courage, character, and grit like nothing else. Others will tell you of how hardship and loss renewed their levels of perspective and appreciation for things the rest of the world seems to take for granted; or how it opened new doors and changed the entire direction of their lives. Most notably, though, you will discover that such individuals now travel through life with no trepidations, no hang-ups—their motto being: *If I can overcome that, I can overcome anything.*

In spite of all the good that can come from painful experiences, you need to be reminded one last time that it won't always be easy to get back on your feet; that there will be those occasions when you feel utterly overmatched and tempted to give up. Fortunately, life experience has shown that it's usually just at these moments of battle weariness that the momentum begins to shift back in your favor. And you can always draw strength from those who have overcome hardships before you. Have not slaves, POWs, and countless other "survivors"—some of whom you may know personally—imparted an eternal example of just how powerful and resilient the human spirit is capable of being? Indeed they have.

Remember then, my student, the combination of a positive attitude, courage, faith, and the resiliency of the human spirit can empower you to overcome any pitch thrown your way...*so challenge yourself to handle life's curveballs*. You can do this.

LIFE APP

REFLECT ON THOSE TRYING TIMES IN YOUR OWN LIFE WHEN IT FELT AS THOUGH YOUR WORLD WAS COMING TO AN END.

1. HOW DID THINGS TURN OUT?
2. COULD YOU HAVE PREDICTED THE ULTIMATE OUTCOMES?
3. DID THE WORST YOU ANTICIPATED EVER COME TO BE?
4. DID YOU SURPRISE YOURSELF BY HOW CONFIDENTLY—AND COMPETENTLY—YOU WERE ABLE TO HANDLE THE CURVEBALL?
5. DID YOU LEARN SOMETHING OF VALUE—ABOUT LIFE OR YOURSELF—FROM THE EXPERIENCE?
6. DID YOU EVENTUALLY DERIVE SOME TYPE OF INSPIRATION FROM THE PAIN?

RECALL THIS INFORMATION WHENEVER YOU FACE ADVERSITY IN THE FUTURE...FOR YOUR OWN ANSWERS REPRESENT LESSONS FOR LIFE.

WEEK 35

Staying Active

To keep the body in good health is a duty...otherwise we shall not be able to keep our mind strong and clear.
—Buddha

He who has health has hope; and he who has hope has everything.
—Arabian Proverb

Do you know a young person or two who could be labeled as a couch potato? Based on the results of the Surgeon General's physical fitness report, I'd venture to guess you do. It states that 65 percent of our nation's kids cannot pass minimum-level fitness tests—relatively easy physical challenges.

What's most disturbing about statistics like these, my student, is that inactive, unhealthy kids ultimately become inactive, unhealthy adults. And let's face it, the world doesn't need any more noncontributing, lazy people. These folks think that they've found a fun, relaxing, easy way to live. But in fact, this couch-potato lifestyle is stripping them of their potential, robbing them of nothing less than future opportunities and fulfillment.

Fortunately, it's never too late for a young person to change. Plus, there is much incentive for making the choice to get off one's couch and onto one's feet. Specifically, those who exercise have healthier hearts, healthier skin, stronger muscles, and stronger bones. They have more efficient digestive systems and brains. They enjoy more energy and stamina, more flexibility and explosive power, better coordination and balance....Want more?

Being active *also* helps to prevent obesity and can defend against serious diseases. In fact, the American Heart Association reports that inactive adults are more prone to cardiovascular disease, strokes, and other serious afflictions. (You probably don't think of your physical activity as heart attack prevention, but in part, that's what it is.)

On top of all the physiological benefits, exercise can greatly enhance our levels of emotional health as well. As you may already know, upon completing any type of workout a sense of pride and personal accomplishment leaves us feeling more efficacious and confident about ourselves—with what is commonly referred to as a "ready to take on the world" mind-set. The power of such emotions can't be overstated, either; we are, after all, talking about an acute sensation of well-being and on many occasions, an all-out, all-natural feeling of euphoria.

Amazingly enough, people still come up with all kinds of excuses for not exercising. Here are just a few, with my responses to them:

1. *A lack of time.* An old Spanish Proverb says it best: "A man too busy to take care of his health is like a mechanic too busy to take care of his tools."
2. *A lack of self-discipline.* Discipline isn't so tough when you write out goals (complete with *hows, whys,* and *if I don'ts*) and tape them to your bathroom mirror for a daily motivator.
3. *A lack of energy.* There's no "chicken or the egg" controversy to debate here. It has been revealed many times over that exercise does indeed spawn increased levels of energy. Put another way, the reason you lack energy in the first place is partially due to the fact you're not exercising!

And then there's the other reason—*a lack of a good example.* Studies have shown that kids raised in homes with inactive adults are likely to be/become inactive themselves. But it does not have to be this way, my student. Sure, parental influence has much to do with how we turn out, but why should it be the be-all, end-all factor for so many individuals? It ain't easy, but we all need to rise above any shortcomings our parents may have...by taking responsibility for our own lives.

As an example: It's been documented that adolescent boys who view two hours or less of television a day are much more physically fit than those who take in more than four hours per day. So, if your parents aren't imposing TV (or Internet) limits, *you* need to limit yourself. That's right, you're certainly old enough now to look out for your own best interest. No parent is perfect, so you need to take charge—especially when it comes to establishing a healthy lifestyle for yourself.

Regardless, then, of what's been modeled, the bottom line is you can make the personal choice to get up off the couch. And once you do, you'll have little trouble figuring out your next move:

Among many other things, you can shoot hoops, rollerblade, join a martial arts class, throw a frisbee around, walk the dog, take up a new sport such as lacrosse or field hockey, head to the driving range, train to be a lifeguard, join a school team, hike, take dance classes, hit at the batting cages, set a goal to someday complete a marathon—and start working (jogging) toward it, mountain bike, play tennis....Need I go on?

Remember then, my student, making up your own mind to become physically fit is an empowering, life-altering choice—one that will fill you with far more than mere physical strength...*so challenge yourself to stay active*. You can do this.

LIFE APP

WHEN IT COMES TO LIFE APPS, I TYPICALLY MAKE A POINT OF PROVIDING YOU WITH OPTIONS. BUT I FEEL SO STRONGLY ABOUT THIS ONE PHYSICAL ACTIVITY THAT I'LL MAKE AN EXCEPTION HERE.

SO, YOU'RE WONDERING, WHAT'S THIS EXERCISE THAT'S GOT MR. G SO HYPED UP? WELL, SCAN THE FOLLOWING CLUES AND TRY TO FIGURE IT OUT FOR YOURSELF:

1. JUST ABOUT ANYONE CAN DO IT.
2. IT'S WIDELY KNOWN TO BE ONE OF THE BEST OVERALL WORKOUTS AVAILABLE.
3. YOU CAN PURCHASE THE EQUIPMENT FOR LESS THAN THE COST OF A CD—OR EVEN MAKE YOUR OWN.
4. ATHLETES FROM JUST ABOUT EVERY SPORT ARE NOW INCLUDING IT IN THEIR TRAINING REGIMENS.
5. GYMS ACROSS THE COUNTRY ARE BEGINNING TO OFFER CLASSES SPECIFIC TO IT.
6. IT CAN BE DONE JUST ABOUT ANYWHERE—INDOORS OR OUT.
7. YOU CAN DO IT TO MUSIC, TOO.
8. THERE ARE TOO MANY HEALTH BENEFITS ASSOCIATED WITH IT TO LIST HERE.
9. WITH PRACTICE, YOU CAN GET SO GOOD THAT TOUGH TRICK MOVES WILL BECOME ROUTINE.

HAVE YOU GOT IT YET? YOU'RE RIGHT IF YOU SAID *JUMPING ROPE*. START OFF BY DOING IT FOR A MERE 15 MINUTES, 2 OR 3 DAYS A WEEK. THEN STICK WITH IT, FOR JUMPING ROPE IS AN EMPOWERING HABIT—THE RARE TYPE THAT WILL BENEFIT YOU FOR A LIFETIME.

WEEK 36

Getting Involved with the Arts

Art enables us to find ourselves and lose ourselves at the same time.
—Thomas Merton

I am an artist…I am here to live out loud.
—Emile Zola

The essence of all art is to have pleasure in giving pleasure.
—Mikhail Baryshnikov

Art teaches nothing except the significance of life.
—Henry Miller

To be truthful, having grown up in a community that regarded sports above all else, I was never exposed to much in the way of the arts. I guess you can say I was arts-deprived, even arts-ignorant.

But now that I'm older, my student—and a bit more worldly—I've begun to see just how much I missed out on. And because of my ever-increasing awareness, I now make it a personal priority to incorporate the arts into my day-to-day life. (Better late than never, eh?) While I won't bore you with the details surrounding my experiences (e.g., clay sculpting, a wildlife photography course, and a newfound love for theater), I will say this: *The arts have enriched my life immeasurably.* And that's saying a lot for a guy whose sports roots still run deep.

Fortunately for those in your generation, there have never been more "art opportunities" available to young people. In a growing number of states, for instance, magnet schools with an arts-centered approach are popping up. In a majority of communities, a growing number of local artists are offering dance, painting, sculpting, piano, and acting classes, among others. And even in an era when some school districts are being forced to cut art and music classes, a growing number are greatly expanding their role within the regular curriculum.

It's clear that you can involve yourself with the arts in one way or another—if you so choose. And while I'm sure many young people have already done so, those who have not just don't know what they're missing.

If you happen to be one of these individuals and you're feeling like something's lacking in your life, it could very well be due to this lack of involvement in the arts. After all, no other activities create more chances to discover, and to then express, what resides deep inside you. I'm talking about such all-important things as hidden talents, hopes and ideals, and fears and inhibitions.

Quite often in school I see "noninvolved" students—with so much to say and so much to get out—experience nothing but frustration, day after day after day. They just haven't found an outlet in their lives through which they can express and release all of what's swirling around inside.

As for the relative few who do get involved, this very frustration is often transformed into sheer exhilaration. Can you relate? Many of these individuals literally come alive. Their comfort levels with themselves and others skyrocket. Their overall attitude toward learning shifts as they become more serious and goal-oriented about the arts, as well as their regular classroom work. I've even witnessed a handful of students who struggled mightily prior to getting involved, go on to earn college art scholarships. What these impressive individuals did, in essence, was to use the arts as a springboard for creating a new and improved way of life—a life many of their own parents and grandparents had never known.

In addition to the advantages I've observed firsthand, it's been established that those who get involved with the arts, irrespective of personal background, benefit in many other ways, too. (After examining the following lists, you may finally understand why it is so many parents push their kids into piano lessons, dance classes, etc.)

All participants...

1. Are provided a personal connection to the past, present, and future world.
2. Learn firsthand about discipline, initiative, and patience—traits that greatly enhance one's character.

3. Acquire time-management and creative problem-solving skills that will serve them for a lifetime.
4. Gain unique insight into important life issues.
5. Gain unique insight into other cultures.
6. Access more intricate and complex forms of thinking (while acquiring their "new language").

Allow me to now switch gears and detail some of the less formal types of benefits:

1. The arts can be a whole lot of fun.
2. The arts allow you to lose yourself in an activity you absolutely love.
3. The arts provide something different and positive to channel your energies into.
4. As with sports, the arts offer you the chance to work and connect with others who share your passion.
5. Through your commitment to the arts, you gain a voice—a voice that provides the opportunity to tell your own story and to state as loudly as you want, "Here I am world, this is what I'm capable of!"
6. The arts make it possible for you to learn things about yourself that you never knew existed.
7. And again, as it is with sports, there is glory to be had; whether you win a championship or bring into being something original, it serves as a way to leave your personal mark—a way to imprint your distinct talents and efforts—on the world.

You should also know that, for many, these profound payoffs prompt the pursuit of an actual career within the arts field. For example, some—after receiving a corresponding college degree—fulfill their dreams by making it to Broadway as a dancer or costume designer; to Hollywood as an actor or writer; to Nashville as a singer or an instrumentalist; or to any school district as a music or art teacher.

If you come to develop similar aspirations, do not expect an easy road, however. No, my student, as it is with any worthwhile life journey, there will be many challenges, many bumps in the road to overcome (critics, serious competition, and self-doubt just to name a few). It is all the more crucial, then, that you commit yourself now to fully developing the special gifts you possess.

Among other things, this may translate to waking up each morning with purpose and a plan, allotting a significant amount of time each day for practice/self-improvement, and going to bed each night truly expecting to someday succeed. Those who come to develop this kind of inner drive invariably find they're now equipped to get over the inevitable bumps in the road, and to fend off all oncoming dream-doubters.

Perhaps the greatest reward for all the hard work you put in will come the day you actually make it. That's right, a career within the professional arts arena can set your spirit soaring like nothing else. (I've heard it most fittingly described as "a labor of love" and "the hardest job you'll ever love.") I mean think about it, day after day after day, you'll be doing what naturally flows from deep within. You're thus able to express yourself in ways most people will never ever know (and earn a paycheck while doing it!).

You're also able to connect with others in the rarest and most genuine of fashions. Indeed, I have attended performances in which I've literally been transported to another dimension, a spiritual place where peace of mind and pure inspiration reside. And it was all a result of the artists on stage doing their thing, touching those present with unique, finely tuned abilities as well as pure, penetrating passion.

Even if your future does not include an arts-related career, you can rest assured that opportunities to stay involved will remain available; and that even when life's hectic pace precludes you from making time for them, your past experiences will continue to serve and nourish you.

That's right, as you grow older you'll find you're more apt to notice and ponder even the smallest details of the world around you, more capable than most of enjoying and appreciating each of your life's present moments, and more inclined to develop a broader perspective of what it truly means to be human.

On top of *all this*, any experiences within the arts will also serve you upon entering the adult world of work:

1. Will not the confidence and self-trust gained from onstage performances come in handy during a job interview?

2. Isn't the ability to manage your time—acquired from fitting practice session after practice session into your schedule—a must for anyone involved in the rat race of day-to-day existence?
3. Won't your grasp of the role patience and cooperation play in life enable you to continue being a valuable team member?
4. Aren't the levels of persistence and commitment you demonstrate inherent to the type of worker *any* company would desire?
5. And in a world and job market evolving at an unprecedented rate, isn't the attribute one most develops within the arts—creativity—downright indispensable?

Remember then, my student, the world of the arts provides a lifelong vehicle to discovering, and a lifelong voice to expressing, *who you are…so challenge yourself to get involved with the arts*. You can do this.

LIFE APP

WHAT COULD BE BETTER THAN APPLYING YOUR PERSONAL GIFTS WITHIN THE ARTS TO THE TASK OF HELPING OTHERS? I'VE LISTED A FEW SUGGESTIONS HERE FOR YOU, BUT FEEL FREE TO GENERATE SOME IDEAS OF YOUR OWN.

1. DESIGN HOLIDAY PLACEMATS FOR NURSING HOME RESIDENTS AND HAVE LOCAL ELEMENTARY SCHOOL STUDENTS DO THE COLORING AND DECORATING.
2. JOIN A CHORUS OR A SYMPHONY THAT PERFORMS FOR THESE SAME FOLKS. (IT DOESN'T HAVE TO BE DURING A HOLIDAY SEASON, EITHER.)
3. PRODUCE A RADIO PROGRAM FOR YOUR SCHOOL—IF YOUR SCHOOL IS FORTUNATE ENOUGH TO HAVE ITS OWN STATION.
4. PERFORM SKITS THAT IMPART POSITIVE VALUES TO YOUNG CHILDREN.
5. WRITE CARDS TO SEND TO HOSPITALIZED WAR VETERANS.
6. SEW STOCKINGS, MITTENS, AND/OR HATS FOR HOMELESS KIDS.
7. MANUFACTURE SCARVES AND DONATE THEM TO A HOSPITAL'S CHILDREN-WITH-CANCER WARD.
8. PRODUCE A FUN, UPBEAT PUPPET SHOW FOR THESE SAME KIDS.
9. DESIGN AND CONSTRUCT A FLOAT FOR AN ANNUAL TOWN PARADE.
10. VOLUNTEER TO PRODUCE BANNERS AND POSTERS FOR THE PURPOSE OF ADVERTISING COMMUNITY OR SCHOOL EVENTS.

THE POSSIBILITIES ARE TRULY LIMITLESS.

WEEK 37

Saying No to Tobacco

When possible make the decisions now, even if action is in the future. A reviewed decision usually is better than one reached at the last moment.

—William B. Given

Tobacco is the only legal product that, when used as directed, kills.

—C. Everett Koop, MD, Former US. Surgeon General

The only thing more inconceivable than tobacco companies knowingly selling a product proven to have deadly effects, is the number of people who actually choose to buy and use it. In fact, my student, so many make this fateful choice that each and every year smoking snuffs out more lives than car accidents, AIDS, murders, fires, alcohol, and drugs *combined.*

In case you're wondering, that's 400,000 deaths—as if the September 11th tragedy were played out a staggering 100 times in 1 year.

Meanwhile, each and every year the tobacco industry—a.k.a. Big Tobacco—spends billions of dollars advertising and promoting their products, while still raking in enormous profits. How is this possible? From my perspective, the answer is clear: effective marketing strategies. That's right, their well-funded ad campaigns continue to succeed at getting lots of young, gullible people to buy their product.

Certainly, my intention here is not to label or put down members of your age group; it's just that 90 percent of all smokers do, in fact, start before they turn 18 years of age.

And don't think for a second that Big Tobacco doesn't know it. Why do you think they regularly use confident, attractive, athletic figures as bait in their advertisements? Clearly, they are intent on hooking and then reeling you in, at a time when you're still impressionable and image-conscious. And as previously stated, their approach is working. It's working so well that over 3,000 American kids start smoking every day.

I would be guilty of oversimplifying matters, however, if I were to suggest that every one of these kids started up solely because of the glamorous images depicted in cigarette ads. Of course, additional reasons for making the fateful choice exist.

For one, many young people see it as a way to strike back at, or break free from, authority figures in their lives. *The ironic thing about their plan is they end up hurting themselves far more than they hurt anyone else.*

Others partake because of peer pressure. If those they hang with are doing it, they conform so as to stay accepted. *If only they recognized that real friends would respect their choice to be their own person.*

Then there's the popular "it's cool" rationale. Most young smokers still think others are impressed by their craziness and willingness to take dangerous chances. *I don't know about them, but when I was a teenager, I looked at those who smoked as fools. Now that we know—via research—that one out of three smokers eventually dies as a result of the habit, it's hard to argue with my choice of terms.*

I've also heard many smokers claim that they smoke because it helps them to relax and unwind. *Wrong again. Nicotine—the drug in cigarettes—is a stimulant, and as such, has just the opposite physiological impact. I guess we can convince ourselves of just about anything if we want to believe it badly enough.*

Other smokers simply don't think much with regard to their future. They are living only for today. *When you're young, it really is hard to imagine being older. But make no mistake, once young smokers reach the unimaginable age of 30, 40, or even 50, their long-forgotten choice to start up will come back to bite them. And if they think they can quit anytime and make everything right again, they should think twice; I personally know people who have been struggling to quit for more than 10 years.*

Having considered several of the motives behind why people light up in the first place, let's now discuss more of the other side of the story. Hopefully, these facts will serve as potent reminders of why we should not be deceived by tobacco companies, or by the so-called friends who urge us to try smoking.

FACT: Tobacco contains upwards of 4,000 chemicals—and of these, at least forty are known to cause cancer.

FACT: Smoking stains and discolors teeth.

FACT: Ninety percent of all lung cancer cases are directly linked to smoking.

FACT: Tobacco use can also cause emphysema, heart disease, and strokes.

FACT: One cigarette contains up to 101 poisons.

FACT: Nicotine, a poisonous compound found in all tobacco products, is physically addictive and makes your heart beat faster.

FACT: Smoking gives you bad breath.

FACT: Smoking damages your complexion.

FACT: Carbon monoxide is only one of the many toxic gases inhaled when smoking a cigarette.

FACT: Just about every family has lost a relative or friend to a tobacco-related illness.

FACT: Whether our minds can grasp it or not, vital organs do in fact exist beneath our outer shells—many of which are irreparably damaged by smoking.

FACT: Over time, the tar in cigarette smoke will actually cause a smoker's lungs—as well as the tubes leading to their lungs—to turn black.

FACT: A recent study indicates that the younger you are when you start smoking, the more likely you are to end up with cancer.

FACT: Cigarette ads are effective. It has been proven that young smokers tend to purchase the brands most widely advertised.

FACT: Because tobacco products are so expensive, the habit hits hard in the wallet as well.

FACT: Many individual members of the tobacco industry are wealthy. In the year 1999, for example, the 4 major cigarette companies reported domestic profits alone of $7.8 billion.

FACT: One out of three will die from his or her addiction to smoking.

Remember then, my student, Big Tobacco has only its own interests in mind, and continues to reel in big revenues only because young, impressionable people continue to fall for the bait...*so challenge yourself to say no to tobacco*. You can do this.

LIFE APP

IN ADDITION TO TAKING A PERSONAL STAND AGAINST SMOKING, HELP OTHERS AVOID MAKING THE FATEFUL CHOICE TO LIGHT UP.

CONSIDER, FOR EXAMPLE, JOINING AN ANTISMOKING GROUP. ONE IN PARTICULAR, TATU (TEENS AGAINST TOBACCO USE), SENDS TEENAGE ROLE MODELS INTO ELEMENTARY SCHOOLS TO EDUCATE AND INFLUENCE YOUNGER KIDS. A GREAT WAY TO MAKE A DIFFERENCE.

WEEK 38

Handling Life's Pressures

Life is a grindstone. Whether it grinds us down or polishes us up depends on us.

—Thomas L. Holdcroft

There are two ways of meeting difficulties: You alter the difficulties or you alter yourself to meet them.

—Phyllis Bottome

Because adults face so many pressures of their own—bills, traffic, parenting demands, and job deadlines, among a host of others—they sometimes forget that young people like you are also under siege. Make no mistake, though, while your pressures—peer, parental, academic, etc.—may be different from theirs, they are nonetheless very real and equally as challenging.

So yes, it's true that no one is immune; that pressure is simply a naturally occurring side effect of life. What counts most then, my student, is not the amount or the kind of pressure we all face—but rather the ways in which we learn to deal with them. Indeed, how you come to handle pressure can determine nothing less than how productive and rewarding a life you'll lead.

Let's first consider the negative ways of dealing with pressure: yelling and screaming, letting little things become big annoyances, biting people's heads off, not sleeping well, even acting violently. Now is this any way to live?

What's noteworthy about all such behaviors is they are symptomatic of the very same bad habit: that of holding too much in. And whatever the reasons for holding stuff in, it is *not* something we want to be developing into a habit. Just as a pressure cooker is capable of exploding when left unvented and unchecked, so are we. On any given day, examples can be found of people who, in the process of holding all their troubles in, have blown their tops in one form or another.

At the very best, this choice allows feelings of tension, frustration, and inner turmoil to become permanent life companions. And at worst, can lead to personal explosions capable of tragic, life-altering consequences.

The good news is that for all the formidable pressures there are in life, there exist just as many ways to release them. Your job, then, is to simply make these a part of your personal repertoire *before* you boil over. (You'll be glad to know you've likely already started taking this proactive approach.)

Getting outdoors, for example, is one outlet you may already enjoy. Mountain biking, jogging, hiking, rollerblading, etc. are all challenging and fun—and therefore, ideal activities for letting off steam. Organized sports can also help to channel your pressures in a positive direction. Track and field, football, field hockey, wrestling, soccer, swimming, etc. all require high levels of physical and mental exertion—and are therefore extremely beneficial.

Even those competitions unrelated to the realm of sport can provide a healthy, fun release. Case in point: I have, at one time or another, started up clubs devoted to debate, chess, theater, and mathematics. In each instance, the members got so wrapped up in learning the intricacies of the activity and improving upon their performance levels, that they were able to transform even their most nagging pressures into purely positive energy.

Another effective way to handle pressures involves the process of "attacking" each one individually. This requires that you first determine what's within your circle of control, and then act on it.

Case in point: As you know, many young people experience anxiety over the future. They worry and agonize over questions like: *What career path will I follow? Am I capable of living up to everyone's expectations? Will I get into a good college? Do I have what it takes to succeed in the world?*

Well, if this considerable weight is ever to be lifted, these worriers must focus their energies on what they can influence, on what they can do to relieve the pressure. After all, we cannot control the specifics surrounding our future lives, but we are capable of doing what is necessary now—day to day, week to week—to provide ourselves the best possible chance for future success.

Take school, for example. You can choose to study for tests, do your homework, pay attention in class, and do all the things that make for a successful high school career. The rest will follow.

I am constantly preaching such advice to my students. I let them know that the greatest reward of working hard and giving strong effort now is they don't have to worry about what the future holds for them. Things simply have a way of working out for those who commit to establishing good habits and consistently strive to live up to their potential. So, the secret to any effective attack, my student: Take care of what is in your control now, for this is exactly what prompts what is out of your control to later take care of itself!

Another pressure this plan of attack can be applied to involves your generation's concern over the present condition of the world.

Day after day, we hear unsettling news of senseless violence and serious environmental troubles, to name just two. It's certainly understandable why young people would come to experience feelings of anxiety and distress; but the fact remains, feeling such as these serve no purpose—they are only good for building up more pressure in one's life. And again, the only way to lighten this load is to concentrate on what it is you can control—on what you can do to make a difference.

You better believe that 100 percent of those young people working to prevent violence (e.g., by becoming a peer mediator in their school) or to raise environmental awareness (e.g., by heading a recycling campaign in their community) will tell you they're now far less likely to feel stressed out about such issues. What they've done is to find peace in the knowledge that, while they cannot control all of the bad going on in the world, they are at least doing their part—adding to the mix their own small, but extremely meaningful, measure of good.

This kind of proactive "What can I do?" approach to handling pressures has become an integral part of how I now choose to live. I've come to understand and finally accept that pressure is simply a normal part of life. Accordingly, I now go through each day in a way that leaves me best prepared to manage and cope with it. This boils down to the good habits of getting to bed earlier than most, watching what I eat, exercising regularly, and refraining from drinking coffee or alcohol, and from smoking cigarettes. I've also experimented with a "new" type of pressure-relieving behavior called relaxed concentration, which combines a bit of meditation, some visualization, and a few deep-breathing techniques. It has not only served to keep me more even-tempered, but has also contributed to a clearer focus and higher levels of positive energy.

As you can see, I speak from experience when I say that being consistent with clean, healthy living habits can leave you feeling capable of handling any and all pressures life throws your way.

In addition to taking the many proactive steps we've covered thus far, you'll be glad to know there exist even more ways for you to better deal with pressure. You do need to recognize, however, that no matter how hard you try to cover all the bases and do everything right, there will still be moments when life gets the best of you. This is why I have included both proactive and reactive responses in the following advice list. The reactive ones are intended to help you find relief from, and perhaps even propel you past, some of the most pressure-packed of personal times.

1. Accept the fact that life includes stress and pressure.
2. Keep your pressures in perspective; we tend to blow our own out of proportion.
3. Talk to someone when feeling overwhelmed; don't ever hesitate to ask for help.
4. Recognize that pressure can have a positive purpose, too. In the way, for example, that coaches and teachers push you to take your abilities to the next level.
5. Write about your pressures in a daily journal or diary.
6. Make time to relax and recharge—no matter how hectic things are for you.
7. Always make your own choices, and fall back on your own values, when pressured into making tough decisions.
8. Plan something you can look forward to enjoying. Do this each and every day.
9. Figure out what your personal limits are, and then make a point of not biting off more than you can chew.
10. Get out of the house to take a walk or a bike ride.
11. Escape in a good book.
12. Laugh it off—when at all possible.

13. Recall all those past pressures you've proven capable of overcoming.
14. Listen to music—and crank up the volume.
15. Help others you know to battle through the pressures they're presently facing.
16. Utilize positive thinking and *fully expect* pressure-causing circumstances to turn out for the best.
17. Invest in a punching bag or revert back to your pillow-fighting days more often.
18. Utilize positive language and talk about how you want things to turn out.
19. Let more of the "little things" slide.
20. Observe and learn from those who cope admirably with pressures of their own.

Remember then, my student, for all of life's pressures—and there are many—there exist just as many ways to deal with them…*so challenge yourself to handle life's pressures*. You can do this.

LIFE APP

THIS WEEK, IN ADDITION TO BECOMING MORE PROACTIVE WITH YOUR APPROACH TO HANDLING LIFE'S PRESSURES, REFLECT UPON THE SPECIFIC ONES YOU ENCOUNTER EACH DAY. UTILIZE THE FOLLOWING QUESTIONS TO ASSURE THAT YOU TAKE SOMETHING OF VALUE FROM EACH EXPERIENCE.

1. WHO OR WHAT WAS THE UNDERLYING CAUSE OF THE PRESSURE?
2. WHY EXACTLY DID I FEEL SO PRESSURED?
3. WAS IT A SITUATION TRULY WORTHY OF MY EMOTION OR DID I OVERREACT?
4. WAS THERE MORE I COULD HAVE DONE TO BETTER "PREPARE" MYSELF?–AND MOST IMPORTANTLY,
5. AM I SATISFIED WITH THE WAY IN WHICH I DEALT WITH THE SITUATION–THIS PARTICULAR PRESSURE–OR WILL I HANDLE IT DIFFERENTLY NEXT TIME?

Seeing School in a New Light

The roots of education are bitter, but the fruit is sweet.
—Aristotle

Education is the most powerful weapon which you can use to change the world.
—Nelson Mandela

I find the harder I work, the more luck I seem to have.
—Thomas Jefferson

When you feel discouraged or simply lazy, as is bound to happen sometimes, remember the millions of people in the world who have not had your privilege…
—Jehan Sadat, widow of President Anwar el-Sadat of Egypt,speaking on the privilege of an education

Frankly, my student, I'm amazed by the lack of interest and enthusiasm some young people demonstrate toward their education.

The type of individuals I'm referring to perceive school as some big drag or nuisance—even as a "prison sentence."

Well, it's quite clear that American culture has greatly contributed to this perplexing set of circumstances. Just consider, as an example, the number of back-to-school commercials contrasting the ecstatic reaction of parents with the anguish of their kids. While the humorous intent is not lost on me, the message certainly does its part to perpetuate the "school is a downer" mind-set.

The time has come to finally set the record straight—to shed a little light on the dim-witted perspective still packing so much clout. (Mind you, if it were at all possible, I'd have the following declaration also signed by our forefathers and heralded from every rooftop in the land.) Here goes: *You are not in school for your parents, you are not in school for your teachers, you are not there for anybody other than yourself—it's your future at stake—yours and yours alone.*

As you allow this concept to take hold, allow me to elaborate.

The first time I shared this observation, a young man with whom I was working responded by saying, "Yeah I know, Mr. G, if I don't start taking my education more seriously, I won't be able to get much of a job when I'm older." As relieved as I was that he'd acknowledged a connection between his present and future, I informed him that the purpose of an education goes far beyond getting a job—that his time, as well as your time in school, can best be described as preparation for life.

Truly, it's about discovering the joy of learning, and at the same time, discovering yourself. It's about expanding your mind so as to expand your horizons. It's about picking up skills and attributes that will empower you to attain your individual potential, both as a student and as a person. And yes, if you respect the school experience, you will someday secure a good job, one that will likely turn out to be more rewarding than you can now know.

This happens to be an especially important point considering that only a relative few careers can be labeled as challenging, enjoyable, *and* well-paying. Moreover, these are the same rewarding careers that provide the greatest opportunity to do good and make an actual difference in the world. You just can't underestimate the value and significance of someday securing such a job. Truth be told, to love and appreciate what you do, day in and day out, is something only a select few people ever get to experience in life.

As you're probably beginning to figure, seeing school in a negative light can certainly dim one's prospects for future fulfillment. Believe it or not, though, there are already a large number of young people who don't need me, or anyone else, to help them figure this out—perhaps you're one. They already know and have known for quite a while.

I have spent time in communities where education is valued above all else, where parents and teachers are wholly dedicated to instilling positive attitudes toward learning. Accordingly, their children, from a very early age, come to see hard work and success in school as *the* ticket to a good life. (Can you see what a huge advantage they enjoy?)

All of this early awareness and clear focus makes for a school atmosphere never experienced by many young people—including myself as a past student. Kids who intently listen to their teachers as well as to one another. Students with vision and direction who routinely go the extra mile because they know it will help get them where they want to go. Students who do not groan when a major project or report is assigned, but rather view it as a chance to learn something new and grow from a challenge. And students who take full advantage of the opportunities presented to them by taking lead roles in clubs, committees, and other extracurricular offerings. (You may think I'm exaggerating here, but I assure you such actions are far more the rule than the exception in these unique places.)

In a perfect world, my student, all young people would approach their education with similar interest, passion, and vision. But as reality has demonstrated over the years, this is simply not how it works.

Instead, a large number of students do things like skip class, concentrate solely on sports, choose to be bored, act out, daydream at all the wrong times, and do only what it takes to squeak by. (The slackers I grew up with would be quick to tell you how much they enjoyed themselves back in school, but now, 20 years later...well, let's just say they're not having nearly as much fun.) If only such students would open their eyes to all their misguided approach is costing them. Indeed, the real world that awaits each ill-prepared young person can be quite unforgiving.

If you're starting to view school with greater clarity, you should know that it's not too late to turn things around—even if school has never been your cup of tea. You see, many young people mistakenly assume that just because they're not the smartest, most prolific students, they cannot be successful. Consequently, they don't even try.

These are the kids who don't listen to much of anything in class, study last second if at all, don't take pride in the work they do hand in, and act like they could care less whenever they flunk. They think not trying at all is better than trying and coming up short, which would be embarrassing. They are afraid of looking dumb.

In order to steer the students in my own classes away from this path, I make them aware—from day one—that ability level and grades mean nothing to me. Yes, you read correctly. What matters most is they learn to give their strongest effort on a consistent basis. This way, upon leaving me, they will have acquired more skills and more knowledge, sure. But most significantly, they will each possess something of far greater value: the habits of a prideful, hard worker.

I also let them know it's true that not every single thing on the blackboard or in their textbooks is really going to matter in their lives; but again, that the habits with which they come to approach such tasks certainly will. Let me be clear: Success and fulfillment hinge on sound, strong habits—sound, strong habits.

The young people who figure this out the quickest invariably benefit the most. Perhaps that's why so many average and below-average students in my classes have responded so positively—and promptly. They see it as a chance to finally excel...the one way they can come to outshine even the highest ability students.

As part of their transformation, they begin to do things like read every day, study harder and longer, ask more questions, and even assign themselves extra work. In essence, they start putting into practice the habits of a prideful, hard worker.

It's also worth noting that in the process of doing so, these students earn the respect and admiration of adults and fellow students alike. (It truly is a privilege to work with them.) After all, there are many in the world who recognize just how tough it can be to bust your butt, and yet reap only average results. Indeed, it takes extraordinarily high levels of courage and resiliency to push oneself day after day under such circumstances.

And because it's so difficult, many others become disheartened and fail to stay the course. Little do they realize, with just a bit more time their efforts would have most assuredly paid off. Heck, even if the A's and B's never came, their new work ethic alone would have helped to ensure a good job and a rewarding future. Does it not make sense that when you've established yourself as someone who consistently gives strong effort, you will become the best student you can be...your grades will become the best they can be...and your future will become as bright as it possibly can be?

Any student who does stay the course shouldn't be surprised if they end up with the last laugh. Oh yes, the world is teeming with individuals who struggled, yet persisted through school, only to go on to become huge successes in life.

Would you believe that even when going head-to-head for top jobs, many such people get hired over former "A" students? It's easy to understand why, when you consider their rare capacity to work hard. Plus, many top students who receive A's do so without having to give much effort, and this often prompts the tendency to rest on one's laurels. They simply stop pushing themselves and resist any attempts by their parents and teachers to do so. Such complacency then becomes the breeding ground for—you guessed it—lazy habits. (If you were a boss, who would you hire?)

My final attempt to refocus your lenses requires you actually transport yourself to the years beyond all graduations. Whether you can fathom it yet or not, this will likely be a time when you look back on your school days with real feelings of fondness and nostalgia.

There will be thoughts and recollections of powerful bonds you formed with certain classmates; extracurriculars which gave rise to life passions; certain teachers who reached you on the deepest level; and interesting classes through which you gained empowering insights.

You'll soon discover that there really are enough positives associated with school to negate all of the bad stuff. And who knows, this new perspective or altered vision may even be enough to get you to appreciate school *now*—while still serving your so-called sentence.

Remember then, my student, it's your future that's at stake—yours and your alone...*so challenge yourself to see school in a new light*. You can do this.

LIFE APP

THIS WEEK, BEGIN TO TAKE YOUR PERSONAL PERFORMANCE AT SCHOOL TO THE NEXT LEVEL. FOR STARTERS, YOU CAN CONSIDER EMBRACING THE FOLLOWING STRONG-STUDENT HABITS:

1. CATCH YOURSELF IN CLASS WHEN THE DAYDREAM BUG BITES. *WE TEND TO FALL PREY AT THE VERY MOMENTS IT'S MOST NECESSARY TO FOCUS.*
2. ASSIGN YOURSELF WHEN YOU HAVE LITTLE TO NO HOMEWORK. *INITIATIVE IS A KEY INGREDIENT OF SUCCESS AND FULFILLMENT.*
3. GET YOURSELF TO THE LIBRARY MORE OFTEN. *THERE IS NO OTHER ENVIRONMENT MORE CONDUCIVE TO GOOD, HARD BRAIN WORK.*
4. DON'T JUST FOCUS ON WHAT YOUR TEACHERS HAVE TO SAY; ALSO LISTEN INTENTLY TO CLASSMATES. *THERE'S A BUNCH OF INSIGHT BEING MISSED OUT ON AS THEY'RE ASKING QUESTIONS, OFFERING RESPONSES, AND DEBATING ISSUES.*

LIFE APP

5. GO THE EXTRA MILE, EVEN WHEN YOU DON'T FEEL LIKE IT. *THIS KIND OF SELF-DISCIPLINE WILL SERVE YOU FOR AN ENTIRE LIFETIME, WHILE CONVERSELY, THE HABIT OF "DOING JUST ENOUGH TO GET BY" WILL LIMIT YOU FOR A LIFETIME.*
6. WHENEVER POSSIBLE, STUDY IN ADVANCE; YOU'LL FIND THAT EACH SUCCESSIVE TIME YOU LOOK AT THE MATERIAL, IT BECOMES MORE FAMILIAR AND UNDERSTANDABLE—THANKS IN LARGE PART TO THE INCREDIBLE POWERS OF THE SUBCONSCIOUS MIND. *THIS IS HANDS DOWN THE MOST EFFECTIVE—NOT TO MENTION, LEAST STRESSFUL—WAY TO STUDY AND SUCCEED.*
7. MOST IMPORTANTLY, READ EVERY DAY. THIS, ABOVE ALL OTHER FACTORS, EMPOWERS YOUNG PEOPLE TO IMPROVE IN EVERY SUBJECT AREA, AND SUBSEQUENTLY, TO ACHIEVE TO THEIR INDIVIDUAL POTENTIAL. *IT DOESN'T MATTER IF IT'S A MAGAZINE, THE SPORTS PAGE, A NOVEL, A BIO, ETC.—JUST READ.*

THE BIG PAYOFF FOR FOLLOWING THROUGH ON SUCH ADVICE IS THAT YOUR FUTURE WILL TAKE CARE OF ITSELF. YOU'LL ACTUALLY BE ABLE TO LOOK FORWARD TO IT MINUS ANY PANGS OF WORRY OR TREPIDATION. SIMPLY TRUST THAT THE STRONG HABITS YOU DEVELOPED, THE EXTRA TIME YOU INVESTED, THE THOROUGH KNOWLEDGE YOU GAINED, AND THE MANY SKILLS YOU ACQUIRED HAVE, IN TOTAL, PREPARED YOU TO ANSWER ANY AND ALL FUTURE CHALLENGES.

WEEK 40

Resisting the Body-Image Takeover

I think it's more important to be fit so that you can be healthy and enjoy activities than it is to have a good body.

—Rachel Blanchard

Beauty is in the heart of the beholder.

—Al Bernstein

Outside show is a poor substitute for inner worth.

—Aesop

Have you ever looked at your body in the mirror and been left feeling frustrated, even disgusted? Well, you're not alone. These days it's a rare individual indeed who loves and accepts everything about his or her appearance.

Why is this so? I guess with so many body parts involved—ears, feet, eyes, stomach, hair, nose, legs, hands, lips, etc.—something *is* bound to turn out less than ideal. (For me personally, it's the first two on the list that are most imperfect.) But more than that, my student, is the fact we've grown up in a culture known to place too much—way too much—emphasis on outer appearances.

For proof, all anyone has to do is turn on a TV or flip through a fashion magazine. Almost immediately, you'll find yourself being bombarded by images of physical perfection, carefully selected to model this and promote that. But "this and that" also serve to promote a terribly false illusion: one of a world populated by attractive, ultra-thin, or ultra-muscular individuals. It's simply an impossible standard of appearance to live up to, yet one society seems intent on shoving down our throats. And because of all the misleading hype, huge numbers of young people—unable to match up—are becoming dangerously critical of their bodies.

With such circumstances in place, it's clear you have some important personal choices to consider.

Choice Number One: *You can continue experiencing negative emotion whenever you look into the mirror.* Have you noticed that museums the world over are full of paintings and sculptures of nude women with voluptuous thighs? Well, it's because that was once considered the "perfect" body for a woman. And while today's advertisers have certainly set in stone a different standard of appearance, the reality of the matter remains the same: someone else is telling you what to think.

In order to continue feeling inferior and even ugly each time you gaze at your reflection, you need to continue blindly buying into society's present-day definition of beauty. More specifically, you need to swallow the notions that inner qualities count for little, if anything, when compared to outer appearances; that skinny, shapely bodies are not out of the ordinary but rather representative of the average, everyday person; and that others should decide for you what is attractive and worthy of imitation.

One sidenote: You also need to be aware that adhering to society's narrow definition of beauty can trigger much more than negative emotion. Diagnosed eating disorders are more prevalent now than at any other time in history. If you *ever even begin to think* you have an eating-related problem, talk to a trusted adult in your life about it.

Choice Number Two: *You can learn to accept what is out of your control.* As you know, physical attributes such as height, bone structure, nose, and shoe size are genetically predetermined, having been passed on to you from your parents, grandparents, and down the line. This, of course, leaves you with no say in such matters. Does it not make sense, then, to accept your imperfections as a part of who you are at the core, a part that connects you to your personal ancestry, a part that makes you a unique, one-of-a-kind individual—rather than be frustrated and even disgusted by them?

Moreover, when an "attitude of acceptance" is embraced, it can spawn a magical kind of domino effect in one's life. I say this because self-acceptance, more than anything else, is responsible for fostering feelings of inner peace and joy. And once someone has achieved peace with himself, true beauty—the kind that emanates from within—is allowed to flow freely forth.

Keep in mind, however, that individuals—particularly those given to gaining weight easily (like me)—sometimes misconstrue this concept of acceptance. For example, I once equated a "hey, my physique is what it is so why bother" mind-set with self-acceptance. In reality, though, all I was doing was providing myself free license to not exercise when I didn't feel like it, and to keep eating what I wanted when I wanted. That's a cop-out. Accepting one's hefty size and shape does not mean one should forget about making healthful choices. According to studies, heavier people who exercise are actually more healthy than thin people who do not. You read correctly; so even if you're not losing weight from working out, be assured that all-important body functions like your immune system, your heart muscle, and your lungs are benefiting tremendously from your efforts. Encouraging, isn't it?

Choice Number Three: *You can commit to change what is within your control.* Many young people fail to recognize that "I don't like my body" is far too broad an assertion to make. Instead, these individuals need to break their feelings down, determining exactly what is unsuitable about their appearances. They must then ask themselves, "Which of these aspects are unhealthy and capable of being changed?"

In many instances, my student, the key to creating overall physical change will come down to eating right and exercising. But despite how simple and straightforward this advice may sound to you, mistakes are often made when attempting to apply it.

With regard to physical activity, the most common mistake—by far—is trying to do too much too fast. It stands to reason, does it not, that if someone is suddenly engaging in long, grueling workouts, it won't be long before he detests them enough to quit. I mean think about it; even an extraordinarily fit athlete training for a marathon must start off slowly. Typically, he will begin by doing shorter runs, then step up the distance little by little each time out.

Indeed, when striding toward any body-change goal, *consistency* above all else will be the key to progress and ultimate success. (If you have any doubts about this, simply look to the physical condition of those who have consistently not exercised.)

Of course, eating right is also a part of the winning equation. But just as with physical activity, there exist both right and wrong ways to go about doing it.

Consider, for example, the high percentage of people who try to lose weight by dieting. While it's understandable as to why they diet—when the number of calories consumed is less than the number of calories burned, weight is lost—it's the methods they use that so often create problems. Many times, their approach equates to nothing more than eating one or two types of food only once or twice a day. Sounds more like fasting than dieting.

One of the problems linked to this type of self-deprivation is the body responds by slowing down its internal fuel-burning rate, a.k.a. metabolism, thus allowing us to live on fewer and fewer calories. This means that in spite of the drastic measures, it becomes increasingly difficult to lose body fat. And what's more, with little to no quality fuel coming in, muscle tissue of all things gets burned for energy. Needless to say, you can eventually be left looking emaciated and sickly—and feeling much the same.

What are the alternatives? you wonder. Well, there do exist a few simple measures proven effective over the years.

First, you need to limit the amount of junk food you consume. Cravings for sweets are often rooted in feelings other than hunger; perhaps it's hopelessness, anxiety, or anger that's really eating at you. As you become more and more in tune with the underlying causes—and work to address them, the solution (resisting junk) becomes more and more attainable.

Second, you need to eat more fruits and veggies. Many people—young and old alike—are surprised to learn that the number of daily portions recommended to maintain a balanced diet is five to six. A whole lot of us aren't even getting close to this amount. Well, here's a simple solution: Consider substituting a fruit or veggie for any sweet snack you've grown overly reliant on.

Lastly, you need to eat more frequent meals—that's right, more. This keeps your body's metabolism fired up and running at a steady rate. Just be sure to pay attention to portion size and calories, as you'll now be eating up to six times a day, rather than the more customary two to three times.

When I myself committed to change what was within my control, this commonsense approach—consistently applied—enabled me to go from 29 percent body fat to 12 percent body fat in two short years. And it's worth noting that despite doing nothing to alter my ears or feet, I felt—and still feel—great about myself and what I was able to accomplish.

Remember then, my student, feeling good about your body comes from feeling good about yourself...*so challenge yourself to resist the body-image takeover*. You can do this.

LIFE APP

THIS WEEK, GENERATE A LIST OF EXACTLY WHAT YOU NEED TO ACCEPT ABOUT YOUR BODY AND WHAT YOU'D LIKE TO CHANGE. JUST KEEP IN MIND THIS SINGLE CRITERION WHEN STRIVING FOR ANY TYPE OF PHYSICAL CHANGE: IS IT HEALTHY? TALK TO YOUR FAMILY DOCTOR ABOUT NORMAL WEIGHT AND BODY FAT PERCENTAGES. THEN EAT RIGHT, EXERCISE REGULARLY, AND ACCEPT THE RESULTS.

IN ADDITION, TURN THE CHANNEL AND DITCH THE FASHION MAGS—OR AT THE VERY LEAST, LEARN TO LAUGH AT JUST HOW OUT OF TOUCH WITH REALITY THE IMAGES THEY PROMOTE ARE.

AND LAST, BUT MOST IMPORTANT OF ALL, START SMILING AT THE UNIQUE ONE-OF-A-KIND INDIVIDUAL STARING BACK IN THE MIRROR!

WEEK 41

Considering Consequences

There are no rewards or punishments—only consequences.
—Dean William R. Inge

Every great mistake has a halfway moment, a split-second when it can be recalled and perhaps remedied.
—Pearl S. Buck

We are each responsible for our own actions. It's been preached countless times before but most often when someone is already facing a serious consequence. Well, if I had my way, the expression of choice would be changed to: *We are each responsible for anticipating the outcomes of our actions.*

This is what I call "consequence thinking." And it's pretty simple to do, my student. All it really entails is learning to pause when faced with a tough decision to think about what could happen if you were to follow through. You then ask of yourself the all-important questions, *Am I prepared to accept the possible consequences?* and *Is it really worth it?* While I can't make any guarantees, it does stand to reason if your gut is answering no to either question, you'll be far less likely to follow through.

Just as we learn to read, hit a baseball, ride a bike, or, to later, drive a stick shift, consequence thinking is a skill that must be developed. In essence, the process only requires—as it does with all of the above activities—that you practice and hone the techniques involved until the behavior becomes second nature, a habit or reflex.

The relative few individuals who've already developed this habit certainly earn the distinction of being the most responsible and fulfilled among us. Primarily, and simply, because they travel through life making fewer mistakes—and as a result, are less likely to ever suffer the anguish brought on by a serious lapse of judgment.

You see, when people insist on paying no mind to consequences, it is only a matter of time before they are shocked and dismayed by their own actions. And when that day comes, thoughts like *What have I done?* and *How could I have been so stupid?* immediately establish their haunting presence. Consider, for instance, the outrageous number of drunk drivers who have killed innocent people; teens who have gotten pregnant; and school-shooters who are now rotting in jail. They are indeed living, suffering proof.

Of course, people don't always make the connection between their actions and the consequences. For many kids, especially, this is not a naturally occurring process.

I'm talking about, as an example, the kid who misbehaves in school, and as a result, receives a detention or in-school suspension from the principal. The idea that he is responsible for the consequence will likely never even cross his mind. Instead, he'll be angry with the principal and perceive his predicament as yet another adult "out to get him" handing down yet another punishment. Do you know anybody who thinks in such a way?

Being a teacher, I have experienced scenarios like this many times over; fortunately, I've had a lot of success empowering such individuals to better make the connection.

Each and every time a young person messes up, I point out his choice as being what brought about the consequences he is now facing. The punishment would've never come to be if it hadn't been for *his* decision to act—hence, there is no one to blame but himself. I then attempt to lend some encouragement and perspective by saying, "While I don't enjoy handing down this penalty, I care way too much about you and your ability to make future decisions for yourself, not to. Remember, ultimately you will always be free to make your own choices, but life will not always give you that same say when it comes to the consequences. And whether you ever come to acknowledge the connection or not, you remain ultimately responsible for your life circumstances."

There are two other points I want to make clear. Number one: *There is great honor in acknowledging a consequence as something you have brought into being.* And two: *There is equally high honor in learning enough from a bad choice so as to never again repeat it.*

You may have heard of a study contradicting my assertion that kids can learn consequence thinking. This particular study revealed that during the teen years, the part of the brain in control of emotions experiences a dominating amount of activity. In light of these findings, the report went on to state that young people were, physiologically, less able than older people to think about consequences. Interesting, eh?

However, my student, while the inner workings of the brain may indeed contribute to the teenage "I'm invincible; it won't happen to me" mind-set, it must be viewed as a factor that nevertheless can be overcome. Basic logic does reveal that many bad choices could be avoided if more individuals—young and old alike—were to simply think ahead and follow their instincts. And as previously discussed, this is well within any brain's, and gut's, control.

If nothing else, such findings should serve as dual motivation, first prompting adults to more aggressively cultivate the skill, and second, compelling young people like you to focus more on developing it.

I have also heard reports about the causes of school shootings. Some have attributed the behavior of the shooters to a lack of love and emotional support, the fact they were mistreated and ostracized by peers, and their overexposure to violent shows and video games. My reply to such arguments: While these unfortunate circumstances may well play some role, they do not get down to the root of the issue. If they did, how could it be that thousands upon thousands of other young people, subjected to similar circumstances, have not resorted to similar extreme measures? Could it be that the consequences of taking another's life actually enter into the minds of most?

Indeed, the vast majority of young people—even the most angry—never consider carrying out such an act, partly because they're aware of the very real and severe ramifications. Make no mistake, we are talking about a lifetime of regret and pain caused to all involved families, not to mention a lifetime of jail—a place in which the individual, while forced to give up just about every freedom he's ever known, also subjects himself to daily terror and abuse. Now do you honestly think these young perpetrators were willing to accept such consequences? No way—tragically, they never even thought about 'em.

Remember then, my student, the simple habit of thinking before acting will not only make your own life far more fulfilling, it will also eliminate an untold amount of the world's pain and suffering...*so challenge yourself to consider consequences*. You can do this.

LIFE APP

THIS WEEK, WORK ON BECOMING A MORE SKILLFUL PREDICTOR OF OUTCOMES. MORE SPECIFICALLY, WHEN FACED WITH A TOUGH CHOICE, ACTUALLY LIST THE CONSEQUENCES OF ACTING ONE WAY OR THE OTHER.

ONCE YOU DO GET YOUR THOUGHTS ON THE MATTER DOWN IN WRITING, YOU'LL FIND YOU'RE FAR BETTER EQUIPPED TO ANSWER THE ALL-IMPORTANT QUESTIONS, *AM I PREPARED TO ACCEPT THE POSSIBLE CONSEQUENCES?* AND *IS IT REALLY WORTH IT?*

WEEK 42

Keeping Music in Your Life

There is no feeling, except the extremes of fear and grief, that does not find relief in music.

—George Eliot

The effects of good music are not just because it's new; on the contrary music strikes us more the more familiar we are with it.

—Johann Wolfgang Von Goethe

Music is the language of the spirit. It opens the secret of life bringing peace, abolishing strife.

—Kahlil Gibran

Magical. Powerful.

These are the two words I kept coming back to when attempting to best capture the essence of music. No matter how long I spent trying, no other options fit the bill quite as well.

Music *like nothing else in the world* is, after all, capable of putting our problems into perspective, changing our mood, bridging differences between people, enhancing brain functioning, pumping us up before a big event, and ushering in memories. Music manages to accomplish all this, my student, by traveling beyond our conscious mind down to the very core of our being—to the realm of spirit, if you will. Magical and powerful, indeed.

Just ask those who, while battling through tough times, have been touched by its deep-reaching energy. It is a true companion. Someone, for example, who has had healing chills run up his spine as a result of "Taps" being played at a loved one's funeral. Someone who has had the weight of the world lifted off her shoulders by simply blasting the lyrics of a favorite song. Or someone who has been moved to the point of tears by the distant sounds of a single bagpipe. Even those who get so caught up in the moment that they crowd-surf and slam are a testament to music's positive, penetrating reach.

Because so many different styles of music exist out there—each one magical and powerful in its own right—our opportunities for healing and enjoying are literally endless. There's pop, country, jazz, rock, classical, hip-hop, New Age, and oldies. And while it's true what you currently choose to embrace is part of what makes you an individual, we could all enrich our lives further by expanding our musical tastes.

If you are willing to try, it will be imperative that you remain patient and open-minded. Allow me to explain why.

Have you ever had the experience of hearing a song on the radio for the first time and not liking it, but then, after being exposed to the same tune a few more times, it actually winds up being one of your favorites? What happens in this type of situation is you gradually become more familiar with and appreciative of a particular song's lyrics, beat, tempo, etc. It "grows on you" because rather than turn the station, you give it a chance. Are you starting to see where I'm going with this?

When trying out a whole new genre of music, this is the type of process we should come to expect. More times than not, however, a final decision is based solely on the initial exposure. The second, third, and fourth listens, from which a greater appreciation of the music usually develops, never get their chance. It's certainly safe to say that many people—young and old alike—have missed out on the intricacies and gifts of a different style of music for this very reason.

I know, too, because at one point in my own life, I scoffed at anything other than rock and roll. It wasn't until a college friend—a talented jazz musician—exposed me to "her music" that my tune finally changed. In only a short period of time, I came to appreciate just how rich and artful jazz music really is. And the experience compelled me to try out other styles as well. Now I can say, in all honesty, that I enjoy just about every kind of music out there—and that each one in its own unique way has managed to enrich my life. In fact, my student, I have come to see evolving as a music lover as an essential component to evolving as a human being.

For now, though, you may be content to continue worshiping the more popular and mainstream music of your time—completely understandable considering that many before you have done the same.

Just remember, it might be in your best interest to be somewhat selective. Pop music is a huge industry, and the bands that routinely glamorize destructive behaviors in their lyrics and videos are only in it for the money. Concentrate on the music—whether it's good or bad in your own mind—and ignore all of the crazy things performers do to make a buck.

As your perspective expands, so too may your desire to try out other kinds of music. When this day comes, I'd advise you to give yourself a jump-start on the process by getting to one magical and powerful place—Broadway. Take it from me—a person who once laughed at the mere mention of musical theater—it is the ideal venue for opening yourself up to new and less mainstream forms of music. The passion and vibe conveyed from performer to audience member make for a truly life-enriching experience. Not once have I left a production without my spirits being lifted, my dreams being validated, and above all, my love and appreciation for music being broadened.

Knowing now just how positive a life force music is, it may be hard for you to imagine ever living without it. But be forewarned, my student, including it in your daily round may actually require a conscious effort someday. That's right, because things in the adult world have a way of monopolizing one's time and attention, many get weighed down and turn their backs on some of life's most precious treasures—music included.

At about the age of 25, I myself was so caught up in the daily grind that music no longer played in my life—not at home, not at work, and not in my car. Even when stuck in a traffic jam, the old, beloved music box was instead tuned in to political talk shows, news and weather updates, or a sports program. Of course, there's nothing wrong with any of these options, but my unconscious choice to exclude music was symptomatic of my losing touch with not only a cherished part of myself, but also with what is truly important in life.

Clearly, my priorities were changing as I continued to harden and lose perspective. In fact, I was guilty of ignoring one of the cardinal rules to creating a rich, fulfilling life: Take care of your spirit, too.

I'm grateful to report I finally came to recognize the error of my ways and now arrange to work music into every single one of my days. This means my car radio's primary job is to once again play tunes.

My wife and I also listen more at work, while on breaks, and at home at a variety of times. Every Saturday morning we pop in the *Rent* or *Les Mis* CD, crank the volume, and proceed to give the house a cleaning. The ritual has actually turned a job we never enjoyed into something with which we now have fun. And at night, after a long, pressure-packed day, we, like so many, have found music to be the perfect medium for unwinding. (Even at your young age, I'm sure you can relate.) It has single-handedly made our nights together more revitalizing, more upbeat, and naturally, more harmonious.

Remember then, my student, anything that is best described by the words *magical* and *powerful* needs to be prioritized accordingly…*so challenge yourself to keep music in your life*. You can do this.

LIFE APP

DURING THE COURSE OF THIS WEEK, TRY LISTENING TO A NEW AND DIFFERENT TYPE OF MUSIC. ONCE YOU DECIDE ON WHICH ONE IT'LL BE, DEVOTE A PORTION OF YOUR TIME AND ENERGY TO IT. TALK TO SOMEONE YOU KNOW WHO POSSESSES A DEEP APPRECIATION FOR IT, DELVE INTO ITS HISTORY, FIND A STATION ON THE RADIO THAT PLAYS IT, AND ABOVE ALL, GIVE IT A CHANCE TO GROW ON YOU. IF IT DOESN'T TURN OUT TO BE SOMETHING YOU CAN GET INTO, DON'T LET IT STOP YOU FROM TRYING OUT OTHER STYLES IN THE FUTURE. BUT IF IT DOES, LISTEN AS OFTEN AS YOU CAN AND CELEBRATE THE FACT THAT YOU'VE JUST ENRICHED YOUR LIFE FURTHER.

LASTLY, WORK TO MAKE MUSIC AN EVEN BIGGER PART OF YOUR LIFE. YOUR OPPORTUNITIES TO DO SO ARE MANY: ATTEND A CONCERT; PLAY AN INSTRUMENT; BLAST YOUR STEREO; SING—IN THE CAR, IN THE SHOWER, IN A CHOIR, ETC.; GET TO BROADWAY (OR ATTEND A MUSICAL AT A LOCAL THEATER); WRITE A SONG OF YOUR OWN; WHISTLE WHILE YOU WORK; PLAY MOZART WHILE YOU STUDY; USE A DISCMAN WHILE YOU EXERCISE—AND ON AND ON.

WEEK 43

Thinking and Talking More About Television

...television is not so much interested in the business of communications as in the business of delivering audiences to the advertisers. People are the merchandise, not the shows. The shows are merely the bait.

—Les Brown

Advertising may be described as the science of arresting the human intelligence long enough to get money from it.

—Stephen Butler Leacock

I maintain that there is now more good television available than there is time to watch. But, if you looked at it all, you'd be a passive spectator of life, not a participant...the trick is to be selective.

—Bill Moyers

As a young person, you're likely being excluded from all the important "TV talk" going on in adult circles. It's a funny thing, too, considering that all the fuss is about people your age watching and being exposed to too much.

Well, I'm now going to let you in on some of the data being shared and discussed. By doing so, I am providing you the opportunity to decide for yourself whether TV is something you should be thinking and talking more about.

The following info was gleaned from a variety of sites intended for—you guessed it—adult research. Check it out:

1. The average American home has a television turned on for more than seven hours per day.
2. The average young person spends an average of 30 hours a week in front of the tube, but less than 45 minutes a week conversing with a parent.
3. There exists a strong correlation between excessive TV-watching and low reading scores.

4. The primary purpose of TV is to sell products and services. And the trend is to show just about anything—no matter how graphic and inappropriate—to get you and your money to tune in.
5. TV in America is now more violent than in any other place in the world.
6. By the age of 18, the average American kid will have witnessed over 200,000 violent acts including 30,000 murders. (This equates to about 12,000 acts of violence observed every year.)
7. American kids see between 150 and 200 hours of commercials annually. This translates to having viewed about 350,000 commercial messages by the age of 18.
8. Every year, young people are exposed to over 1,000 beer and wine commercials—and this number is rising steadily.
9. Per capita intake of beer and wine in America has risen 50 percent since 1960. In Sweden, on the other hand, per capita consumption is down 20 percent since 1976 when they banned the advertising of alcohol.
10. Through television, the youth of our country are exposed to over 14,000 references to sex each year—and even this high number is rising steadily. (America has the highest teen pregnancy rate of all western countries.)
11. There exists a strong link between how much TV young people watch and how much they weigh. (The obesity rate of young people in America has increased since 1980—to the point that obesity now ranks as the most common nutritional disease among our nation's youth.)
12. Of all the developed western countries, ours is the only one not to require commercial networks to air at least one hour per day of educational programming for young people.
13. Other potential-sucking behaviors that have been linked in some way to TV viewing include: aggressiveness, pessimism, boredom, short attention span, passivity, desensitization to violence, low grades, promiscuity, eating disorders, and lack of enthusiasm for both physical activity and learning.

Whether or not your parents, or any other adults, have detailed the threats, it's clear that TV can have a very real social, emotional, psychological, and even physical impact on you.

In light of so much troubling information, one might think all parents would be setting limits on the amount and kind of television that their kids can watch. It ain't happening, though. In fact, my student, more than half of all young people now have sets in their own bedrooms.

It stands to reason that no matter how much viewing is allowed in your home, *you* may want to rethink your position on the matter. You may conclude that your time spent in front of the television really is something to take more seriously.

Much of what I've detailed thus far has admittedly focused on the negative aspects of television. This is not to imply, however, that there's nothing positive about it. In all actuality, the list of positives one can associate with TV is both lengthy and impressive. Where else can you be brought up-to-date on important news the world over, take in your favorite sporting events, gain insight into any number of topics, be inspired, be challenged, be entertained, etc.?

Truth be told, I look forward to time spent in front of the tube. Any day of the week I know I can find good television that can enrich my life. Quality stations like Discovery, Wisdom, the Learning Channel, PBS, Travel Channel, National Geographic, and Tech TV all offer programming that is both enlightening and entertaining.

Even when I'm watching, enjoying, and relaxing, however, I still make it a point to reflect on what I'm taking in. For example:

1. If I'm watching a program about an endangered species or an environmental problem, I consider whether I'm doing anything in my life that might be making the problem worse.
2. If I'm watching a comedy about a bunch of young adults with few career aspirations, I ask myself whether it's realistic they'd live in such an expensive home and wear such expensive clothes.
3. If the bad guy in a crime movie is from a particular ethnic group, I think about whether the film has stereotyped people of that ethnic group.
4. If I'm watching a drama, I consider the choices each character makes. Would I make the same choice in the same situations?

The point is that TV is not reality, and if we are to guard against the thousands of unhealthy and manipulative messages it bombards us with, we need to start thinking about it in the context of reality.

Although watching in this "active" manner can be both compelling and fun, it's not something most young people are accustomed to. Even so, as awareness of television's possible influences spreads, more and more people—of all ages—will decide to do more reflecting while viewing.

While thinking more about television is good, talking more about it is even better. Any form of discussion—with parents, teachers, or friends—can provide different perspectives and serve to further provoke thought. More specifically, those with more worldly experience and maturity can help you see that the behaviors television portrays as normal, natural, and okay, often aren't. And make no mistake, this awareness is critical for you to possess, especially when so much of what's being broadcast (e.g., on music television, trash talk shows, etc.) is serving to create the illusion that everyone thinks and acts in these same crazy ways. The truth of the matter is while some in the world do, many more don't.

The big question to ask in your discussions, then, is why networks seem so intent on hyping and glamorizing every irresponsible behavior that exists. Then again, maybe you already know the answer: Boring, old reality doesn't make for strong ratings. Who, after all, would continue tuning into programs that always focused on the realities of life, e.g., on the consequences associated with routine TV behaviors like sex and violence? Story lines highlighting jail time, AIDS, and unplanned pregnancies certainly wouldn't make for appealing, feel-good viewing, now would they?

Chats with others can also assist you in understanding how the specious world of television advertising works.

For instance, you may not know that the celebrities making all those straight-faced endorsements on TV usually do so not because they believe in or use the product, but because they want to earn yet another paycheck with lots of zeros attached to the it. Big business has always relied on the simpleminded notion that if a star says he prefers a certain brand of soda or jeans or credit card, well then, golly gee, all of his fans wanting to be more like him will blindly prefer the product, too.

A similar concept applies to all those commercials showing confident, good-looking, athletic types of people partying and having a great time drinking certain brands of alcohol.

The corporations who pay big bucks to air these advertisements are banking on your connecting their brands with the notions of having a positive self-image and a whole lot of fun. In other words, they want you to believe that by drinking their product, you too will feel and be perceived as fun, confident, attractive, and athletic. You can probably figure out the upshot of such historically successful ad campaigns: You and millions of others are left feeling a lot more willing—eager, even—to fork over your money. So really, don't believe the hype.

Remember then, my student, whether someone has pointed it out to you or not, there are very real consequences associated with excessive and mindless TV viewing—consequences that can compromise your potential as a human being...*so challenge yourself to think and talk more about television*. You can do this.

LIFE APP

FOR EACH HOUR OR SO YOU SPEND IN FRONT OF THE TUBE THIS WEEK, GENERATE AND JOT DOWN AT LEAST ONE THOUGHT FOR DISCUSSION. IT CAN INVOLVE WHATEVER IT IS THAT STRIKES YOU WHILE WATCHING–SOMETHING ABOUT A SHOW'S STORY LINE, A CHARACTER'S CHOICE, OR A COMMERCIAL'S INTENT. YOU CAN ALSO SHARE–OR COMPARE–WITH A FAMILY MEMBER ANY SELF-TALK YOUR BRAIN GENERATED WHILE VIEWING.

IN ADDITION TO WORKING ON THIS NEW HABIT, ALSO TRY REDUCING THE OVERALL TIME YOU SPEND IN FRONT OF THE SET. A WHOLE LOT OF US, AFTER ALL, NOW SIT DOWN TO WATCH OUT OF HABIT–WITHOUT EVEN THINKING OF OTHER ALTERNATIVES.

SO THE NEXT TIME YOU FIND YOURSELF GRABBING FOR THE REMOTE, CONSIDER WHAT ELSE YOU COULD CHOOSE TO DO: LISTEN TO MUSIC, GET OUTDOORS, CALL A FRIEND OR RELATIVE WITH WHOM YOU'VE LOST TOUCH, READ A BOOK OR MAGAZINE, GET AN EARLY START ON A SCHOOL ASSIGNMENT, PLAY WITH YOUR PET, ETC. YOU'LL SOON DISCOVER THAT LIFE WITH LESS TV HAS A MOST POSITIVE AND LIBERATING FEEL TO IT!

WEEK 44

Stemming the Tide of Violence

The main goal of the future is to stop violence. The world is addicted to it.
—Bill Cosby

All that is necessary for evil to triumph is for good men to do nothing.
—Edmund Burke

Violence is not strength and compassion is not weakness.
—King Arthur *(in Camelot)*

Like so many violent encounters it started off as a minor conflict, only to quickly snowball and take on a life of its own. A group of four teenagers was upset with another young man over a girl. Or maybe it had something to do with his spitting near one of their cars. Or was it a combination of both? No matter, because nothing warranted what happened next. As you may have already guessed, the four decided to put a beating on the kid. They saw violence as the answer, the only solution to their problem.

Perhaps their intent was to teach him a lesson, to show him and others that nobody was going to mess with them and get away with it. Whatever the rationale, they made their point many times over...by beating him mercilessly. One of the assailants even went so far as to smash a 40-ounce beer bottle over the victim's head as he lay curled up in the fetal position. The brutal assault left the young man bedridden and severely brain-damaged—a mere shell of the smiling, baseball-loving brother and son he once was. Can you imagine the depth of pain and despair that his family and friends were left to endure?

After spending years lying contorted in a hospital bed, and shedding tears each and every time a family member he could not even speak to left for home, Matthew—mercifully—died. As for the attackers who chose violence, all of them now wake up where they belong: behind bars and electric fences in a truly violent world. Their own loved ones having been left behind, too, to suffer and forever wonder why.

This incident occurred when I was in college. But unfortunately, my student, violence is even more prevalent today. Its impact has certainly been felt in your schools, in your neighborhoods, in our places of business, and even in some of our own homes. Its presence is also more palpable on our highways, in our theaters, on our television screens, and yes, even in some of our own hearts.

Violence is so rampant, in fact, that it has influenced many in your generation—not to mention many in mine—to give up all hope of ever living in peace. And who could blame these people? Violence seems to be a completely unavoidable aspect of life, and as such, something that's far too big for any one person to do anything about. Even you would have to agree with that—right?

Wrong. For in truth, this is the very type of defeatist attitude that serves to embolden those who act violently—and in so doing, allows violence to prosper and spread. Let me be as explicit as I've ever been: We cannot accept violence of any kind—to accept it is to encourage it. Instead we must *each* take responsibility for learning how to steer clear of its reach, and then model and promote nonviolent behaviors for the rest of society. By focusing on our own choices, our own actions, and our own example, each of us really can stem the tide. Indeed, what is most maddening about violence—the fact that it results from personal choice—is exactly what offers us the greatest hope and opportunity for change!

Think about it; other options or ways to respond obviously exist. Options that can enable us to stop small stuff from escalating, help us handle confrontations nonviolently, and keep us from becoming victims ourselves. It's just that these different, more positive choices need more attention brought to them—more individuals to point them out and bring them to life. And yes, together we can get this done. (In case you're thinking there's no way we can expect to eliminate all violence from the world, I understand. But make no mistake, if we each do our part in our own schools and communities, we can certainly impact present and future circumstances.)

Are you ready to fight the good fight—we'll do it in the name of Matthew, and the millions of others who have suffered needlessly. Excellent; then check out the following list of "options." You'll soon realize that the existence of violence really does hinge upon each individual's most basic either/or decisions, and that this insight alone will leave you not only more apt to make sound choices, but will also make you a positive role model for untold numbers of others.

You can...

1. Continue to see violence as a solution *or* recognize that it serves only to create more problems and more pain—for you and the rest of the world.
2. Spend time in violence-prone areas *or* find your own safe spots in which to hang out.
3. Seek out somebody to help you when you're feeling threatened *or* go it alone and risk further victimization.
4. Allow alcohol to take over your ability to think straight *or* recognize that countless people have lived to regret the life-altering choices they made while under the influence.
5. Take personal issues and frustrations out on another *or* search out alternative ways to release the pressure. (Every young person on the planet should have a punching bag and/or loud speakers in the basement.)
6. Get loud and intimidating *or* use a civil, respectful tone of voice.
7. See situations through your eyes only *or* make a point of considering the other person's position, too.
8. Remain stubborn or bitter about a situation even when you were in the wrong *or* summon the strength of character to admit fault and then apologize.
9. Get caught up in the hype and glamour of violence on TV and the big screen *or* understand that those making these types of shows, videos, and movies are likely to be laughing all the way to the bank.
10. Use fists, guns, knives, and bats to solve conflicts *or* make words, perspective, intelligence, and controlled emotion your weapons of choice.
11. Keep believing that acting tough and getting physical will earn you respect *or* realize that this type of ill-earned esteem will mean little the day you wake up behind bars and electric fences.
12. Perceive the choice to walk away from a fight as being chicken *or* view it as not only a mark of being smart, strong, and secure in

yourself, but also as a way to safeguard your future life.

13. Lose control and pay the consequences *or* maintain awareness of your emotions and keep them in check. (The vast majority of people don't realize just how often even the common fistfight has led to tragic circumstances. A single punch can cause a bone in the nose to penetrate the brain, or in the process of knocking someone off his feet, lead to the person falling down and cracking his skull. It happens.)
14. Use your voice to cheer and encourage violence in sports (e.g., "professional" wrestling and hockey) *or* use it to speak out against the very real influence it has on society.
15. Fail to communicate at all, leaving it up to others to mind-read *or* convey to them what it is that's upsetting you.
16. Hurl insults and threats at the beginning stages of a conflict *or* stick to the issue at hand and talk it through.
17. Automatically go into "ignore mode" dismissing everything the other person has to say *or* keep an open mind and hear him or her out.
18. Seek revenge and retaliate for being wronged *or* chalk it up to experience and get on with the business of living your life to the fullest.

In light of recent events, I'm also adding this critical option:

You can brush off ominous threats made by others *or* you can play it safe by immediately notifying an adult of anything that remotely resembles one. Does the town of Butler, Pennsylvania, ring any bells with you? I didn't think so. You see, just prior to the Columbine High incident in Littleton, Colorado, an anonymous tip enabled Butler authorities to avoid a similar tragedy. (A rifle was found hidden in some bushes outside one of the schools.) Because someone took personal responsibility and made the sound choice to report what he had heard—a choice that by all accounts saved lives—the small town of Butler was able to elude the far reach that we've all come to associate with violence.

Remember then, my student, creating hope and the opportunity for change starts with each of us—our own choices, our own actions, our own example...*so challenge yourself to stem the tide of violence.* You can do this.

LIFE APP

GETTING THE MESSAGE ACROSS TO KIDS EARLY ON IN LIFE IS OBVIOUSLY A BIG KEY TO STEMMING THE TIDE.

WITH THIS GOAL IN MIND, FIND OUT IF THERE'S A VIOLENCE PREVENTION PROGRAM IN YOUR SCHOOL SYSTEM, AND IF THERE IS, VOLUNTEER TO HELP OUT IN THE ELEMENTARY GRADES. (IF THERE ISN'T, CONSIDER STARTING UP ONE OF YOUR OWN.) IF YOU DECIDE TO FOLLOW THROUGH ON THE IDEA, KNOW THAT YOU'LL BE PUTTING YOURSELF ON THE FRONT LINES—A PLACE WHERE MANY OPPORTUNITIES TO MAKE A DIFFERENCE EXIST.

SPECIFICALLY, YOU CAN BRING AWARENESS TO THE EITHER/OR OPTIONS THAT THE YOUNGER CHILDREN WILL SOON BE FACING; YOU CAN SHED LIGHT ON POSITIVE, PROACTIVE WAYS TO RELEASE LIFE'S PRESSURES (SEE WEEK 38); AND YOU CAN SHARE KNOWLEDGE PERTAINING TO CONTROLLING ONE'S ANGER (SEE WEEK 12).

SKITS, OR MINI-DRAMAS, ARE AN EXCELLENT VEHICLE FOR IMPARTING SUCH LESSONS. FOR EXAMPLE, TRY CREATING ONES IN WHICH VIOLENT RESPONSES AND THEIR NONVIOLENT ALTERNATIVES TAKE TURNS TAKING CENTER STAGE.

IN THE PROCESS, YOU MAY ALSO WANT TO HIGHLIGHT THE DIFFERENCES BETWEEN THOSE INDIVIDUALS WHO CAN WALK AWAY FROM A FIGHT AND THOSE WHO CANNOT. MAKE IT CRYSTAL CLEAR TO THE KIDS THAT A NONVIOLENT RESPONSE REQUIRES NOTHING LESS THAN INTELLIGENCE, CONVICTION, AND STRENGTH OF CHARACTER...WHILE A VIOLENT ONE IS CLEAR EVIDENCE OF AN INDIVIDUAL'S LACK OF COURAGE, LACK OF PERSPECTIVE, AND LACK OF SELF-RESPECT.

WEEK 45

Thinking with Purpose

Do not think that what your thoughts dwell upon is of no matter. Your thoughts are making you.
—Bishop Steere

Sooner or later, those who win are those who think they can.
—David Bach

...What the mind dwells upon, the body acts upon.
—Denis Waitley

Thoughts have power; thoughts are energy. And you can make your world or break it by your own thinking.
—Susan Taylor

Tiger Woods stands at the first tee of the Masters. He is fully expecting to, again, win this prestigious tournament. He is ready to put into action his game plan—rehearsed many times over in his mind—to master this hole, and the next one, and all that remain. He truly believes he's going to finish with the lowest score, hear the crowd cheer for him, and don the green jacket on Sunday. Tiger Woods has a true winner's mentality. In fact, my student, Tiger and many other athletes know full well, *you are what you think.*

This may be common knowledge in the professional sports world but not so in the real world. Most people are completely unaware of just how deep an impact habits of thought have on their lives. Did you realize that your own thoughts are at the root of all you do, experience, and will become? I'm not exaggerating. A direct link has indeed been established between a person's thinking and the most crucial aspects of his or her life. Are one's level of self-confidence, quality of choices, quality of relationships, degree of inner peace and happiness, future earning power, work ethic, and overall attitude enough to get your attention?

Your first order of business, then, should be to become more in tune with how and what you tend to think. (Obviously, I'm not talking about examining every thought of the thousands you have in a day.) Pay particular attention to what runs through your mind when setting goals or contemplating your future, when faced with a challenge, and when experiencing feelings of inadequacy.

As you start becoming more and more in tune, it's important that you understand the only limits facing you in these areas are the ones your own mind has worked to create. Thoughts like, *That's too big a dream for me, I'm not smart enough, Why would they want to hang out with me?* and *What's the point of even trying?* only become beliefs if they are "practiced"—many times over. And because of the rather fascinating way in which our brains work, such internal messages, although flawed and misguided, still manage to ring true and do damage.

It's easy to understand why, when you consider that whatever we consciously—and repeatedly—think to be true becomes reality on a subconscious level. Or to put it more simply, our minds don't know the difference between what is factual and what we believe to be factual! Fascinating, indeed.

The great news is that this can all be worked to your personal advantage (à la Tiger). The trick to doing so is first to align your thoughts with exactly how you want circumstances in your life to be—and then to "practice" thinking such thoughts. Allow me to elaborate.

The subconscious mind has no choice but to act on positive ideals—empowering thoughts like *The combination of my brainpower and work ethic will enable me to succeed at anything I put my mind to; I am more than capable of proving myself worthy of their friendship;* and *I have what it takes to make it big in life*—even if you have no concrete basis for believing them to be true!

Are you beginning to grasp the possibilities here? Why not go all out, then? More specifically, start making it a point to think of yourself as a strong, self-assured person who can come through in even the most trying of situations. See yourself pridefully bouncing back from any failures or misfortune. Imagine others now looking to you for guidance and leadership. Visualize yourself ignoring and laughing off the next insult thrown your way. Expect to evolve into a competent, self-reliant individual. And believe that you *will* make your life extraordinary.

As you should be beginning to piece together, my student, becoming a true winner is largely dependent on one's chosen state of mind. Those who have worked to create positive thought energy, or "a winner's mentality," consistently envision things in their lives working out for the best. Again, consider as an example their mind-set leading up to an important life event like a big game or big performance. Unlike most others, they make a point of conceptualizing the exact scenarios they want to have play out.

This habit of thought involves first taking the time to create a state of relaxation, and then focusing on the details of their upcoming performance: their bodies maneuvering with skill and precision; their minds remaining mentally tough amidst even the most tense moments; their confidence levels soaring to new heights; the crowd creating loud, well-deserved applause; and their own sense of exhilaration upon achieving the desired outcome. Such positive thoughts and images are self-empowering in the truest sense.

If you develop into someone with a similarly proactive mind and can-do attitude, you can expect much good to come from it. For when an aura of confidence and self-belief comes to surround you, it attracts into your circle people and events that are equally positive and favorable. Put another way, good fortune and good people actually find their way into your life!

And while some in the world would have you believe this phenomenon—officially referred to as the "law of attraction"—is more a matter of luck or coincidence, you can rest assured in the knowledge that it's no accident. In fact, *you* can become another example—more living proof—of how thinking with purpose can draw great things into one's life.

Start making a habit of expecting to achieve your goals. Believe you'll come through in the clutch. Think you can overcome obstacles. Know you can beat the odds. And most importantly, deem yourself worthy of love, happiness, friendship, and extraordinary success.

Finally, let's consider the experiences of individuals who not only lack such a mentality but have unknowingly developed the exact opposite habits. I'm talking about the many who, by failing to think with purpose, have "thought to fail."

They're the ones prone to thinking powerlessly about themselves and their future prospects for success. Moreover, they've never worked at becoming more aware of these weak, negative thoughts so as to try to change them. As a result, they've unwittingly brought into being an aura of pessimism and self-doubt that accompanies them wherever they go.

With such thought energy in tow, it's certainly not difficult to guess what kind of people and circumstances they attract, either. I know several individuals who fit this description (to a tee). And let me tell you, it never ceases to amaze me just how often negative events occur in their lives—it's as if an ominous black cloud of bad luck floats over each of them. But again, it's not a result of happenstance.

Let's not make any mistake about it—if you convince yourself you're destined for failure, you will be. If you think others won't like or respect you, they won't. If you believe your day will be long and hard, it will be. And if you deem yourself unworthy, thinking that your life won't amount to much of anything, it won't.

Remember then, my student, your thoughts are at the root of all you do, experience, and will become...*so challenge yourself to think with purpose.* You can do this.

LIFE APP

BECAUSE THOUGHTS OF THE POSITIVE VARIETY, TOO, DO NOT BECOME DEEPLY HELD BELIEFS UNLESS REPEATED MANY TIMES OVER, YOU SHOULD GET STARTED ASAP.

THAT SAID, WHY NOT ALLOT A SPECIFIC PERIOD OF TIME THIS WEEK–A MERE 10 TO 15 MINUTES PER DAY–FOR THE PURPOSE OF "PRACTICING" THINKING WITH PURPOSE. SIMPLY FIND A NICE, QUIET SPOT IN WHICH TO RELAX AND FOCUS–AND AGAIN, REMEMBER IT'S A TIME TO ALLOW ONLY STRONG, POSITIVE THOUGHT ENERGY TO TAKE ROOT.

YOU CAN BEGIN BY MENTALLY LISTING ALL YOUR PERSONAL STRENGTHS, BY RECALLING ALL THOSE WHO LOVE AND RESPECT YOU, AND BY THINKING ABOUT ALL THE GOOD DEEDS THAT YOU'VE CARRIED OUT IN THE PAST. THEN MOVE ON TO ENVISIONING YOURSELF ATTAINING A GOAL, SEEING YOURSELF ACTING IN CONFIDENT AND ASSERTIVE WAYS, EXPECTING A PROBLEM IN YOUR LIFE TO WORK OUT, OR IMAGINING–AS IF IT WERE REAL–YOUR BIGGEST DREAM COMING TRUE.

BEFORE LONG, YOU'LL DISCOVER THAT WITH POSITIVE THOUGHT HABITS IN PLACE, THERE REALLY ARE NO LIMITS TO WHAT YOU CAN THINK UP...NO LIMITS TO WHAT YOU CAN COME TO BELIEVE...AND ULTIMATELY, NO LIMITS TO WHAT YOU CAN DO!

WEEK 46

Searching Out Heroes

If I have seen farther than other men it is by standing on the shoulders of giants.
—Isaac Newton

Goal achievement is hero's work.
—Earnie Larson

The legacy of heroes is the memory of a great name and the inheritance of a great example.
—Benjamin Disraeli

The general feeling among adults is that your generation doesn't have enough extraordinary people to look up to...not enough individuals meeting "hero standards." But you know what, I don't buy it. Extraordinary people have and always will exist; I believe it's more a matter of young people themselves not realizing just how invaluable it is to search out and have heroes. That said, my student, allow me to now increase your awareness, and in the process, to point out where to start such a search.

When you hear the term "hero," who or what comes to mind? For me, it's anyone—famous or not famous—whose example inspires others to live with increased passion and purpose. (My own heroes include Bill Cosby, Christopher Reeve, Jimmy Valvano, my Little League baseball coach, and my eighth-grade teacher.) Invariably, it is an individual who lives life to the fullest, aspires to personal excellence, wants to lead and have a positive impact on the world, always stays true to his or her personal values, and is intent on being an all-around good person (a.k.a. *a winner by any standard*).

It's simply not possible for me to overstate the value of finding such a person. A hero, after all, is not just someone to model yourself after, but also living, breathing proof that it's entirely possible to create a fulfilling life—that one's grandest of dreams can come true.

So where to look? Heroes are actually easy to find. Even in the high-profile world of sports, for example—a place where stories of greed, disloyalty, and irresponsible behavior among athletes emerge daily—there still exists those of indisputable hero status.

Consider as a case in point, the one and only Lance Armstrong.

Here was a man who had long dedicated himself to becoming the greatest cyclist in the world. But in 1996, just as he was beginning to realize his lofty dream, he was diagnosed with cancer—and given only a 50 percent chance for survival. Imagine Lance's subsequent state of mind; one of the strongest and most well-conditioned athletes in the world being told chances were good he'd die!

Lance, however, was accustomed to facing uphill challenges, and with the love and support of his own hero—his mom—he summoned the deep levels of courage, will, and optimism required to beat the cancer odds.

But he was not finished accomplishing great things. Lance still wanted to win the Tour de France (the world's most grueling of all bike races)—an unlikely dream indeed for a man recovering from the effects of cancer treatment. Again, though, he demonstrated extraordinary levels of commitment and self-belief, and to the astonishment of all went on to win five consecutive (and counting) Tours de France—a first for an American! His example proves above all else that human resolve makes *anything* possible.

If you and I were to take the time to analyze others within the sports world, we'd find the list of heroes goes on and on.

Cases in point:

1. Venus and Serena Williams who, while ascending to world-class levels, overcame gang violence, run-down tennis facilities, physical injury after injury, and a general lack of respect from those in the sometimes intolerant tennis world.
2. Tiger Woods who, off the course, has helped launch a noble organization for young people called Start Something, and on the course, continues to breathe life into the virtues of competitive fire, mental toughness, personal honor, and humility.
3. Derek Jeter, Nomar, A-Rod, MJ, Mia Hamm, Shaq, and Lisa Leslie—among many others—who have all sacrificed money, and more

importantly, time, for the purpose of making a difference in their local communities.

Heroes can also be found in our own country's rich history. That's right, the choices and actions of those from past generations often teach lessons and provide inspiration that manages to endure for all time. For you, it might be...

1. A courageous slave who took enormous personal risks and made great sacrifices for the sake of future generations.
2. A virtuous political figure who approached each issue or crisis with superior levels of wisdom and foresight.
3. A tormented war general who proved to be both a strategical mastermind and a loyal patriot.
4. A cutting-edge inventor who overcame failure time after time only to change the way the world itself would forever operate.
5. Or anyone, who upon learning of how they chose to live and of what they accomplished makes you stop and say, "Yes, *that's* the type of person I want to be...*that's* the type of impact I want to make."

Truth be told, my student, extraordinary people who do extraordinary things exist in all walks of life.

There are...

1. Medical research heroes working to cure the now incurable.
2. Educational heroes committed to finding new and more innovative ways to teach.
3. Environmental heroes intent on preserving our planet's precious resources.
4. And public servant heroes dedicated to fighting crime and fires so as to make their small corner of the world a safer, better place.

You may also know a politician, a coach, a local businessman, a nurse, etc. who fits the mold. Heroes still exist. All you have to do is look.

Remember then, my student, they are out there—and their example is invaluable…*so challenge yourself to search out and have heroes*. You can do this.

LIFE APP

AS YOU BEGIN TO ANALYZE THE LIVES OF OTHERS, USE THESE QUESTIONS TO NARROW YOUR PERSONAL SEARCH FOR A HERO:

1. DOES SHE HAVE GOALS AND DREAMS? HAS SHE MADE SACRIFICES IN ORDER TO ATTAIN THEM?
2. IS HE A LEADER IN HIS FIELD?
3. DOES BEING AN ALL-AROUND GOOD PERSON SEEM TO BE A PERSONAL PRIORITY?
4. DOES SHE POSSESS A STRONG WORK ETHIC?
5. HOW DOES HE HANDLE HIMSELF WHEN FACED WITH ADVERSITY?
6. DOES SHE ACT FROM A POSITION OF STRENGTH, BUT STILL MANAGE TO TREAT OTHERS WITH RESPECT, COMPASSION, AND KINDNESS?
7. IS HE COMMITTED TO MAKING A POSITIVE DIFFERENCE IN THE WORLD?

WEEK 47

Building Up Your Own Levels of Self-Esteem

Until you value yourself you will not value your time. Until you value your time, you will not do anything with it.
—M. Scott Peck

Low self-esteem is like driving through life with your hand-brake on.
—Maxwell Maltz

Outstanding leaders go out of their way to boost the self esteem of their personnel. If people believe in themselves, it's amazing what they can accomplish.
—Sam Walton

Take a look in a mirror—it doesn't have to be a real mirror, a mental one will work—and ask yourself these questions: *What are my values? What are my dreams? What do I like about myself? What don't I like about myself? What do I do well? What don't I do well?*

Knowing the answers to these questions, my student, is the first step in building your levels of self-esteem.

What exactly is self-esteem? Well, in case you haven't heard for a while, it's how you see and feel about yourself—deep down. More specifically, it's believing at your core that no matter what anyone else may say or think, you *are* a unique and valuable individual. It's accepting yourself for who you are—your every strength as well as your every weakness. And it's knowing in your heart of hearts that you are worthy of all the best in life—friendship, love, good fortune, and fulfillment.

Here's more:

1. Without self-esteem it is simply not possible to create a happy, successful life—no way, no how.
2. Self-esteem serves as a protective shield that no negative comment, situation, or look can penetrate.

3. Self-esteem makes for the fertile ground from which your true personality grows strong, shines brightly, and eventually flies free.
4. Self-esteem, or a lack thereof, can come from within—by way of your own thoughts and actions.
5. Just about every person out there—young and old—could benefit from a boost to their self-esteem levels.
6. Every little extra bit of self-esteem makes a difference in adding to the quality of your life.

Powerful stuff, indeed.

To more clearly understand its power, consider how those individuals who possess low self-esteem compare to those with high levels.

Among other things, "lows" tend to be pessimistic and lazy, avoid risk, give in to peer pressure in order to gain acceptance, get down on themselves, let their physical appearance slide, allow criticism and disapproval to eat away at them, put others down, and easily give up on their dreams (if they had any in the first place).

"Highs," on the other hand, think and act much differently. They tend to be positive and enthusiastic, are open to trying new experiences, stay true to themselves by making their own choices, bounce back from failures and mistakes, eat well and exercise, don't permit others to bring them down, bring others up, and have very real goals and dreams.

Quite a difference in terms of quality of life, eh? Well, the fantastic news is that you as an individual are capable of increasing your levels of self-esteem *on your own.*

You need to start by getting in the habit of self-reflection, taking the time to look in the mental mirror and knowing yourself. You can even write down your answers.

This process of self-reflection will help you whenever the negative voice in your head pops up and persists in pointing out personal faults. After all, you've already acknowledged these weaknesses, and when possible, are working to improve upon them. What's more, you'll now be better prepared to counter this inner critic—and thus build, or at least protect, your self-esteem levels—by reminding him of the many strengths you also happen to possess.

Once the habit of self-reflection is established, there are a variety of other things you can do to continue building up and protecting your self-esteem levels. (Consider the following list among the most valuable you've encountered.)

1. Regularly remind yourself of your strengths, and work to improve upon those weaknesses capable of being changed (see Week 1).
2. Tune in to the type of thoughts that you tend to have—*awareness* is the first step in the process of changing your thinking from more negative to more positive (see Week 45).
3. Act as if you already possess high levels. Put another way, do what the "highs" do. At first this will require conscious effort and courage, but in time, will enable you, too, to become a "high."
4. Stop expecting perfection from yourself—it puts you squarely in a no-win situation.
5. Choose and act in accordance with what you truly value (see Week 8).
6. Be your own person—the rare type who is true to herself and stands up for what she believes.
7. Hang out with people who appreciate and respect you, not those who manipulate and degrade you (see Week 21).
8. Recall any kind, positive things said about you, and finally allow yourself to forget all the mean, nasty stuff.
9. Get involved in extracurriculars—sports or otherwise—that provide a fun, positive outlet and challenge you to grow (see Weeks 29 and 35).
10. Regularly remind yourself of all the good that you've done in your small corner of the world.
11. Do even more good in the world (see Week 7).
12. Remind yourself of the trying times that you've already managed to overcome.
13. Have goals and dreams and do what it takes—persistently—to attain them (see Weeks 27, 28, and 31).
14. Rather than be immobilized by criticism, view it as valuable feedback from which you can learn and grow.
15. Give yourself a pat on the back for any job well done—and avoid the habit of beating yourself up whenever you fail.
16. Make your own choices (see Week 2).

17. Be more assertive (see Week 23).
18. Take responsibility for your actions—both the good and the bad (see Week 4).
19. Resist the body-image takeover (see Week 40).
20. Learn something from each mistake you make (see Week 9).
21. Take more positive risks (see Week 31).
22. Stay active and healthy (see Week 32 and 35).
23. Make good use of your sense of humor (see Week 26).
24. Don't *allow* others to bring you down (see Week 15).
25. Bring others *up* (see Week 7).
26. Regularly remind yourself that you, too, are as worthy as anyone, of all the best in life: friendship, love, good fortune, and fulfillment.

Make no mistake about it, the payoffs associated with learning to build up and protect your self-esteem are unparalleled. (Remember the "highs" and "lows" differences in quality of life?)

Indeed, doing so will ultimately lead you to think positive, self-empowering thoughts: *I can do it; I deserve to be treated better; Hey, we all screw up; This is my choice to make; I'll just have to work on that; He must have a personal problem to be treating me in such a manner; I'll act my way through it; I know what kind of heart I have; I deserve it.*

This will in turn lead you to make positive, self-empowering choices: *standing up for yourself; taking risks; sticking with it; walking away from false friends; doing good in the world; trying again; holding on to dreams; speaking your mind; resisting pressure.*

Which will lead you to develop positive, self-empowering habits: *perseverance, self-reliance, optimism, humility, self-respect, creativity, pride, responsibility, open-mindedness, virtue, resiliency, empathy, wisdom.*

Which will lead to happiness and true success becoming a reality in your life!

So, it's quite clear that you have an important choice to make—each and every day. Will you be the type of person who thinks and acts in ways that short-circuit the growth of your own self-esteem, or will you do what it takes to build up and protect your personal levels?

To be even more specific:

1. When having a bad hair day, will you beat yourself up and let feelings of ugliness and inadequacy ruin your day *or* shrug your shoulders and say, "Hey, it happens to the best of 'em; today, I'll just have to shine extra brightly from within."
2. When being pressured to drink/smoke/do drugs, will you relinquish your power and right to choose out of the need for acceptance *or* stay true to yourself and your values—and work to find other friends?
3. When presented with the opportunity to try something new, will you pass, fearing disapproval and humiliation *or* think, *What's the worst thing that could happen*? and just do your best.
4. When criticized or rejected, will you allow it to hurt, thinking there must be something wrong with you *or* let it bounce off, realizing that those who need to criticize and reject are the ones with the problems?
5. When contradicted, will you shift your position in order to agree and be accepted *or* stand your ground even if it causes tension and ill feelings?
6. When complimented, will you feel undeserving and "explain it away" *or* simply say "thank you" and give yourself a pat on the back?
7. When you fall on your face and fail, will you use it as reinforcement to not take future risks *or* get right up, dust yourself off, and move forward with a sense of pride in yourself for trying?
8. When experiencing success and good fortune, will you consider it a fluke—something that won't, and shouldn't last *or* think to yourself, *My hard work is paying off—I'm worthy of all the good that comes my way.*

No matter the number of real life applications, the choice is yours and yours alone to make each time.

Remember then, my student, every little extra bit of self-esteem makes a difference—and without it, you'll never know true happiness and success...*so challenge yourself to build up your own levels*. You can do this.

LIFE APP

ONE OF THE MOST EFFECTIVE (AND REWARDING) WAYS TO BUILD UP YOUR OWN SELF-ESTEEM IS TO BUILD UP THE LEVELS OF OTHERS. BY WORKING TO TOUCH PEOPLE IN POSITIVE WAYS, EVERYONE INVOLVED REAPS BENEFITS—AND THE WORLD ITSELF BECOMES A BETTER PLACE.

STARTING THIS WEEK, MAKE MORE OF A POINT TO ENCOURAGE OTHERS TO FOLLOW THEIR DREAMS; TO GIVE OUT MORE COMPLIMENTS; TO PRAISE ALL JOBS WELL DONE; TO REMIND SOMEONE WHO IS DOWN ON HIMSELF OF HIS UNIQUE STRENGTHS; TO TELL HIM YOU, TOO, HAVE BEEN THERE AND CAN RELATE TO HOW HE'S FEELING; TO TRULY LISTEN AND CARE; TO POINT OUT ALL THE GOOD THAT SHE'S DONE; AND MOST IMPORTANTLY, TO LET OTHERS IN ON THE FACT THEY CAN BUILD UP THEIR *OWN* SELF-ESTEEM LEVELS.

AGAIN, EVERYONE INVOLVED WILL BENEFIT!

WEEK 48

Embracing Differences

Civilizations should be measured by the degree of diversity attained and the degree of unity retained.
—W. H. Auden

Learn never to conceive a prejudice against others, because you know nothing of them. It is bad reasoning, and makes enemies of half the world.
—William Hazlitt

The test of courage comes when we are in the minority; the test of tolerance comes when we are in the majority.
—Ralph W. Sockman

I recently attended a parade, along with thousands of others, to celebrate the University of Connecticut's national championship basketball season. I'm not sure how many of the other fans noticed it that day, but in every direction, people of all backgrounds were celebrating as one—talking, laughing, high-fiving, hugging, etc. It filled my heart with intense feelings of pride and joy. And it also aroused in me the recognition that we *can* all get along, that we *don't* have to let our differences get in the way and keep us from connecting. In fact, my student, that rare experience actually served as the inspiration for this advisement.

No one can dispute the fact that hatred, ignorance, and bigotry are learned behaviors. If you've ever witnessed the natural manner in which toddlers (not to mention, certain parade participants) of different races or religions interact, you know this firsthand.

Over time, though, these same innocent minds are often influenced by the worst in others. The process usually begins in the home and is then carried on in the neighborhood, at school, and on television. For many, stereotyping evolves into an ingrained way of reacting to our complex world. And since it allows people to keep things simple and categorized, it's not the type of behavior that is likely to ever be worked on.

Such circumstances have helped to create a society where those who stand out—due to race, religion, ethnicity, social class (even size, shape, or clothes)—are routinely grouped and judged in a negative light. Again, such differences automatically spark feelings of disrespect and incivility because, at some point, it was learned.

This means you as an open- and right-minded individual may want to relearn, or refocus, if you will, the lenses through which you see others. In order to do so with maximum clarity, you must consider some frequently overlooked insights.

First, it needs to be stated that some who are different do in fact deserve to be disrespected and even feared. By all means, if any *individual* is mean-spirited, crude, or criminal-minded, see him for what he is and stay away. The utter ignorance comes in judging entire groups on outer qualities alone—thinking, for example, that all Muslims are anti-American, all people of color are criminal-minded, or all wealthy folk are elitists. (Some people actually think in such blanket terms.) The bottom line fact: good and bad people exist in every religion...every race...and every social class.

Next, with regard to outer appearances, did you ever learn why humans exist in varying shades of color? Interestingly, it's a simple matter of where in the world one's descendants lived. That's right, a factor as arbitrary as this is responsible for creating one of the most ignorance-inducing differences: skin color. Those who lived in climates of intense sunlight experienced a physiological adaptation in which their bodies produced more of the chemical, melanin—the more sun, the more melanin (a.k.a. nature's sunscreen); the more melanin, the darker the skin pigment.

So yes, we do in fact come in varying shades of color, and share different customs, accents, and family histories as well. But the basis for our physical uniqueness comes down to this one uncomplicated factor. Besides, on the inside where it counts—in terms of blood, guts, and emotions—we are all very much the same. Surely then, we need to do a better job of focusing on our common bonds, not to mention our common future, rather than on our far less significant differences.

When the cynical among us hear this type of plea, they instinctively go into questioning mode: "Why, what's the point? There have always been disharmony and prejudices of this nature, so what makes you think things need to change now?" And indeed, people used to be able to go through life in ignorance of others who were not like them. But now, my student, we live in a diverse, global world where every day we see and must interact with those who are different from us.

Did you know, for example, that the American workforce of today is a giant melting pot of diverse peoples whose ancestors or parents came from Europe, Africa, Asia, the Caribbean, South America—you name it? The percentages are historically unprecedented. And what it means to you, personally, is that your chances of achieving future success may well hinge upon your ability to coexist within such a work populace. But more than any individual motivation, it remains downright unjust and immoral to reject or alienate another human being for merely being different. (And believe me when I tell you, ignorance of this nature has caused an immeasurable amount of suffering and torment to fellow humans throughout history.)

To be clear, I'm not claiming that the notions of tolerance and acceptance will suddenly be adopted by the masses. No, but what I do believe is if more people were reminded of the fact that we are all immigrants (with the exception of Native Americans) and all human, it would help in providing a window of opportunity. Then, if we could get your generation—more than any generation before—to see the awesome promise associated with the embracing of diversity...well then, unprecedented strides could well be made.

To this end, I have compiled a compelling list of the potential positives. Reflect on each one.

1. Without question, embracing diversity can make the world a better place to live. For each of us, this translates to a more harmonious home life, school life, and community life. Case in point: the UCONN parade.
2. In a world filled with individuals committed to tolerance, the hurtful practice of stereotyping will finally be reduced to a rare, rather than routine, act.
3. In a society full of individuals committed to acceptance, none of us will ever again have to experience the awful feeling associated with being an outsider.
4. When we see past outer appearances, we make it possible to discover the person within; some have even discovered the soul's color to be that of a rainbow.

5. Many people hang with those similar to themselves because there's a built-in comfort level. But based on personal experiences, anyone who is open to diverse friendships, and is willing to put in the time and effort required to develop a comfort level of their own, will be rewarded by a host of rich and enlightening moments—ones that countless others have missed out on.
6. If you're open to sharing with and listening to those whose backgrounds are different from your own, you will learn things that you otherwise would not have. This ensures that you will continue to grow and evolve as a true individual.
7. Young people being educated in a diverse environment now enjoy a number of special advantages. First and foremost, they will be in a better position to prosper in a society that is itself becoming more and more diverse. Indeed, interacting across racial, religious, socioeconomic, and cultural borders will have become second nature for many of them. And such experiences, along with the interpersonal skills and attitudes they cultivate, happen to be exactly what most employers want. (Many corporations now actively seek out these individuals because an adaptable workforce is a must to gaining an edge in a global marketplace.)
8. Coming together—truly coming together as individuals—can enable any group to achieve a common goal, even when it's against all odds. How many times has an underdog sports team, consisting of players from diverse backgrounds, proven this very point while displaying rare levels of respect and camaraderie? (You may be starting to see the promise this holds for the game of life, too.)
9. Would it not be another giant leap for mankind if those who are different automatically triggered the responses "I respect you," "I appreciate your uniqueness," and "I can learn from you"—rather than sentiments such as "I am superior to you" and "You are not worthy of my respect"?

Let it be known that people who respond to differences in positive ways represent nothing less than the future—and lead by example we will.

Remember then, my student, we're all in this thing called life together, as one race—the human race—*so challenge yourself to embrace differences.* You can do this.

LIFE APP

CHANCES ARE YOU'VE BEEN PRESENT AS A RACIAL, RELIGIOUS, OR ETHNIC JOKE HAS BEEN TOLD. JUST ABOUT EVERYONE HAS, AS JOKE-TELLING WITH THE INTENT TO DEMEAN IS AS WIDESPREAD NOW AS IT'S EVER BEEN. WELL, THE NEXT TIME SOMEONE DECIDES TO CONTAMINATE YOUR AIR WITH SUCH A JOKE, TAKE A PERSONAL STAND. YOU CAN WALK AWAY, STARE BLANKLY, OR EXPLAIN TO HIM THAT HE'S BEING INCREDIBLY IGNORANT. HOWEVER YOU DECIDE TO RESPOND, REALIZE THAT SUCH SMALL ACTS OF COURAGE *CAN* COLLECTIVELY CHANGE WHAT'S WRONG AND UNJUST IN THE WORLD.

WEEK 49

Following Your Dreams

Don't be afraid of the space between your dreams and reality. If you can dream it, you can make it so.

—Belva Davis

You are never given a dream without also being given the power to make it true. You may have to work for it, however.

—Richard Bach

The future belongs to those who believe in their dreams.

—Eleanor Roosevelt

Every mountain climbed, every CD recorded, every trophy won, every law passed, every major accomplishment you can think of, started out as a mere glimmer in someone's imagination. Indeed, my student, behind every truly great success is an individual who first had, and then chose to follow, a dream.

Some of my favorite examples of dreams coming to life include: Michael Jordan crying as he cradled his first NBA championship trophy; Rosie (O'Donnell) overwhelmed with similarly deep emotions as she welcomed her hero, Barbara Streisand, onto her own show; Tara Lipinski and then Sarah Hughes—as teenagers—exulting in the glory of their pressure-packed Olympic gold-medal performances. And Billy Gilman—as a 12-year-old—belting out Christmas songs on his own TV special. Each one created something truly great in their lives by choosing to follow a dream. And each one, as captured live on camera, declared to the world, "It's a dream come true!"

So yes, dreams do come true, but they don't come true easily. There will always be some people who do their best to convince you that having dreams, especially big ones, is naive and foolhardy. Such individuals are notorious for pointing out reason after reason as to why dreams—particularly yours—won't come to be. And often, their doggedness prompts your own inner critic to chime in with thoughts like, *Get real, having a dream come true is something that only happens to other people* and *They're right, this is just too big.* I often tell my students in class, though, that if a particular dream seems like it'll be a long, hard road—one littered with dream doubters and potential setbacks—then they've got a worthwhile dream on their hands.

The journey of anyone who has achieved a dream of their own, including any of the five stars just mentioned, would serve as an ideal case in point. Such individuals understood that if extraordinary efforts weren't required of them, then the end result wouldn't have been nearly so rare and meaningful an achievement.

To be clear, the term "extraordinary efforts" breaks down into several qualities—all of which you need to be aware:

> For one, the dreamer has to be willing to commit enormous amounts of time and energy to practice and preparation. *Week after week, year after year, they will be found intently working to perfect their abilities.*
>
> Naturally, this requires that the dreamer also be willing to sacrifice. *Normal relationships and normal routines won't always be possible—it's just that simple.*
>
> Those who pursue greatness also understand that trying times, which will occasionally leave them feeling demoralized and even defeated, are to be expected. *Because of this unique insight, they are never duped into giving up but instead know to apply perseverance, hope, and self-belief in the face of such adversity.*
>
> Just as uniquely, dreamers recognize the importance of talking about and visualizing their ultimate aim. *Both practices provide a true advantage as both help to make what they've always desired more tangible—more real.*
>
> And lastly, whenever possible, effective dreamers study the lives of those who have already achieved something big. *Any lesson learned, any secret to success uncovered, any perspective gained can, after all, make the ultimate difference in one's own dream quest.*

Because of the many requirements associated with following a dream, there will certainly be many benefits to enjoy. (And the neat thing is that the benefits are reaped no matter how your dreams ultimately turn out.)

1. By following a dream, you discover not only what you're made of, but also what you're capable of. Countless people have surprised even themselves by accomplishing dreams considered to be overly ambitious and idealistic (even naive and foolhardy).
2. When working toward something you hold near and dear, day-to-day life becomes more precious and enjoyable.
3. Dreams tie all of humanity together. This means that by having one you become connected to every other individual—past, present, and future—who has ever dared to.
4. Carrying a dream within keeps you grounded and focused—even when things around you seem to be falling apart.
5. By following a dream, you will become known as a person of ideals and action.
6. Dreams guide and keep you in touch with your priorities, your values...and your true self.
7. Following a dream makes certain that you'll continue growing and evolving as a human being.
8. Following a dream fosters a strong work ethic and unshakable resolve—both of which will serve you for life.
9. The leaders of every generation—including the next millennium's—are those who dare to dream big. By having your own, you put yourself squarely in position to inspire and lead others.
10. The feelings experienced once you realize that your dream is no longer a far-off possibility, but rather a real probability, will rumble through you like nothing else.
11. Having dreams keeps the fire inside burning with rare intensity.
12. Those who dare to dream will live a life with no regrets.

Remember then, my student, someday it can well be you accomplishing amazing things and declaring to the world, "It's a dream come true!"...*so challenge yourself to follow your dreams*. You can do this.

LIFE APP

NOW THAT YOU'RE FAMILIAR WITH WHAT IS REQUIRED TO ACHIEVE GREAT THINGS, LET'S DISCUSS YOUR PERSONAL DREAM OPTIONS. THE GOOD NEWS FOR YOU—AND YOUR ENTIRE GENERATION—IS THAT THERE'S LITTLE, IF ANYTHING, YOU CAN'T DO. THAT'S RIGHT, OTHERS WHO CAME BEFORE YOU HAVE FOUGHT TO OPEN SO MANY DOORS THAT *NO DREAM* CAN BE CONSIDERED IMPOSSIBLE ANY LONGER.

TAKE THE AREA OF SPACE EXPLORATION AS AN EXAMPLE. NOT ONLY HAVE FEMALE ASTRONAUTS BROKEN NEW GROUND, BUT NASA AND THE FEDERAL GOVERNMENT CONTINUE TO MAKE CLEAR THEIR COMMITMENT TO GO FURTHER AND FURTHER INTO THE FINAL FRONTIER. CLEARLY, WHEN IT COMES TO DREAMING, NOT EVEN THE SKY IS THE LIMIT ANYMORE!

WITH ALL THIS INSPIRATION IN MIND, DON'T EVER BELIEVE SOMEONE WHO DISMISSES YOUR DREAMS AS TOO BIG. THERE'S NOT A SINGLE PERSON OUT THERE WHO CAN KNOWINGLY STATE YOU WON'T ACCOMPLISH AMAZING THINGS IN YOUR LIFE. INDEED, SOMEDAY *YOU* MAY WELL SCALE EVEREST; HAVE A CD GO PLATINUM; WIN A PROFESSIONAL SPORTS TITLE; BECOME A WORLD LEADER (EVEN THE FIRST FEMALE OR MINORITY PRESIDENT); HOST YOUR OWN SHOW; BREAK AN OLYMPIC RECORD; WIN AN OSCAR; CURE A CANCER; OR EVEN WALK ON MARS...THE POSSIBILITIES ARE TRULY ENDLESS.

SO DREAM—DREAM BIG!

WEEK 50

Becoming a Leader

As we look ahead into the next century, leaders will be those who empower others.
—Bill Gates

Leadership and learning are indispensable to each other.
—John F. Kennedy

Do not go where the path may lead, go instead where there is no path and leave a trail.
—Ralph Waldo Emerson

Leadership is action, not position.
—Donald McGannon

We've all heard the expression, "He (or she) is a born leader." And we've all seen what appears to be living, breathing proof of it. (Individuals like JFK and MLK immediately come to mind.) Heck, even in our own small corners of the world, there exist certain friends, siblings, classmates, and teammates who have a seemingly natural way of getting others to respond—to follow. At times, it's enough to make the rest of us think we really weren't born with what it takes to be a leader.

Before you give up on the idea, though, consider all the research refuting this common assumption. That's right, my student. The research says leaders are not born—but made.

It also reveals that anybody—regardless of age, race, gender, etc.—can succeed at this self-making process. Even matters of personality and leadership style were shown to be of little consequence. Some leaders have been effective leading by example, getting things done quietly and efficiently, while others have taken a more vocal approach, using enthusiasm and charisma as their primary tools of influence. What all of this boils down to is you too may have what it takes to lead...you just don't know it yet.

Where exactly should someone who is up to the challenge get started? Well, believe it or not, you've already begun your personal training process right here. That's because several of the advisements in this book help to develop the very interpersonal, intellectual, and emotional traits you'll need to lead.

Traits like...*possessing self-confidence and a positive attitude; being reflective and open-minded; having a sense of humor and a zest for life; knowing what you stand for; thinking with purpose; embracing risk; putting off pleasure; being goal-oriented; bouncing back from failures; being loyal and dependable; being persistent and strong-willed; treating others in sincere, respectful ways; being motivated to make a positive difference; and being open to learn from others.* Each of these is an essential component of leadership.

At your age, the last trait mentioned takes on even greater significance. You see, the longer you are open to learning from others—particularly those in positions of leadership—the more insight and relevant experience you'll be able to acquire. This alone can put you on the inside track to future success and effectiveness as a leader, providing you a very real advantage over your peers.

Now I'm not saying that opportunities to lead and learn aren't presently available to you—they are—it's just that as you're still growing and developing, you will find yourself playing the role of follower more often than not. And to be perfectly clear, this is not a bad thing. In fact, it's crucial for any future leader to learn firsthand what it takes to follow.

Use each experience to your benefit, e.g., to observe how a leader does, or does not, bring out the best in others; to discover what loyalty, humility, and honesty are all about; to figure out how to relate to different types of people and become a team player. Believe me when I tell you, right now there are leaders in your life—a coach, teacher, classmate, or boss—from whom you can learn things of tremendous value...if you remain open and on the lookout.

Of course, there are also things you will need to learn, not by observing others, but by doing on your own. Formal leadership training courses, for example, focus on the development of three critical skills: communication, decision making, and problem solving. Think about the editor of the school newspaper, the captain of the track team, and the president of the student council as you read about these important skills:

1. Communication: If your idea of leadership involves handing down order after order, you won't be an effective leader. It is imperative, my student, that you listen to and "involve" those with whom you're working. This translates to, among other things, regularly meeting to discuss goals and expectations, truly listening to all opinions, and genuinely respecting all input. Indeed, everyone on the team should feel comfortable enough to raise even an opposing viewpoint.

And when problems arise, be equally sure to share and discuss the details with everyone. Great leaders, after all, understand that breakdowns in communication—not the problems that inevitably arise—are what lie at the root of most every group failure.

2. Decision making: Taking responsibility for important decisions also comes with the leadership territory. And while the absolute necessity to involve others in the process still exists, understand that as the leader you will be the one making the final call.

As long as you carefully weigh all pros and cons, and sincerely feel that you're doing the necessary—and right—thing, there is no reason to second-guess yourself. In fact, once a choice is made, never look back, unless of course it's to learn something from it.

One last thing: When your decisions end up working out, spread the credit around. And when things don't turn out well, take more than your fair share of the blame—others will respect you for it.

3. Problem solving: As you already know, problems are guaranteed to crop up when working to accomplish a worthwhile end. How you choose to tackle them will go a long way in defining how effective you become as a leader.

Once again, you'll need to take the all-important team approach. Thinking for yourself is one thing, but if you insist on solving things as a solo act, you will miss out on the fresh and unique perspectives of others, and eventually falter. Together, then, you need to think creatively and critically about the problem at hand. This involves brainstorming possible solutions, as well as being prepared to predict possible outcomes and more potential obstacles.

Once a realistic plan of action is agreed upon, you must then decide who will do what and when. Just be certain each individual is clear on his or her responsibilities—as one breakdown can short-circuit the entire problem-solving mission.

Aside from becoming familiar with the three technical aspects of leadership, a certain state of mind must also be adopted. The following principles help to define the *true* leader's state of mind:

1. Problems are perceived as challenges, as opportunities.
2. You think for yourself.
3. You do not hesitate to speak your mind—even when it goes against popular opinion.
4. Expectations of self and others are set high.
5. Every individual is viewed as someone of unique value.
6. The desire to learn, reflect, and grow as a person always burns within.
7. A hands-on approach, in which you do your share of the dirty work, is taken so as to better earn respect, trust, and loyalty.
8. Because mistakes and failures are inevitable, you are first ready to learn from them—and then ready to move forward from them.
9. It is recognized that anything worth doing does not come easily; that sacrifice and perseverance will always be required.
10. To reinforce your never-say-die attitude, you adhere to a never-say-die vocabulary (in other words, no "I won'ts" or "I can'ts").
11. It's understood that no matter how confident and capable an individual you may be, you cannot do it all on your own.
12. And lastly, the focus is never on getting others to follow your lead. If you believe in what you're trying to accomplish—and are passionate about it—they *will* rally behind you.

With all that is required of a leader, you may be wondering why anyone would choose to go this route in the first place. Well, the answer is quite simple: Leading is a tremendously virtuous and gratifying way to travel through life. Consider, if you will, just a few of the rewards:

1. As a leader, you are in position to bring about positive change. And when you do succeed at improving a situation—no matter how small—you've succeeded at making the world a better place.
2. You have a much greater opportunity to influence individual lives. That's right, because of your specialized abilities and prominent

role, others—more than you'd ever imagine—will look up to you as a person worthy of respect and loyalty.

3. The experience of transforming a personal vision into reality is something that enriches one's life irrevocably.
4. You're able to fulfill what many, including me, consider to be a high-ranking priority: giving something back to society in recognition of all the ways you've been blessed.
5. You earn the privilege of serving as a beacon of light—a person in position to provide direction, inspiration, and hope to other people—a person who helps others to feel more confident about themselves and what they can accomplish!

Remember then, my student, you may not know it yet, but you too may well have what it takes...*so challenge yourself to become a leader*. You can do this.

LIFE APP

WHETHER YOUR FUTURE INCLUDES A CAREER IN MEDICINE, POLITICS, EDUCATION, SPORTS, ENGINEERING, OR BUSINESS, POSITIONS OF LEADERSHIP WILL BECOME AVAILABLE TO YOU.

IT STANDS TO REASON, THEN, THAT THE MORE EXPERIENCES YOU AMASS NOW, THE BETTER THE LIKELIHOOD OF SECURING SUCH A ROLE LATER. AND AS FATE WOULD HAVE IT, THERE PRESENTLY EXIST FOR YOU A WIDE VARIETY OF OPPORTUNITIES FROM WHICH TO CHOOSE—IN YOUR SCHOOL, ON YOUR TEAM, AND IN YOUR COMMUNITY. THE WORLD IS ALWAYS IN NEED OF PEOPLE WILLING TO STEP UP AND TAKE CHARGE.

OFTEN, THIS NEED GETS FILLED IN THE NAME OF A GOOD CAUSE. WHEN I WAS IN SCHOOL, FOR EXAMPLE, A CLASSMATE STARTED AN AFTER-SCHOOL PROGRAM FOR KIDS AT A LOCAL ELEMENTARY SCHOOL. TO MAKE A LONG STORY SHORT, HER TRAIL-BLAZING EFFORTS HAVE MADE A DIFFERENCE IN THE LIVES OF HUNDREDS—AND ALTHOUGH THE FACES HAVE CHANGED, THE PROGRAM IS STILL GOING STRONG SOME 15 YEARS LATER.

SO NOW, IT'S YOUR TIME TO PICK UP THE TORCH AND LEAD OTHERS IN A POSITIVE DIRECTION. THE OPPORTUNITIES TO DO SO ARE ABUNDANT, AND INCLUDE DIRECTING A FUND-RAISING DRIVE FOR A CLASS PLAY OR TEAM TRIP, INITIATING A PICKETING OR LETTER-WRITING CAMPAIGN ON BEHALF OF THE WORLD'S RAINFORESTS, ORGANIZING A VOLUNTEER EFFORT FOR A LOCAL SOUP KITCHEN, OR STARTING UP A CLUB NEW TO YOUR SCHOOL.

WHATEVER YOU DECIDE, THE INSIGHT GAINED FROM THIS ADVISEMENT, IN COMBINATION WITH A PASSION FOR WHAT YOU WANT TO ACCOMPLISH, PROVIDES ALL THAT IS REQUIRED TO TURN YOUR PERSONAL VISION INTO REALITY!

WEEK 51

Embracing the Olympic Ideal

The most important thing about the Olympic Games is not to win but to take part, just as the most important thing in life is not the triumph, but the struggle. The essential thing is not to have conquered but to have fought well.

—Olympic Creed

Elite athletes who have dreamed, sacrificed, and persevered in the pursuit of excellence. Spectacular opening/closing ceremonies that celebrate diversity, patriotism, and expression through music and the arts. An "eternal" flame that burns in the name of peace and spirit. Competitions that spotlight intense effort, honest emotion, and rare displays of sportsmanship. A torch passed from country to country, person to person, that emanates hope for a better, brighter tomorrow. The rings representative of all athletes and all people joining together as one. This is what the Olympic Games are all about.

Make no mistake, my student, no other occasion on earth is so capable of uniting us the world over, and no other occasion on earth so embodies all that is glorious about life. In fact, and not coincidentally, the Olympics underscore the value of all we have covered together in this book.

As the world eagerly anticipates the next round of Olympic Games, let's first reflect on some compelling moments from the past—moments that in addition to providing true enjoyment, also serve to guide and inspire. (While I realize the examples closest to my own heart may seem like ancient history to you, they are representative of the extraordinary stories that come with every Olympics...and touch every generation.)

Let's start with the 1980 U.S. men's hockey team in Lake Placid, New York. It was at the most tumultuous point of the already tumultuous Cold War Era, when by chance, or perhaps fate, a bunch of our college kids were paired up to play the best professionals on the planet—the Soviet Union. (A team, mind you, that had recently dominated the NHL All-Stars.) The young, dare I say naive, Americans seemed undaunted though in their approach to the challenge. And against overwhelming odds, they—or should I say, we—did manage to overcome the perennial champions, eventually going on to win gold. Commentator Al Michaels' question, "Do you believe in miracles?!" resonated over the airwaves and up and down the spines of millions. Indeed, it was a moment of glory that will endure for all time. Truth be told, my student, this unlikeliest of gold medals was a miracle: the direct result of all-out hustle and intensity; an absolute trust in, and love for, one another; the highest degree of mental toughness; and a deep sense of national pride and honor. This, after all, is the stuff miracles—and this team's legacy—are made of.

One cannot write about the value and magic of the Olympics without also including the journey of Dan Jansen. In 1988, having established himself as the top speed skater on the world circuit, Dan entered The Games as everyone's pick to claim gold. But as you already know, things in life don't always go as expected.

You see, back at home DJ's biggest fan, his sister Jane, was stricken with leukemia. Knowing just how dire the situation had become, he wanted desperately to win in her honor. But on the very day he was to race, she lost her valiant battle. Hours later, not even a world-full of support and goodwill were enough to stop Dan from falling and skidding helplessly off the track. It was just heartbreaking to watch.

A full four years later, the world again rallied around Dan in hopes he would finally achieve his dream. But again, it was not meant to be.

By the time the 1994 Olympics rolled around, Dan was nearing the end of his career. But thanks to his deep resolve and desire for redemption, he did manage to make the American squad. All hopes were dashed, though, as *again* he failed in his best race. Down to the final Olympic event of his life, yet another fateful twist took shape. You see, although the 1,000-meter was far from Dan's strongest race, he found a way to win—*in world record time*—and at last laid claim to his gold medal. During his victory lap, my student, the world watched and wept as he carried in his arms his baby daughter—Jane.

DJ had battled through personal tragedy, huge expectations, world-class competition, and a decade of worldwide disappointment, on his way to the top. His journey is a true testament to the resiliency of the human spirit...and Olympic Ideal.

I could go on and on with inspirational accounts of past Olympic champions (e.g., Jim Shea, Jr., Carl Lewis, Bonnie Blair, Kerri Strug, Bjorn Daehlie, Eric Heiden, Ian Thorpe, Happy Harada), but there is another story equally as meaningful. It involves those Olympians who have never set a record, never won a medal, and never achieved world fame. Heck, many of them trained their entire lives only to fall short of even making their actual Olympic teams. And of those who did make it, some ended up finishing near, if not in, last place.

Yet, by having strived to be the best they could be and by having given all they had to give, they paid ultimate tribute to what the Olympics—and life itself—are all about.

I grant you, my student, finishing on top does taste great, but clearly, what matters most is the process—the struggle—that leads up to the opportunity to participate. Just think about the process every one of these athletes, from the gold medalist to the last-place finisher went through: They, among other things, *dared to dream...believed in themselves...put off pleasure...took risks...set and visualized lofty goals...committed to an intense physical regimen...refused to quit...learned from failures/mistakes...handled pressure-packed situations...surpassed previous limits...mentally prepared for victory...and truly succeeded in life.* Any sound familiar? They should, for these are the exact qualities we've been saying will enable you to create a rich, fulfilling life.

Knowing just how extraordinary every Olympian's journey is, it's tough for me to see any of them respond to not winning by hanging their heads. Sure I can understand the bitter disappointment of defeat, but I hope they eventually come to recognize that if their absolute best effort was given, then it does not matter if they've won or lost.

Consider the aforementioned hero, Dan Jansen. Would he be any less worthy of holding his head up if he had lost his final race? Of course not. Here was a man who carried on year after year, had his will tested over and over again, fought through trying time after trying time, yet continued to strive and sacrifice for another crack, another opportunity to participate.

Characteristics such as these make him a winner, a winner by any standard. And the same holds true for you in life. Aspire to someday boast, "I lived life the way it was meant to be lived, approaching every day with perspective, determination, and passion. And while I faced my share of difficult times and made my share of mistakes, I never gave up; instead, I chose to grow and push forward with head held high. I take great pride in the knowledge that I was an active participant in life, a true individual—a winner by any standard."

With all we have discussed in mind, you too may be eagerly anticipating the next round of Olympic Games. No one could blame you, as it's clearly a life experience to be cherished. Following are just a few more of the reasons why:

1. Each new Olympic venue serves as an opportunity to become acquainted with another amazing area of the world. By merely watching on TV, you can learn a lot about the history and culture of the country's people, as well as the awe-inspiring topography of the land. In addition, you can marvel in and be encouraged by the level of hospitality and national pride the hosts invariably demonstrate.
2. The Olympics provide each one of us a chance to join the vast collection of human beings who come together—either in person or over the airwaves—to share a rare life experience. (And who knows when the next "miracle" will be witnessed and shared the world over.)
3. The faces and emotions of those athletes who appeal to us on a personal level will remain forever etched in our minds and hearts.
4. Where else do you get to witness—on a daily basis no less—just how sweet it is for someone to achieve a goal he has poured his heart and soul into. And where else do you get to see firsthand how world-class athletes, unaccustomed to losing, handle bitter defeat and disappointment?
5. You can count on each Olympic venue as being a place where new stars will emerge and true heroes will be born.
6. It's both heartening and inspirational to see the fiercest of competitors reach out to one another in victory, as well as in defeat.

7. The competitions and incredible levels of athleticism provide the ultimate thrill for any sports fan. Whether you prefer gymnastics, swimming, skiing, snowboarding, figure skating, track and field, rowing, softball, or another of the dozens of Olympic sports, you're ensured of experiencing more than your fair share of captivating moments.
8. And finally, as a result of embracing The Games, you may find yourself becoming more in tune to your own personal dreams, as well as more motivated to begin travel down your own road to greatness. This, after all, is how the Olympic Spirit works. Empowering, yet fleeting, it can free us from getting caught up in life's more trivial matters, while sustaining the sense of purpose and passion required to accomplish something great...something extraordinary. Carry it within!

Remember then, my student, there is much to appreciate and learn from an event featuring those who, in the process of living life to the fullest, have chosen to answer the call to glory...*so challenge yourself to embrace the Olympic Ideal*. You can do this.

LIFE APP

EVEN THE OLYMPIC GAMES HAVE PROVEN SUSCEPTIBLE TO IRRESPONSIBLE AND DISHONEST ACTS. THE MOST CURRENT SCANDALS INCLUDE DRUG USE AMONG CHEATING ATHLETES, COLLUSION AMONG JUDGES, AS WELL AS ALLEGATIONS OF BRIBERY INVOLVING TOP OLYMPIC OFFICIALS AND POTENTIAL HOST CITIES.

MAKE NO MISTAKE, SUCH ISSUES POSE A VERY REAL THREAT TO EVERYTHING GOOD AND PURE ABOUT THE OLYMPICS. BUT IF WE WERE TO LOOK AT THE SITUATION IN A MORE POSITIVE LIGHT, IT COULD ALSO BE SEEN AS WHAT WILL SERVE AS THE CATALYST FOR REFORM.

AS INDIVIDUALS WHO CARE ABOUT AND UNDERSTAND THE TRUE VALUE OF THIS HISTORIC EVENT, IT IS BOTH YOUR AND MY RESPONSIBILITY TO GET INVOLVED. THAT'S WHY I'M SUGGESTING YOU WRITE OR E-MAIL THE UNITED STATES OLYMPIC COMMITTEE (WWW.USOC.ORG) AND/OR THE INTERNATIONAL OLYMPIC COMMITTEE (WWW.OLYMPIC.ORG).

LET THEM KNOW, AS A REPRESENTATIVE OF THE WORLD'S YOUTH, JUST HOW CONCERNED YOU ARE. URGE THEM TO STEP UP THEIR EFFORTS IN THE BATTLE TO ELIMINATE ANY AND ALL CORRUPTION. AND BE CLEAR THAT THE MATTER IMPACTS MORE THAN THE REALM OF IMAGE—THE OVERALL INTEGRITY OF THE GAMES IS AT STAKE!

WEEK 52

Truly Succeeding in Life

Success without honor is an unseasoned dish; it will satisfy your hunger, but it won't taste good.
—Joe Paterno

He has achieved success who has worked well, laughed often, and loved much.
—Elbert Hubbard

Your best shot at happiness, self-worth and personal satisfaction—the things that constitute real success—is not in earning as much as you can but in performing as well as you can something that you consider worthwhile. Whether that is healing the sick, giving hope to the hopeless, adding to the beauty of the world, or saving the world...I cannot tell you.
—William Raspberry

Here's a question for the ages, my student: What constitutes *true* success?

Certainly, the answer you'll hear depends on who you ask and how that particular person happens to keep score. From my own life experiences, though, it's evident that two predominant schools of thought—or scorecards—exist on the matter.

The first, which happens to be the more widely followed of the two, conveys a narrow definition in which securing external things such as money, promotions, and praise—at any cost—scores big points. The other, which happens to be the more balanced but less adhered-to viewpoint, also values working hard to earn external rewards but ranks inner accomplishments and personal character far higher. Accordingly, things like loyalty, courage, laughter, humility, and concern for others rack up big numbers.

As you read on, contemplating how you yourself define true success, keep in mind that those who live by this second definition are a special breed of people. They are the relative few working to create sound, balanced lives by combining worldly success with authentic success—a rare combo, indeed.

More specifically, they make time for family, friends, and personal pursuits. They treat those who work with them—or for them—with dignity and respect. They apply their skills and intellect to charitable causes (matters of the heart) in addition to business matters. And they live each day with overflowing enthusiasm, which for them translates to lots of laughs, love, and personal growth. Within these lifestyle parameters, many have gone on to prove that it is, in fact, possible to make it to the top of their class or chosen field and, at the same time, be a top-notch, class human being. Perhaps you know a special someone like this.

Again, though, keep in mind that such individuals represent a rare and dying breed of people. I say this because countless more in the world grow up to live with an alarmingly narrow perspective, their true stripes being revealed by none other than their typical actions: neglecting even the most important people in their lives; treating clients and colleagues as mere pawns or stepstools; knowingly placing the well-being of their wallets over the well-being of the environment; or starving their own spirits via materialism and cynicism.

It shouldn't surprise you that such people come a dime a dozen, either. After all, the society in which we all grow up does promote an obscenely narrow definition of success. A definition that has helped to create the following types of circumstances:

1. External attributes and possessions are now widely viewed as the be-all, end-all gauge for judging who's winning in life and who isn't.
2. Greed is now widely viewed as an acceptable, even commendable notion.
3. Personal advancement at the expense of family, spirit, and the common good is becoming nearly instinctual behavior for many.

Indeed, it's now clear that we as a lens-clouded society are so consumed with succeeding to get ahead, we've lost sight of the ultimate test...the ultimate aim...the ultimate challenge: to succeed as human beings.

With this unsettling thought in mind, my student, I have worked to outline a standard of success that few, if any, would call into question (and even fewer would view as an overly narrow definition). If you can someday look back on your life and honestly say you aspired to each of these ideals—even while working toward worldly success—

then you will have certainly attained true success. (Many of the following entries may sound familiar to you—and they should, for there are more than 52 in all.)

1. Did I treat my fellow human beings with respect and compassion?
2. Did I keep the promises I made to myself?
3. Did I communicate to others that I am a person of dignity—and expect to be treated as such?
4. Did I take risks and make personal growth a top priority in life?
5. Did I care for my physical self by eating well and staying active?
6. Was I an honest, loyal, and trustworthy friend?
7. Did I have heroes? And did I hold myself up to similarly high standards?
8. Was I able to maintain perspective on what's truly important in life?
9. Did I resist the urge to judge and criticize others?
10. Was I there for those in need?
11. Did I develop an undying belief in my unique capabilities?
12. Was I able to rise above others' pettiness and mean-spiritedness?
13. Did I come to see the presence of failure in my life as the positive indicator it truly is?
14. Did I learn something from each of my mistakes?
15. Did I make "giving strong, persistent effort" a life habit?
16. Was I able to build up self-esteem on my own?
17. Will others someday remember me as a caring, compassionate individual?
18. Did I learn to accept myself—faults and all?
19. Did I have dreams...and did I pursue them with passion?
20. Was I up to the challenge of constructing enduring relationships?
21. Was I able to bounce back from inevitable heartache and loss?
22. Did I appreciate both the big and small wonders of our world?
23. Did I develop my self-confidence and consistently act from a position of strength?
24. Did I make the effort to connect with all kinds of people in all types of situations?

25. Was I open-minded enough to try new experiences and weigh even opposing viewpoints?
26. Did I live each day with zest and enthusiasm?
27. Did I avoid the ever-alluring temptation to take the easy way out?
28. Did I choose optimism and search for the bright side of every situation?
29. Was I able to look in the mirror and see the inner beauty?
30. Did I come to recognize that worry is the most worthless of habits?
31. Was I able to make sacrifices in the short term so as to benefit in the long term?
32. Did I treat those who are different from me as equals?
33. Did I work to become a responsible, self-disciplined individual who considers consequences before acting?
34. Did I continue to grow by utilizing the power of goals?
35. Did I leave it all on the field?
36. Did I develop the attitude wherein I *expected* things in my life to work out for the best?
37. Was I loyally devoted to my family...to my pets...to my friends...to my country...to my God?
38. Was I open to learning something from everyone?
39. Did I do my part to take care of the environment?
40. Did I take achievement in stride, always striving to act with humility?
41. Did I learn and apply a variety of strategies so as to better manage the stress and pressure of day-to-day life?
42. Did I make a conscious effort to include music in my daily round?
43. Was I able to hold on to my sense of humor?
44. Did I develop the capacity to live in, and appreciate, the present moment?
45. Did I make choices that were consistent with my values?
46. Did I learn how to control my emotions rather than let them control me?
47. Did I remember to pay attention to, and care for, my spirit?

48. Was I open, assertive, and not afraid to stand up and speak my mind?
49. Was I able to impact others' behavior in leading by example?
50. Did I allow outside forces (e.g., TV, peers, etc.) to compromise my personal values and choices?
51. Did I make time to pursue my life passions?
52. Did I work hard to overcome obstacles and never give up?
53. Did I focus on all that I had to be grateful for—rather than on what I lacked?
54. Could I look myself in the eye at the end of each day?
55. Was I able to make a difference in the life of another?
56. Lastly, could I state with sincerity and conviction one of the most profound of all ideals: After a well-intentioned life, *I wouldn't change a thing.*

When such questions can be reflected on with pride and honor, you will have unequivocally earned the title, **A Winner by Any Standard**—indeed, no one could declare otherwise!

Remember then, my student, there's a vast difference between becoming a winner by society's standards and becoming a winner as a human being...*so challenge yourself to truly succeed in life*. You can do this.

LIFE APP

REFLECT ON EACH OF THE QUESTIONS ABOVE—ONE AT A TIME. YOU CAN EVEN USE THEM TO EXTEND YOUR WEEKLY-CHALLENGE REGIMEN FOR AN ADDITIONAL YEAR!

To dream anything that you want to dream. That's the beauty of the human mind. To do anything that you want to do. That is the strength of the human will. To trust yourself to test your limits. That is the courage to succeed.

—Bernard Edmonds

Afterword

Congratulations on having completed your unique yearlong journey.

Whether you realize it or not, my student, the simple fact you chose to read such a book speaks volumes to the kind of person you are. Already you have picked up on things that only a relative few ever figure out. First and foremost, you understand that growing and evolving as a human being is what life's truly all about. Sure, sacrifice and hard work are required to live in such a way, but as you've come to recognize, the price of coasting—unchallenged—through life is far steeper.

What's equally impressive is you sense that, while having fun and being happy are worthy aims, there is far more involved with why we are each here. To ultimately stand for something, to become one's own person, to build meaningful relationships, and to have a positive impact on the world are what make for a truly fulfilling existence.

Having armed yourself with this rare knowledge—at such a young age, no less—means you are now ready to employ the kind of choices that can make effective living a reality. It's no small accomplishment, either. Especially when you consider that effective living and the personal fulfillment that results, are two things many people never come to experience.

I'm hopeful, though, that together we can work to change such circumstances. Who knows, together we may even be able to transform the less traveled path to true success into the path of common choice. You see, because superior levels of insight and inspiration are now yours, you enjoy a real advantage over the majority of your peers. But rather than look down from the elevated land of enlightenment, you can instead lead by example and help lift others up to equally high levels.

In the process, you will demonstrate to them that there really are no limits to how high one can climb *if* the choice is made to challenge oneself, and that while this may be an uphill path to follow at times, it is worth every ounce of the struggle. For the struggle is precisely what infuses our lives with meaning—and empowers each of us to become extraordinary in our own way...winners by any standard.

In parting, let me say that it's been an absolute privilege connecting with you—as an individual and as a fellow world citizen. May you continue to make your life journey everything it can be, and in the process, to make the world we share everything it can be.

Respectfully,

Mr.G

P.S. You did it.

About the Author

ROB GAROFALO, JR. is a renowned teacher from Berlin, Connecticut—a place where he enjoys the reputation of being an efficacious facilitator of not only academic learning, but also life learning. In fact, Mr. G, as his school community refers to him, is widely thought of as that special kind of teacher and role model that comes around once in a lifetime. A past congressional scholarship recipient and state Teacher of the Year award winner, he possesses a gift for imparting ideals to young people in a way that gently guides them to see the value of these ideals for themselves.

Having inspired countless students to live with more passion and purpose, Mr. G hopes his first book, *A Winner by Any Standard: A Personal Growth Journey for Every American Teen,* will become a life manual that empowers young people everywhere to realize they possess the power to shape themselves, their future lives, and the world itself.

As a dedicated educator, Mr. Garofalo has taken advantage of professional-development opportunities throughout his career. Most notably, he has received federal training in the areas of esteem building and drug and alcohol intervention. This training led to his becoming involved with the nationally recognized program, UpBeat, which proactively fosters peer-leadership skills and community involvement among local youth. Meanwhile, on a state level, he has become a respected mentor and has continued his education in such areas as character ed., mastery teaching, conflict resolution, childhood depression, bullying, diversity, student leadership, stress management, violence prevention, and how young people grieve. Organizations to which he belongs include the National Education Association,

Character Education Partnership, the National Parent Teacher Association, Youth Service America, and Start Something.

A skilled and confident public speaker, Mr. G has written, designed, and presented several education-related workshops (e.g., Laser-disc Technology, Expository Writing) to both parents and fellow teachers. He also designed and taught, as part of his town's summer school program, a popular course that promotes sound ideals and social/emotional aptitude, titled "It's All About Choices." And last, but not least, he implemented a Good Citizenship program for his entire school.

Having been long dedicated to growing and evolving on a personal level as well, Mr. Garofalo—a loyal patriot, spirited athlete, avid traveler, animal lover, and music enthusiast—has studied upwards of 120 self-help/inspirational books. The authors he credits most for influencing his life pursuits—including his writing, of course—are Anthony Robbins, Stephen Covey, M. Scott Peck, and Sarah Ban Breathnach. Mr. G's ultimate goal is to become as important and profound an influence for the world's youth as these extraordinary individuals have become for adults everywhere.

Check It Out!

You can write to Mr. G at www.TeenWinners.com—a great website for teens around the world to share their personal growth experiences. Check it out!